Texas Jazz Singer

Number Twenty-Five

Sam Rayburn Series on Rural Life

Sponsored by Texas A&M University–Commerce

M. Hunter Hayes, General Editor

Texas Jazz Singer

Louise Tobin in the Golden Age of Swing and Beyond

Kevin Edward Mooney

Texas A&M University Press   *College Station*

This paper meets the requirements of ANSI/NISO Z39.48–1992
(Permanence of Paper).
Binding materials have been chosen for durability.
Manufactured in the United States of America

Library of Congress Cataloging-in-Publication Data

Names: Mooney, Kevin Edward, 1961– author.
Title: Texas jazz singer : Louise Tobin in the golden age of swing and
  beyond / Kevin Edward Mooney.
Other titles: Sam Rayburn series on rural life ; no. 25.
Description: First edition. | College Station : Texas A&M University Press,
  [2021] | Series: Sam Rayburn series on rural life ; number twenty-five |
  Includes bibliographical references and index.
Identifiers: LCCN 2020042346 | ISBN 9781623499655 (cloth) | ISBN
  9781623499662 (ebook)
Subjects: LCSH: Tobin, Louise. | Women jazz singers—Texas—Biography. |
  Jazz singers—Texas—Biography. | Swing (Music)—History and criticism.
  | LCGFT: Biographies.
Classification: LCC ML420.T624 M66 2021 | DDC 781.65092 [B]—dc23
LC record available at https://lccn.loc.gov/2020042346

All figures from The Louise Tobin and Peanuts Hucko Jazz Collection
are courtesy of Northeast Texas Digital Collections. Velma K. Waters
Special Collections Department, Texas A&M University–Commerce,
Commerce, Texas.

Contents

Foreword

TO PROVIDE AN accurate and detailed account of the importance of female musicians in jazz throughout the twentieth century would seem a daunting and monumental task, requiring multiple volumes; even then, too many voices might remain relatively muted, a consequence of the vicissitudes of popularity inherent to the fluctuating modes of artistic culture. In this biography of Louise Tobin, the first detailed account of her life, Kevin Mooney captures the unique difficulties that women faced as professional musicians, navigating situations where their creativity and desire for popular success clashed with the restrictive assumptions of society, with bandleaders and others in the music industry, and with the demand of husbands and other family members. Shrewdly, Mooney does not attempt to present Tobin as simply an emblem for women in jazz of the big band era, concentrating instead on the story of Tobin's life, her struggles and successes, and the particular sense of grace that resonates throughout each phase of Tobin's career.

While Louise Tobin may have once seemed modestly content for the public to identify her as "just Mrs. Harry James," as Mooney points out, her achievements and contributions to traditional and big band jazz deserve broad recognition and appreciation.

Mooney's sympathetic and instructive analysis of Tobin's "Louise Tobin Blues," among her first performances and recordings with the Benny Goodman Orchestra, uncovers Tobin's skills in simultaneously subverting various cultural expectations of women while refashioning blues conventions to imprint her identity on the American songbook of the twentieth century. Although "Louise Tobin Blues" first served as her novel introduction to Goodman's audience, conveying her journey from rural Texas to the metropolitan big band stages and airwaves, the tune also reveals Tobin asserting her individuality as an artist and not merely as the spouse of a more famous musician.

Tobin's personal life merges often with her musical career, as her marriages to Harry James and then to Michael Andrew "Peanuts" Hucko demonstrate, but she also maintained a lifelong commitment to music, even when younger audiences viewed big band and swing as relics of bygone eras. Throughout her career, Tobin forged pivotal associations with people who endure in the annals of music history, and Mooney keeps Tobin firmly in the spotlight as she encounters dominant figures such as Benny Goodman, John Hammond, and Frank Sinatra.

Texas Jazz Singer: Louise Tobin in the Golden Age of Swing and Beyond is the product of deft research. Mooney's archival research through trade and other publications, the materials housed in the Louise Tobin and Peanuts Hucko Jazz Collection at Texas A&M University–Commerce's Velma K. Waters Library, and Mooney's primary-source interviews with Tobin all help to shape and to inform his account of Tobin's life and career. Less tangibly, perhaps, Mooney buttresses his scholarship through a nuanced understanding of the creative environment Tobin inhabits and that she helped to transform. Mooney's writing here is also the product of his deeply-informed musical perspective, the acuity and sensitivity that he brings to his subject from his own knowledge and experiences as a musician. It seems entirely fitting that a fellow musician would provide the narrative account of Louise Tobin's rich life and career.

The title for Mooney's biographical study, *Texas Jazz Singer: Louise Tobin in the Golden Age of Swing and Beyond*, conveys an evocative sense of Tobin's deep roots in Texas and the jazz idioms through which she shared her talents across the world for decades before retiring and returning to Texas. Along the way Tobin befriended generations of musicians—including many who might have dominated the spotlight but did not compromise Tobin's individuality or musical skills—and established through those associations a wide-ranging sphere of influences. Thanks to Mooney's devoted research, readers now have the opportunity to revisit or to experience anew Tobin's remarkable career, documenting the interplay between her personal life and her professional accomplishments and excursions.

Mooney's *Texas Jazz Singer* is the twenty-fifth volume in the Sam Rayburn Series on Rural Life, and it is a privilege to not only welcome this book to the series but to have it mark such an important milestone in the continuing history of the Rayburn Series. Since its inception in 1997, the Rayburn Series has endeavored to present the diverse cultural, social, and political histories of rural Texas, centering roughly on east Texas. Louise Tobin's fascinating journey from Aubrey and the then-small town of Denton—decades before it would become a major city within the Dallas-Fort Worth Metroplex—to the portion of fame she received as a successful singer during and after the heyday of the big band era, and then to her return home to suburban Dallas, constitutes an essential part of this history. Tobin's life and artistic achievements enhance the state's cultural heritage, and readers may regard her as an indispensable contributor to the evolving history of jazz.

—**M. Hunter Hayes**
General Editor
Sam Rayburn Series on Rural Life

Acknowledgments

TO LOUISE TOBIN, for graciously sharing her story, her time, and her enthusiasm, I express my heartfelt thanks and deep appreciation. Equally committed to this project were Mike Kubiak and Deborah Porter, both of whom accompanied me on most of the in-person interviews and both of whom arranged to secure the Louise Tobin and Peanuts Hucko Jazz Collection at Texas A&M University–Commerce. The writing of this book also benefited from the many interviews that Deb transcribed and the photos she took of documents from the collection. I extend my appreciation to Harry James Jr., whose smile and kind welcome always greeted me on my arrival for an interview. Thanks, Harry, for listening to our interviews and for sharing your perspectives.

Without Andrea Weddle, head of Archives and Special Collections, Velma K. Waters Library, Texas A&M University–Commerce (Andrea archived and inventoried the Louise Tobin and Peanuts Hucko Jazz Collection); Adam Northam, Digital Collections librarian, Texas A&M University–Commerce; Kennith R. Kimery, director, Smithsonian Jazz Masterworks Orchestra; John Edward Hasse, curator of American Music, Smithsonian Institution; Dan Morgenstern, director, Institute of Jazz Studies, Rutgers University; Donna M. Arnold, music reference librarian, and Maristella Feustle, music special collections librarian, both at University of North Texas Library; Graham Pass, BBC Radio; and Mark Blair, music librarian, Schneider Music Library, Texas State University, this book could not have been written.

My sincere thanks go to M. Hunter Hayes, general editor of the Sam Rayburn Series on Rural Life, for his foreword and continued commitment to the series and to the Louise Tobin project.

For his continued support and enthusiasm for my work on this book, I express my gratitude and appreciation to Thomas Clark, director, School of Music, Texas State University. This came with the support of my colleagues Cynthia Gonzalez, Ludim Pedrosa, John Schmidt, and Nico Schüler. My research also benefited from the work of three graduate research assistants, Brent Ferguson, Wesley Peart, and ShaoYing Ho.

I also want to thank musician, arranger, and Louise Tobin fan, Karl Wingruber. He generously shared his knowledge of Louise's discography and *Camel Caravan* performance history.

I thank all of the editors at Texas A&M University Press—Thom Lemmons, for your expertise, guidance, and patience, and Dawn Hall and Patricia A. Clabaugh, for bringing this project over the finish line. I extend a huge thank you to designer Kristie Lee for her stunning jacket design. Thanks also is due to M. Hunter Hayes and Jonathan Hooper, both of whom reviewed the entire manuscript and offered insightful and encouraging suggestions for improvement. Nevertheless, I take full responsibility for any shortcomings that might remain in this book.

For their all-around cheerleading and wisdom, I am indebted to Jan Whitener, Ezra Heitowit, John Hubner and Sarah Brown, Wendy Goldstein, Delbert McClinton, Delaney McClinton, Kimmie Rhodes, Diana Finlay Hendricks, and Sandra Tenorio.

Finally, I wish to express my thanks to my husband Jaston Williams and our son Song for their unbounded love and support. This book is dedicated to them.

Texas Jazz Singer

Introduction

THIS BIOGRAPHY documents the life and music of jazz vocalist Louise Tobin (b. 1918) and also, with the benefit of hours and hours of interviews, presents *her* story of the jazz legends with whom she had contact from the early 1930s through the twentieth century.

When listening to Louise talk about her first date with Harry James, or how she and the other orchestra wives snuck backstage at Carnegie Hall for the infamous Benny Goodman concert in 1938, when she shares personal stories about John Hammond, George Simon, and Frank Sinatra, or Ben Pollack, Eddie Condon, and Bobby Hackett, or Lionel Hampton, Charlie Christian, and Fletcher Henderson, or Louis Armstrong, and . . . the list seems endless—it is easy to be seduced just by being in the presence of someone who has known firsthand so many of the history makers of jazz. What could be missed, however, is *her* story, *her* life in music, *her* career. In the words of her first son, Harry Jr., "It's hard to get mom to tell stories that feature *her*. She'll tell stories about everybody else. Mom lived it. Her friends were to her just her friends. To everybody else they were giant superstars in the industry."[1] This book is Louise's story.

Seeds of this biography were planted by Mike Kubiak and Deborah Porter, both of whom were instrumental in compiling the Louise Tobin and Peanuts Hucko Jazz Collection at Texas A&M University–Commerce, and both of whom brought me into the project, arranging my first interview with Louise in the spring of 2009.

I had just finished presenting the keynote address at a Texas Music Conference in Dallas, when Deb and Mike approached me as I left the podium.[2] Their introduction came with two objectives: first, to invite me to Deb's presentation later that day on Louise Tobin and Peanuts Hucko and formally announcing the newly acquired Louise Tobin and Peanuts Hucko Jazz Collection.[3] Deb, a musician, author, and entertainer, at the time was a grant writer at Texas A&M University–Commerce, and Mike had produced and remastered a recording for jazz clarinetist, and Louise's second husband, Peanuts Hucko.[4] Their other objective was to solicit my scholarly services, suspecting that they had found a music historian who could formally record Louise's oral history. During the next two months, with Deb's assistance, I prepared for my first meeting and interview with Louise Tobin.

On July 16, 2009, Louise sat with me, Deb, Mike, and a cameraman and told her life story, at least the early years through her work with Benny Goodman in 1939 and her eight-year marriage to Harry James.[5] I led the questioning, with Deb and Mike interjecting a few requests for elaboration. Three-and-a-half hours later, Deb took a couple of photos of Louise and me, and I left with my head spinning with excitement about having just met Louise Tobin, one of the last survivors of the swing era. I knew there was so much more about her life and musical experiences that she had yet to share. Deb and I agreed that we needed to write a book on her life; hence, there would be many more visits and lengthy discussions. Indeed, our interviews became half of the two most significant sources for this biography, the other being the Louise Tobin and Peanuts Hucko Jazz Collection, which includes fifty-three linear feet (plus one media storage cabinet) of documents and other items related to concerts, tours, and other public appearances, correspondence, personal papers and effects, publications, sheet music, photographs and negatives, and audio and video recordings, covering the period from 1925 to 2011. Louise did not keep a diary. A scrapbook, however, compiled by one of her sisters, informally documenting the early years of her career, is in the collection.

My interviews with Louise continued after that summer of 2009, two or three times a year for nearly the ten years following. With a few exceptions, both Deb and Mike were present and contributed to the questioning as well.

Given her two marriages, first to trumpeter and bandleader Harry James and second to clarinetist and bandleader Peanuts Hucko, the significant musical contributions of these two musicians and Tobin's personal perspectives arguably strengthen the depth of this book, and I hope will broaden its appeal. Peter Levinson's *Trumpet Blues* is the definitive biography of Harry James. While we await an extended biographical treatment of Peanuts Hucko, I hope that this book on Louise with a peripheral lens on Peanuts will contribute toward such a biography.

Louise's oral history, like most, is filled with anecdotes and reminiscences. When I first interviewed her, she was ninety-one years old, and in succeeding interviews her memory remained sharp. Nevertheless, I have researched related information for historical accuracy, and I have noted those rare occasions when it was necessary to correct the record.

Chapter one of this volume covers Louise Tobin's early years as a grandchild of north Texas pioneers, her informal music education, singing at home and in high school and for the Saturday evening stage show at what is now University of North Texas, winning a 1934 Dallas, Texas, CBS talent contest, performing at age fifteen throughout Texas on the Interstate Theatre Circuit, and regional and national tours with the Art Hicks Orchestra. It was with this ensemble where Louise first met Harry James. Chapter one concludes with the breakup of Hicks's band in Albany, New York, and Harry and Louise's marriage in 1935.

The second chapter covers the early years of Louise's marriage to Harry, their move to Chicago when Harry went to work with Ben Pollack, and her work with Mike Todd's first successful variety show, *Bring on the Dames*. The chapter also describes Harry's tenure with the Benny Goodman Orchestra, and Louise's dual role as "orchestra wife" and jazz singer.

Chapter three centers on Louise's tenure with the Benny Goodman Orchestra, 1939, life on the road, the records she made with Benny, including a detailed look at the eponymous "Louise Tobin Blues." Louise also recalled her role in bringing Frank Sinatra to the attention of Harry, who was looking for a singer with his new band.

The following chapter covers the 1940s and '50s, nearly twenty years of retirement as she raised her sons. Louise had left Goodman and moved to Hollywood to be with Harry. Ultimately, however, this time was marked by her subsequent divorce from Harry (1943) and the challenges she faced, balancing single-parent family life with such occasional performances as singing with the Ziggy Elman Orchestra at the Hollywood Palladium.

Chapter five covers the 1960s. Louise moved to New York and reignited her career, first singing with Peanuts Hucko at the Connecticut Jazz Festival and shortly after that with George Wein at his 1962 Newport Jazz Festival. This led to more singing engagements with Peanuts. They fell in love, got married, and, after a brief time running a jazz club in Denver, Colorado, performed together both nationally and internationally for another three decades, despite the challenges they faced as jazz musicians from the swing era, trying to sustain their careers in the shadow of rock and roll during the cultural revolution of the 1950s and 1960s.

The final chapter traces Peanuts and Louise's career through the 1970s, '80s, and '90s, when they continued to perform at jazz parties, concerts, dances, clubs, and at jazz festivals in America, Europe, Japan, and around the world.

During one of our interviews, Louise suggested a title for her biography: *Married in Music*. First to Harry and then to Peanuts, to whom she was married for thirty-six years until his death in 2003, Louise was also married to music. She said that she fell out of the cradle singing and that all she ever wanted to do was to sing. While she flirted with writing poetry, briefly posed in the latest outfit for celebrity fashion pages in newspapers, and was devoted to raising her two children, Louise had a monogamous commitment to singing. And it all began in Aubrey, Texas.

1

From Amateur to Professional Songstress, 1918–1935

I fell out of my cradle singing. I never did proper things. I just sang.[1]

MARY LOUISE TOBIN was born in Aubrey, Texas, on Armistice Day, November 11, 1918. Much of the world was celebrating the end of "the war to end all wars." The Tobins were thankful for a healthy baby born amid an influenza pandemic that had ultimately resulted in more deaths worldwide than the First World War.[2] Woodrow Wilson was president of the United States, and William Pettus Hobby was governor of Texas, having succeeded the impeached James Ferguson.[3] Just nine months before her birth, the legislature passed the law allowing women to vote in primary elections and party nominating conventions.[4]

The Tobins were already a large family. Mary Louise was Hugh and Edna Mae's eighth child, and she ultimately would have three younger siblings.[5]

Mary Louise was named after her grandmother, Mary Susan Looper (1842–1934), "a wonderful, old, pioneer lady who came across in a covered wagon from Alabama to Texas [in 1867] and had a baby in the wagon."[6] The baby was Laura Edwards (1867–1919), whose daughter, Bertha Rhoades (1885–?), except for Louise, was another member of her extended family whose life centered on music. In Bertha's case, she was a pianist and organist who taught music lessons in Aubrey, Texas, for the greater part of her adult life.[7] Louise recalled that her grandmother had a small, eighteen-inch waist and wore a black satin dress that went to the ground. "Nobody ever saw her ankles!" Technology frightened her. She refused to put a phone in her house.[8] Louise's mother, Edna Mae (1884–1975), was the baby of the family[9] and remained close to her mother even after her marriage, going home often. When she took her children to their grandmother's, Louise recalled her mother sending them outside to keep them quiet. With a large number of children in the immediate family and numerous cousins nearby, it is hard to imagine there was ever that much quiet time. They played around in one of the two buggies outside: one for Sundays and one for every day.[10] Although the automobile had become common during 1900–1910, her grandparents' attitudes and ways reflected more of a traditionalist view than progressive. On music-making in the Edwards family, Deborah Goin writes in *History of Aubrey, Texas*, that, "Dancing was not allowed, but singings were held at the Edwards home. People from Sanger and other nearby places came to spend the weekend and hear one of the first organs in the country, brought by Edwards."[11]

Louise Tobin's childhood home in Aubrey, Texas. The home was constructed by Louise's maternal grandfather, Lemuel Noah Edwards. (Courtesy of the Louise Tobin and Peanuts Hucko Jazz Collection)

Louise's grandfather, Lemuel Noah Edwards (1837–1910), a Civil War veteran from Alabama, has been credited with founding Aubrey, a town that was first territorialized as a Cherokee Indian village called Onega.[12] According to Jackie Balthrop Fuller in *The Handbook of Texas Online*, Edwards "built the town's second house, a large, imposing, two-story structure, of lumber hauled from Jefferson in 1867."[13] When each of his children married, Edwards deeded a plot of land for the newlyweds' home to be built, all surrounding his own.[14] The Texas and Pacific Railway came in 1881. "After the first businesses east of the railroad tracks burned in 1887, the town was rebuilt west of the tracks, partially [*sic*; 'mostly,' Louise corrected] on land donated by Edwards."[15]

At the time of Louise's birth, Aubrey was home to about 700 residents and a growing number of stores and businesses, including cotton gins, flour mills, a large school, and the Miller Hotel.[16]

Louise's grandfather was very protective of his daughters. He built a well at the bottom of the hill so that men did not have to come to the house to water their horses, keeping the young men away from his daughters.[17] The Aubrey area—situated on US Highway 377, in Denton County, approximately ten miles north of US Highway 380 and twenty miles west of US Interstate 35—was once known for its cotton farming. With the community's decline, peanut crops became profitable. Today the area is known as the horse capital of Texas.[18] The Tobins left Aubrey not long after Louise was born, living for a time in Plainview and later in Denton, following the drugstore business of Louise's family.

In 1929 tragedy struck the Tobin household. Louise recalled how frightened she and her sisters where as they were suddenly awakened at three o'clock in the morning and learned of the accident. Her father had been driving back and forth from Plainview to a town in West Texas in order to start another pharmacy. On March 2, on his way home, Hugh lost control of his car, flipped over, and was killed. Louise recalled that when her mother went to the hospital, "Big Daddy," the father of Edna's brother-in-law, came to stay with the children. "The young girls got up and sat together on his lap in the comfort of his arms."[19] Hugh Tobin (1882–1929) was only forty-seven years old. Louise's mother was nearly incapacitated and long to approach anything resembling recovery. Ultimately, the family was held together by the strength of Louise's older brothers.

The Tobin's were a musical family, "nothing professional, but they all sang."[20] Her sisters were the first to notice that Mary Louise could sing remarkably well for someone so young and lacking formal training. Her short stature contributed to the impression of her being even younger than her years. She could quickly memorize song lyrics, sing in tune, and possessed the innocence and fearlessness of youth. Mary Louise liked the attention and praise she received when she sang for her family, so she expected such accolades when she performed in public. She was rarely disappointed.

Announcements in the local newspapers document Mary Louise's experiences singing in public from age seven to fifteen, when she began to sing professionally. By age seven, Louise was singing at church and Sunday school, and shortly thereafter could be heard on the radio in advertisements for Metzger's Milk on WDAG, the panhandle radio pioneer in Amarillo that began broadcasting in 1922.[21] The March 9, 1930, Amarillo newspaper mentioned an evening celebration with entertainment that included "numbers by Mary Louise Tobin."[22] Her experience was soon growing from local to regional performances. Outside of Amarillo, she "took part in a radio program in Wichita Falls," and the *Denton Record-Chronicle* on June 10, 1930, announced a "Little Mary Louise Tobin . . . who sings over the radio, at the Methodist Church Sunday morning."[23] In February 1931 Louise sang in Denton on the college campus at Mary Arden Lodge for a Washington Day, student-led celebration, featuring a variety of entertainment with "Mary Louise Tobin [who] sang several popular numbers including 'I'm Yours' and 'You're Driving Me Crazy,' and 'Yours and Mine.'"[24] After spending several months living with relatives in Amarillo, Louise had returned to Denton to live with her immediate family and attend junior high school there.[25] She participated in a couple of junior high fundraisers, in April singing "Nobody Cares If I'm Blue" accompanied by local pianist Virginia Woodford, and, about a week prior to her thirteenth birthday in November, at an event where she was crowned queen of Junior High School, she sang "several 'blues' songs."[26]

In addition to singing in church, for junior high school–related activities, and at the college after her move to Denton, Louise began to sing on occasion with a quartet of young, African American musicians, singing "anything and everything [with them]."[27]

Louise learned songs from the radio, mostly, and was particularly drawn to the dance orchestras, singing along with "whatever was popular at the time."[28] She liked the emerging new sounds of western swing, especially the Light Crust Doughboys; she also listened to Ruth Etting and the Boswell Sisters.[29] There was a record player in the house, but Louise could not afford to purchase such extravagances as records.

Following her passion as well as encouragement from her older sisters, Louise sang at every opportunity. Her love for song and performing did not affect her academic studies, at least at first. She made the honor roll in junior high at the North Ward School.[30] About a year later, after having just recently recovered from a case of diphtheria, and still a high school student, Louise sang at a Senior High School assembly in Denton.[31]

The following week Mary Louise participated in an evening of music and dancing at the College Club House of the North Texas State Teachers College. On April 14, 1932, the *Campus Chat*, the college's weekly student newspaper, reported that among the evening's variety of performances by several Denton High School students were "songs by Mary Louise Tobin, the blues singer."[32] Two days later Mary Louise attended a dance given by Froggies' Club.[33] And just a few weeks after that, "Miss Mary Louise Tobin sang, accompanied by Miss Esther Province," for a meeting of the Business and Professional Women's Club.[34] She was becoming a local celebrity. When the *Denton Record-Chronicle* included an article titled "66 Promoted to Senior High School," the newspaper singled out Mary Louise Tobin among those receiving diplomas.[35]

In 1933 Mary Louise spent more time on school-related activities than performing. By late summer of the following year, however, her life as Senior High School student "Miss Mary Louise" would become "Miss Louise Tobin, petite and brunette blues singer from Denton," and about eight months after that, a sixteen-year-old Mrs. Harry James.

As a high school student, Mary Louise was active in various social clubs. In late January 1934, she was elected officer of the Denton High School "Justamere" Club and was also leader of the Hi-Yi Club.[36] During their March meeting, the Hi-Yi Club reportedly discussed "the challenge of leisure time," no doubt a timely topic for Mary Louise, as her time for leisure and school-related activities had become much more limited in 1934.[37] In mid-February she sang as part of a dance program at her high school and soon became a regular feature on Saturday nights with the College Stage Band.[38] In late July of that year, the *Campus Chat* advertised the Saturday performance of the College Stage Band, presenting

Louise Tobin's school photograph from the Denton High School yearbook, 1934. (Courtesy of the Louise Tobin and Peanuts Hucko Jazz Collection)

"Mary Louise Tobin, who has proved herself a find within the past few weeks."[39] The orchestra performed a variety of "song hits of today" prior to projecting a motion picture.

For the 1925–26 school year, the college acquired two moving picture machines. (It took the use of two projectors to avoid interruption during the process of changing the reels.) In 1927, new faculty member and violinist Floyd Graham began directing a pit orchestra made up of college students as well as musicians from the community, supplying music for the silent movies shown on Saturday evenings.[40] In 1929 with the new talking motion pictures, the orchestra was "transformed into a stage band to provide a show before the movie."[41] This ensemble became known as the "Aces of Collegeland," soon to become the "feature attraction of the traditional Saturday night stage shows." The Aces of Collegeland was arguably the catalyst of the One O'Clock Lab Band and planted the seeds at North Texas for what became the first college degree in jazz studies.[42]

Despite her relatively extensive experience singing in public at such a young age, singing with Floyd Graham's Saturday Night Stage Band was the first time Louise sang with such a large ensemble. She learned to listen, not only musically, but to direction as well. "Graham told me what to do, and I did it," she recalled.[43] Louise's performances with the band for several weeks during the summer of 1934 provided her with invaluable experience singing with an orchestra. As with several other budding performers from this ensemble under "'Fessor's'" direction, Louise drew extensively from this experience as she was soon to transition from amateur to professional status.

Louise was not the only musician to benefit from the education and experience available to local, rising stars. Indeed, as her professional career first took her beyond Texas and ultimately to New York with the Art Hicks Orchestra, as described in more detail further on, she was listed among several former members of the organization

> found everywhere throughout the country, from New York to California, and in practically every field embracing music. . . . Bill Ardis, pianist, dancer, and scenic artist, is now studying at Columbia University in New York. Alpha Louise Martin, who sang with the band, is soloist with Don Pedro's Orchestra in Chicago. . . . J. Hobert McLaughlin, violinist in Teachers College for the past three years, is in California. He is a student at University of California. . . . Back to New York, we find Louise Tobin, popular singer while with the stage band, now becoming popular with Art Hicks.[44]

Singing with the Aces undoubtedly prepared her for that longed for, quintessential breakout, historical moment of all dream-to-be professional musicians, performers, artists, and entertainers; nevertheless, it was her success singing for a regional talent contest that ultimately launched her career.

To say that amateur talent contests were the rage in 1930s America—consider Major Bowes Amateur Hour (1934–45), which for television became *The Original Amateur Hour* (1935–70; 1992)—would be to ignore the fact that for centuries spectators have enjoyed observing everyday people doing extraordinary things in the context of a competition.[45] A young Frank Sinatra with the Hoboken Four appeared on Major Bowes Amateur Hour in 1935. He was just eighteen years old.[46] Radio and later television allowed even greater numbers of people to be involved. More recently, look no further than the popularity of *American Idol* and *Dancing with the Stars*. Winners in most cases receive a monetary reward and/or an opportunity to enter into the industry as a professional. The Miss America Pageant winners in the 1930s received Hollywood screen tests, for example.[47]

In the summer of 1934 Mary Louise competed successfully in two contests: a Texas county declamation contest and a national talent contest. The former advanced her to the district contest in Fort Worth the following week, and the latter led to a lifelong career as a professional singer.[48] Her extensive performance experience, talent, and fearlessness no doubt contributed to the successful outcomes of each.[49]

In the late summer of 1934, Louise was surprised to learn that her sister Dora had entered her in a singing contest sponsored by CBS radio broadcasting out of Dallas. Louise's rendition of "Emmaline"[50] impressed the judges, and she won a singing tour on the Interstate Theatre Circuit and the opportunity to perform with a variety of regional society and dance orchestras in Dallas, Houston, and Beaumont.[51]

What about high school? The fall semester was soon to start; nevertheless, Louise and her mother decided to accept the conditions of the tour with the intention of returning to school not too long after the start of the term. Louise and her mother might have sensed but could not have known that Louise's formal education was essentially over. She was leaving high school and transferring to the school of hard knocks.

One of Louise's first teachers in her new school was Fred Patterson, manager of the Dallas Palace Theatre, her first engagement as part of the Interstate Theatre tour. He did not refrain from offering advice and direction and was responsible for Louise's professional name. For most of her childhood, Louise was called Mary Louise—"like one word."[52] "We can't get Mary Louise Tobin on the lighted marquee," Patterson told her, "so let's just cut that down to Louise."[53]

Patterson was kind to the petite, fifteen-year-old Louise and gave her professional guidance. He called her into his office and advised: "You have to be careful with your makeup. When you are a little bit older, you'll learn all about makeup." When she received mush notes from the teenage ushers at the theater, notes like "Can I bring you lunch?" and "I like the way you sing," Patterson told her, "those are just ushers. Now, you can't be dating those boys." She also learned quickly that as a member of the entertainment, she was part of the theater workforce. After she entered in the front door of the theater, Patterson said: "You know, honey, the people who work here don't come in the front door. We have a stage door for that."[54] This was just one of the signs that Louise was now entering a world of professionalism.

The Palace Theatre in Dallas featured weekly motion pictures preceded by an orchestra-led "pit program." The entertainment preceding the featured films typically began with a "classical overture," an orchestral arrangement of melodies ranging from musical theater and operetta to Wagnerian music dramas, all considered "the classical unit of music."[55] Following the overture, the most recent "personality," newly discovered young talent debuting that week, sang popular tunes of the day. One cannot help but wonder whether the draw was hearing the child star hit all the right notes or some other dubious fascination with being witness to a ten-year-old girl sing such numbers as "Out for No Good," "You Nasty Man," and "Kissin' Games."[56] In any case, the prevalence of young, female singers arguably had significant influence on the period's singing style. Linda Dahl, in her seminal book on jazz women, characterized Ella Fitzgerald's voice while singing with Chick Webb, for example, as having had "the 'little-girl' quality that was part of the period's singing style, a quality that in her case always seemed to come from a fresh, ever-youthful spirit."[57]

When Louise arrived at the Palace Theatre for her debut, she entered the stage door as directed, happy to follow the rules and protocol of professional, working performers. The films featured that night were the recently released *The Old Fashioned Way* starring W. C. Fields and Walt Disney's animated short in Technicolor, *The Flying Mouse*, pitching the moral to "do your best, be yourself, and life will smile on you," a sentiment most appropriate for Louise's debut. The Palace Theater Orchestra was under the direction of Hyman Charninsky (1899–1977), a longtime bandleader and lifelong Dallas resident, where he conducted orchestras for more than forty years, mostly during the late 1920s through the 1950s.[58] His orchestras played at the Palace Theatre in the 1920s and 1930s and on radio stations WRR, WFAA, and KRLD.[59] As Louise stood on the side of the stage waiting for her cue, Charninsky directed his orchestra through a collection of opera excerpts, including a march from Wagner's *Tannhäuser*, the *Nibelungen* march from *Das Rheingold*, the quartet and "La Donna è Mobile" from Verdi's *Rigoletto*, and the prison scene from Gounod's *Faust*.[60]

Then it was time to introduce the week's new personality and the debut of a young, petite, and brunette blues singer from Denton.[61] Louise was directed up to the microphone, and she sang her opening number: "Pardon My Southern Accent," a lyric by a young Johnny Mercer, recently made popular by several recordings and radio play.

> Pardon my southern accent
> Pardon my southern drawl
> It may sound funny, but oh my honey
> I love y'all
>
> If you don't like my accent
> If you don't like my drawl
> Then just don't listen, let's start kissin'
> I beg y'all
>
> Come on now
> Let me hear you see myself
> And when I say do you love me
> All you got to say is sure enough
>
> Pardon my southern accent
> Didn't I hear you drawl
> Were you just lying or replyin'
> Honey, I love y'all[62]

The audience exploded in applause and continued their warm and enthusiastic reception after her second number, "I Never Knew." Louise was a hit.[63] She was held over for another week,[64] and her name appeared in the next week's *Dallas Morning News* headline, "Louise Tobin Making Hit on Palace Bill." The article also informed readers that she has never had a vocal lesson in her life. . . . [H]er appearances as a singer have hitherto been limited to amateur entertainments at C.I.A. and the State Teachers' College at Denton, and also over radio. She expects to enter C.I.A. in the fall, where she will study voice.[65]

The Denton paper proudly ran the headline, "Denton Singer Well Received at Palace," over the article stating that "Miss Louise Tobin, daughter of Mrs. Hugh Tobin of Denton, was well received by Dallas audiences, according to report, when she made her debut as a blues singer in Dallas pit show Saturday night. She will appear on the program during the week."[66] The Plainview paper also expressed pride of "Miss Louise Tobin of Denton, formerly of Plainview," quoting from a *Dallas News* article that described "Little Louise Tobin [as a] husky-voiced blues singer." "The personality-plus Tobin girl from Denton and 'first out' in a big town engagement, scores heaviest with 'I Never Knew' after making a distinct hit with her opener, 'Pardon My Southern Accent.'"[67]

It was not unusual for singers with orchestras at the time to be labeled blues singers. Benny Goodman's Helen Ward recalled that, "They billed Benny as the King of Swing and the amusing thing is they called me 'America's Premier Bluestress' . . . 'Bluestress'? This was a new one on all of us, and it just went away."[68] Singer Helen Humes had a similar experience: "I just considered myself a singer, but so many people, they want me to be a blues singer. I sing two or three little blues numbers, but I don't like this down-home moanin' and sad blues. I usually like the little fun numbers."[69] For white bands, labeling your vocalist a blues singer bestowed at least rhetorical connections to one of the most significant roots of jazz.

Regarding her debut, Louise recalled: "I went from wearing short dresses to long formals. . . . Then it kind of changed from me coming on stage waving at the audience to coming on stage from the side. I was presented, so to speak."[70] "I looked about twenty-five [years old]. [She was 15!] I was just having a good time, wearing bought dresses and not having to wash dishes. I didn't realize that I was starting out to become a professional."[71] "I went in as a kid and came out as a grown girl. I have earrings on, and I never wore those as a child. And I had lipstick on."[72]

Louise was soon adding to her fast-growing repertory, singing "Were Your Ears Burning?" "Do I Love You," and "Tell Me I'm Wrong" during her third week at the Palace Theatre.[73]

Louise's next stop on her Interstate Theatre tour was Houston, where she appeared for two weeks with the Metropolitan Theater orchestra under the direction of violinist Lloyd Finlay.[74] An article in the *Houston Post* focused on the musical talents of the young Jal Herod "serious of mein [*sic*] and playing with the gift and art of a master thrills his hearers with his violin solos and his playing . . . a real musician and unspoiled boy." The article did not similarly mention Louise's musical talents and skills. Rather, "Louise Tobin, blues singer, is young and vivacious, her dark eyes and bright smile adding much to her fascination for the younger patrons."[75] The different treatment here is not just related to gender. Vocalists traditionally held a rather low status among the participating members of an ensemble. David Stowe in *Swing Changes* writes that, "'Girl singers,' also known as 'Thrushes,' 'chirpies,' 'canaries,' and 'warblers,' were regarded as an unfortunate concession to commercial taste, and according to many jazz critics at the time, geared primarily toward visual pleasure ('seducing the microphone') rather than aural."[76]

After two weeks in Houston, it was on to Beaumont, performing at the Jefferson Theater with Al Kvala [*sic*?] for two weeks before spending a week off back in Denton with her mother, only to return to Dallas the following week "as 'blues singer' for Hyman Charninsky's Palace Theatre orchestra for an indefinite engagement."[77] During this time a local talent agent approached the Tobin family about wanting to hire Louise as a territory band's singer for regular performances at the end of her talent contest tour.

Bernard Goldberg, an agent around Dallas, had heard Louise singing with Charninsky and wanted to book her for a longer engagement at a new nightclub in Arlington.[78] He had a discussion with Louise's family. At the time, they already had reluctantly accepted the fact that Louise's singing commitments to date would delay her return to school, but there were other concerns as well. Goldberg wanted to put her in a nightclub, a significantly different atmosphere than the more family-friendly theaters at which she had been performing. Louise recalled that her family "was not too happy about that, but times were very tough then . . . and they agreed to let me go into a nightclub between Dallas and Fort Worth, and that was major, because I'd never, not only been in a club, I didn't even, I hardly knew how to get there."[79] "It was a whole new world for me."[80] Ultimately, her family allowed Louise to sing in nightclubs, but only if her older sister Dora was allowed to accompany her as chaperone. Goldberg accepted this condition and hired Louise.

She began by taking the place of Broadway singer Lee Morse and singing during the new floor show with Art Hicks and His Orchestra, who was about two weeks into an extended engagement at the new Sylvan club just outside Arlington.

Since the repeal of Prohibition in 1933, the novelty of sitting and sipping had worn off, and customers wanted entertainment. In the daily column of the *Dallas Morning News* titled "Dining and Dancing," readers learned which hotels and clubs boasted the most appealing entertainment. A survey of these announcements reveals a plethora of dance orchestras featuring crooners (men), torch and blues singers (women), dance teams, and novelty numbers. "Even the smallest hole-in-the-corner has some sort of entertainer all the way from a lone crooner to a four and six-piece band."[81]

The Sylvan supper club, "under the personal direction of Maurice, well-known dancer," was located on the Dallas–Fort Worth pike west of Arlington and had opened on June 28, 1934.[82] The club's entertainment bragged a variety of regional and national stars accompanied by a dance orchestra. Perhaps in an effort to distinguish its entertainment from that of other clubs and hotels as well as to evoke a sense of exoticism, patrons of the Sylvan were greeted at the entrance by a maître d'hôtel named "Nickolas, formerly in the service of the King of Rumania."[83] The Chic Scoggins Orchestra played the opening. The club's location drew audiences from both Fort Worth and Dallas. About two weeks after opening, the Sylvan club was advertised as "Dallas and Fort Worth's joint claim to big-time night spots."[84]

The location and musical entertainment were not the club's only attractions. As Louise recalled, "this club, was a very posh club, because there were some very high rollers in Texas, but gambling was illegal. Now, of course, we didn't know that there was gambling in the back of that club, because we weren't allowed back there, but there was."[85]

In late July, the floor show at the Sylvan featured baritone Gene Almy, a Bing Crosby–like crooner, accompanied by Manny Harmon's fifteen-piece Biltmore Hotel dance orchestra.[86] Harmon had replaced Johnny Maloney as master of ceremonies of the club, and the featured artists included Maurine and Norva "doing their famous ballroom dances,

The Sylvan, Louise Tobin with Art Hicks and His Orchestra, 1935. (Courtesy of the Louise Tobin and Peanuts Hucko Jazz Collection)

with Lillian Barnes singing torch songs and the Roddy Twins dancing specialties."[87]

On September 10, another new floor show at the Sylvan club was announced, featuring Art Hicks and his sixteen-piece orchestra.[88] Sitting first chair trumpet was Harry James, who was tall, had piercing blue eyes, was mature for his nineteen years of age, and full of charm. About two weeks after that, new numbers in the floor show included the soon to become a regular member of Hicks's ensemble, "Louise Tobin, blues singer."[89]

Art Hicks was a violinist, singer, and bandleader from Cincinnati, Ohio, and whose past work included directing Paul Spector's band in New York and fronting the Chubb-Steinberg Orchestra in Cincinnati. The latter was organized by music store partners Howard Chubb and Eli Steinberg, neither of whom performed in the ensemble, as a publicity gimmick for their business in the 1920s.[90] This group performed mostly sweet dance music and novelty numbers. When the Chubb-Steinberg Orchestra broke up in the fall of 1925, Hicks and tenor saxophonist (and law student) Paul T. Omer formed the Omer-Hicks Orchestra. Young cornet player Bill Davison was the only member of the Chubb-Steinberg enterprise that Hicks took with him. Hal Willard, in his biography of Wild Bill Davison, writes:

> They booked a major tour through the East that included the Roseland Ballroom in mid-Manhattan, then the top of the heap. And, the band played opposite what was arguably the best band in the country, Fletcher Henderson's. How a fledgling orchestra from the musical hinterlands managed that booking is lost to history. Omer must have had some connections.[91]

After about six weeks at the Roseland Ballroom, the orchestra played a brief engagement at the Brooklyn Paramount and then moved on to Carlin's Park in Baltimore.[92] The band broke up not long after this tour, with Paul Omer becoming a lawyer in New York and Art Hicks ultimately forming his own orchestra.

Hicks's experience fronting bands no doubt served him well. With financial backing from his wealthy father-in-law, Hicks was ready to organize and front his own orchestra. The few published accounts of Hicks suggest that he was a charismatic, competent leader. His business stationery dubbed him as "The Personality Boy."[93] According to Willard, Hicks "played the violin well and sang at least passably well. He was a good showman with an attractive personality."[94] Louise recalled Hicks fondly: "such a nice guy."[95]

The Hicks orchestra included several young Texas musicians whose musical interests leaned more toward the emerging "hot jazz" styles rather than sweet, popular dance music. Harry James, for example, had been playing trumpet in various dance bands around Texas. Most recently working with Ligon Smith and His Orchestra in San Antonio, Harry joined Art Hicks in the summer of 1934.[96] Other notable members of the band were Jimmy McManus, banjo and guitar player from Dallas, and Jimmy Jackson, pianist who, according to Louise, later arranged for Glenn Miller.[97] Louise recalled that Hicks's orchestra, with such players as James, McManus, and Jackson, "was a good swing band. We would have made it except Benny made it. It's all timing."[98]

Louise sang with Hicks at the Sylvan from late September through most of October, and the first part of November, just prior to her sixteenth birthday.[99] Newspaper announcements for the floor shows continued to emphasize a variety of entertainment and dance with such regional, national, and international references as "an American tango and savage mania dance" performed by the Honey Sisters, a soft shoe dance by Bob Bixley, "formerly with Eddie Cantor's revue," a Romanian waltz presented by dance team Alice Louise and Walter LeMae, and a "flying trapeze" number by Art Hicks and His Orchestra. Billed as the "Denton blues singer," Louise was content to sing "whatever they gave me to sing,"[100] including "I Got Rhythm" and "I Never Slept a Wink Last Night."[101]

Discounting the song's sexual innuendos, "I Never Slept a Wink Last Night," words by Andy Razaf and music by Nat Simon, was a fitting title for Louise during her performances at the Sylvan. The club was about thirty miles from Louise's home, and with the last show starting about 1:30 a.m., she often did not get home until about four or five in the morning. She was having trouble staying awake, despite napping in the dressing room between shows. They decided that Louise and her older sister Dora would stay at a hotel nearer the club in Arlington. Harry was the only band member who had a car, so it was arranged that Harry would drive Louise and her sister to the hotel each night. Louise described the circumstances that brought her and Harry together.

> So, after the show, we would get in Harry's Ford and off we would go to Arlington, downtown. It was about six blocks from the club. Anyway, I always rode in the back seat, because my 18-year-old sister rode in the front seat. She was, I think, she was totally enamored with being away from the small town of Denton and near to the big city of Dallas, and she just was having a wonderful time, so she sat in the front seat with Harry, and one night after he had been taking us back to the hotel for maybe a couple of weeks, she said, "You know, Louise, you're going to have to ride in the front seat with Harry tonight, because I have a date with a piano player, and I am going to be riding with him in the back seat," and by the way that piano player turned out to be Jimmy Jackson, who later was one of the wonderful arrangers for Glenn Miller. I'm sure you knew that. Anyway, that's how I met Harry, and I rode in the front seat for the rest of the tour, as you can understand. That was my first date.[102] Harry was only nineteen. Of course, he had been out on the road, and he was pretty suave, for me anyway. As a matter of fact, my mother didn't allow us to date, and I'd never even had a date, but I had one then! He was very charming, so I said to my sister, "I'm riding in the front seat the rest of the time, and you're riding in the back."[103]

This last sentence is worth repeating: "I'm riding in the front seat the rest of the time, and you're riding in the back." Note the active voice. Up to that point, most of Louise's life and music-making decisions were made for her. Recall her singing with Floyd Graham's Saturday Night Stage Band: "Graham told me what to do, and I did it." Her sister, Dora, entered her in the singing contest, which ultimately launched her career. Fred Patterson, manager of the Dallas Palace Theatre, was responsible for shortening her name from Mary Louise to Louise. Her sisters picked out her performance gowns for her, dressed her up, and helped her with her makeup. Despite the noticeable assertiveness that Louise expressed in declaring her desire to sit in the front seat with Harry, she was still just fifteen years old and fast becoming seduced by Harry's charm, self-confidence, and maturity.

One night, when Dora had fallen asleep in the back seat, Harry leaned over and asked Louise, "Do you want to marry me?" She said, "sure." She later recalled that if he had asked, "Do you want to get a Coke? I'd have said, "sure." "As far as I was concerned, I didn't have to go home. I wouldn't have to wash dishes, *I thought*. It turned out I washed a lot of dishes."[104] Harry expressed the sincerity of his feelings for Louise in a letter to his father, Everette, in Beaumont: "Dad, I met the girl I want to spend the rest of my life with. She's from Texas."[105]

The extended engagement at the Sylvan club offered the Hicks ensemble coveted airtime—they were broadcast on WFAA—and an opportunity to prepare for their upcoming tour outside of Texas that would take them through Oklahoma, Ohio, and, the ultimate goal and destination, New York.[106]

In late November, after one more engagement in Texas (at the Hilton Hotel in San Angelo), Louise and her sister Dora packed their bags, said their goodbyes to their family, and left their home state for the first time in their lives, celebrating Thanksgiving and Christmas on the road.[107]

Their first engagement on the tour was in Oklahoma at the elegant Mayo Hotel in Tulsa, playing for luncheon, dinner, and late supper dancing under four bright chandeliers in the Chrystal Ballroom on the sixteenth floor.[108] Louise thought it was the most gorgeous space she had ever encountered—"very impressive." She was awestruck by the magnificence of the place; it was Louise's "first inkling of what glamour might be."

Reflecting Hicks's effort to advance his territory band to national status and recognition, the ensemble was now calling itself "America's Newest Dance Sensation."[109] The bulk of the tour was ahead of them, and the airtime and enthusiastic reception that the band was getting along the way no doubt contributed to the positive mood of the members of the Hicks ensemble. Louise and Harry continued to discuss marriage, agreeing to actively seek a judge who would officiate their relationship.[110]

Louise Tobin and Harry James on their wedding day, May 4, 1935. (Courtesy of the Louise Tobin and Peanuts Hucko Jazz Collection)

Unfortunately, they learned that the state would not allow them to marry, because of Louise's age. They would have to wait, while the Hicks tour continued east.

The Commodore Perry Hotel in Toledo, Ohio, the band's next engagement, was equally luxurious and impressive, but Louise was more taken with the solid ice and snow outside the hotel. As a southern girl, she had seen snow only two or three times in her life.

Louise recalled that during their breaks six or seven of the guys would go down to the lobby in order to listen to a broadcast of Hal Kemp and His Orchestra. "They probably were particularly taken with the horn section," she recalled.[111] Benny Goodman had hit by this time, and on one night off Louise went up to Chicago with Harry and a couple of other musicians from the band to hear Benny.[112] They could not stay in Chicago very long; Hicks had picked up another engagement in Toledo, this one not nearly as glamorous as either the Mayo or Commodore Perry hotels. In late January 1935, the band presented a program for the automobile show in the Toledo Civic Auditorium. The *Toledo Blade* announced that "Miss Tobin will sing several numbers and Hicks' band will play selections arranged specially for this occasion."[113]

After Toledo, Hicks took his orchestra farther east for an engagement in Albany, New York. As Harry and Louise were intensifying their relationship and still looking for a way to make it official, the band was splitting apart. Shortly after their engagement at Chez Ami, Hicks was finding it difficult to meet the organization's expenses, and he asked the band to take a cut in pay. Not willing to work for less than twenty-two dollars a week, Harry and the rest of the band parted ways. Harry and Louise, however, found a way to get married.[114] On May 4, 1935, Louise and Harry drove from Albany to Millerton, New York, where they found a justice of the peace who would marry them on the spot.[115]

Looking at a photo of them taken on their wedding day, Louise shared her memories of the event.

> What happened was that when we decided to get married, we went to Massachusetts and found that you had to wait three days. On the way coming back we stopped in New York to get a sandwich, and they said, "You can get married here in a day." I remember that [my] dress was navy blue and white. I thought it was such a good-looking dress. Those were navy and white shoes that matched it. I remember Harry

had suspenders, and he kept saying, "Remember, you were born in 1916!" I had to be eighteen to get married. And he was so nervous that *I* was going to forget, and *he's* the one who got mixed up, and said, "I, with this wing, I we thed." He was so afraid I was going to forget. I was born in 1918, but I was supposed to say I was born in 1916."[116]

"I was very lucky," Louise recalled. "Harry could have been an axe murderer. What do you know when you are that age? . . . And those eyes just propelled me along the way."[117] For a single woman traveling with a group of men, marriage offered Louise some security. Recalling its positive aspects, Louise stated that marriage "was the best thing that ever happened to me. It kept me safe. I didn't have to put up with most of the stuff that the other girls who were working did. I didn't have to sleep my way or talk my way to the top."[118] On the negative side, Louise said, "When I got married, the world fell apart. We were so young. Harry was nineteen, and I was going on seventeen. What do you know at that age?"[119]

Louise Tobin and Harry James's wedding day, May 4, 1935, close up. (Courtesy of the Louise Tobin and Peanuts Hucko Jazz Collection)

2

Harry and Louise
Paying Their Dues, 1935–1939

We were more trying to establish Harry
than we were trying to establish me.[1]

BY LATE MAY 1935, neither the news of the breakup of the Hicks Orchestra nor Louise's marriage to Harry had made it back to Texas. On May 22, the *Denton Record-Chronicle* published an announcement of Louise and Dora's impending return home: "Word has been received by Mrs. Hugh Tobin from her daughters, Misses Mary Louise and Dora Tobin, who are in Albany, N.Y., where Miss Mary Louise is singing with Art Hicks' orchestra, that they expect to return to Denton in about two weeks for a short visit. . . . She will continue singing after a short vacation here."[2]

Dora, who just one summer ago had bought Louise her first formal dress and high-heeled shoes, who taught her how to wear makeup, and whose charge had been to chaperone her younger sister, returned to Denton without Louise and informed the family that the band had broken up.[3] Even Dora had been unaware of Louise's marriage. According to Peter Levinson, Louise "kept her marriage a secret from Dora and her family for four months. On finally learning the news, Louise's mother tried to have the marriage annulled, but Louise remained stalwart. When the Tobins finally met Harry, however, they were immediately charmed by him and accepted him as a member of the family."[4]

With their departure from the Hicks Orchestra, both Louise and Harry were looking for the next rung on that ladder of professional fulfillment.

Unfortunately, they had different ideas about what that would mean for them, a disjunction they also shared regarding marriage, they were soon to discover.

Back in Texas, they stayed with Harry's parents, Everette and Maybelle, in Beaumont, at least for a short while as they both found work, Harry with Herman Waldman and Louise with Ligon Smith.

The Herman Waldman Orchestra was in town for a one-night engagement, and Harry learned of an opening for a third-chair trumpet player.[5] Harry auditioned and was hired. "He hated it," Louise recalled.[6]

The Waldman Orchestra was a big-name territory dance band active in the 1920s and '30s and based in Dallas with tours primarily of the South and Southwest. The orchestra boasted extended engagements at the Baker and Adolphus Hotels in Dallas, the Peabody in Memphis, and Muehlebach in Kansas City.[7] Harry was not happy working for Waldman, frustrated at having to play third trumpet and such bland, "sweet" dance music; nevertheless, he was making $55 a week, a significant increase from what Hicks had been paying.[8] Harry first went to Louisiana with Waldman for an extended engagement, while Louise stayed in Beaumont with her new in-laws.

Louise would go out to hear Harry a couple of times, but she was eager to sing again and soon found steady work. Not only had she tapped her past experience singing on the Saturday Night Stage Shows on the university campus in Denton, but also Harry had helped her secure an extended singing engagement with Ligon Smith and His Orchestra at the Sylvan club followed by a short regional tour around West Texas.[9] For the last two weeks in June, Louise had double singing engagements on Saturdays, singing a couple of numbers with "'Fessor" Graham's Aces and then heading over to the Sylvan club, singing the floorshow with Ligon Smith, the latter of which could be heard at ten o'clock over station KTAT.[10]

A column in the college's paper, the *Campus Chat*, "Enthusiastically recommended: the stirring voice of Mary Louise Tobin, redolent of wisteria blossoms, and the whisper of rain on fresh green leaves, and the throb in one's throat when one says good-bye."[11] *The Denton Record-Chronicle* was less poetic: The "pretty, petite, personality . . . Miss Louise Tobin"[12] was heard over the airwaves each night over station KTAT."[13]

After their gig at the Sylvan, Ligon Smith took Louise and his orchestra, now being billed as "the South's finest novelty band," to Lubbock,

Amarillo, and Lake Cisco, returning to Dallas for a two-week engagement at the Ice Parade. But first, having learned of her marriage to Harry,
Louise's family posted an official announcement and hosted a proper
wedding shower. On the Wednesday (July 24) prior to her departure
to Lubbock and West Texas, Louise was back in Denton. Almost three
months after her marriage, the *Denton Record-Chronicle* announced the
"Marriage of Miss Tobin."[14] Her mother and sisters agreed that since
Harry had been working in Louisiana that the marriage would have to
have taken place "in Shreveport, La., July 18."[15] With the announcement
was a description of the reception:

> Mrs. Hugh Tobin entertained with tea and miscellaneous shower.
> [snip] The home was beautifully decorated with Shasta daisies, yellow
> zinnias and marigolds. The dining table was laid with lace cloth over
> yellow satin and lighted with yellow tapers in antique candelabra. A
> matching bowl held daises. Mrs. Byron Henderson poured punch and
> Miss Dora Tobin kept the bride's register. Both are sisters of the bride.
> [snip] Mrs. James went to Dallas today, where she will finish a con-
> tract as singer with the Ligon Smith orchestra. In about 10 days[16] the
> couple will go to Chicago, where James will play with Ben Pollock's
> Orchestra in Lincoln Tavern. Mrs. James also has a contract to sing
> in Chicago. She has won renown as a singer during the past year, and
> has sung in Dallas and other Texas cities and in New York and Shreve-
> port, La. James is a son of Mr. and Mrs. Everett James of Houston [*sic*;
> Beaumont].[17]

Louise expressed her appreciation to her mother and sisters for giving
her such a beautiful wedding shower, and then she was back on the road
with Ligon Smith, heading to Lubbock, for a return Saturday night (July
27) dance engagement at the Auditorium. The local paper advertised
Louise as the "featured blues singer," a former resident of Plainview,
and "well known to a number of people of Lubbock and vicinity."[18] The
Saturday, July 27, 1935, *Morning Avalanche* detailed the Ligon Smith
Orchestra and their program.

> Ligon Smith's return to Lubbock for a dance engagement Saturday
> night at the Auditorium means an inundation of new dance rhythm
> and hits. His orchestra has a repertoire that includes the latest compo-
> sitions heard in new motion picture productions and radio programs.

Smith is bringing with him what has been termed "the South's finest group of novelty entertainers." Miss Louise Tobin, brunette blues
singer, Jimmy Stewart, comic trap drummer, and Jimmy McManus,
Irish tenor, are featured, but every member of the band takes part in
special numbers Smith presents.

Stewart, original drummer of the Smith band who just recently re-
joined it, is famed for his interpretation of "Have You Had Your Corn
Today," which has earned him the moniker of "The South's Greatest
'Hill-Billy' singer."

Smith directs the thirteen-piece orchestra from the piano. The band
carries its own loudspeaker system.[19]

Sunday was a travel day for their well-advertised Monday night performance at The Nat in Amarillo. The *Amarillo Globe* noted that Miss
Louise Tobin, "a Texas girl who has been singing with some of the leading orchestras of the nation during the past year, is the featured female
personality."[20]

After an engagement at Lake Cisco, "Where West Texas Dances," the
Ligon Smith Orchestra returned to Dallas to perform on the *Ice Parade*,
a thirty-minute radio program sponsored by the Southwestern Ice Manufacturers' Association broadcast from the WFAA studio in Dallas.[21]
The *Dallas Morning News* announced that "Louise Tobin, female heart
interest of the Ligon combination, is not just an ordinary blues singer, but
she also knows how to put over a sweet or personality number. She will
make her *Ice Parade* debut singing 'Devil in the Moon.' The song 'Night
Wind,' will serve to introduce the tenor soloist Jimmie McManus."[22]

McManus, "a banjoist by trade," was a well-known, versatile Dallas
musician. He was the "boy" singer with the band. As part of the floor
show, Louise and McManus were featured in a duet arrangement of
"Sunday Go to Meetin' Time."[23] Prior to working with Smith, McManus
was part of the rhythm section of Art Hicks's orchestra, so he and Louise
had experience performing together.

Louise liked working for Ligon Smith, and he liked Louise. She recalled
that he was like a daddy to everybody.[24] In striking contrast, she did not
have kind words for bandleader Charlie Davis. Louise had one more
singing engagement to fulfill before leaving for Chicago and that was
working for Davis.

Without a break from singing with Smith, "the little Denton songstress" joined the floor show at the Adolphus Hotel along with Sally Gay,

the featured entertainer with Charlie Davis and His Orchestra. Gay was scheduled to leave the band the following week "to go to New York to open theater engagements."[25]

Charlie Davis was from Indiana and had formed his dance band in 1923, touring through the 1920s and '30s. Davis and his orchestra boasted national success, having headlined with Duke Ellington at the Paramount Theatre in New York City in 1930.[26]

If Davis hired Louise with the intention to replace the soon-departing Sally Gay as featured singer, his hopes were dashed after about two weeks. Davis's side of the story is not known. He did not mention Louise in his autobiography. Louise would not elaborate, but she rarely spoke derogatively about anyone during interviews. Regarding Davis, however: "I didn't like him. He was a bullish bandleader."[27] Louise benefited from certain advantages working with Ligon Smith that she did not have with Davis. Smith was introduced to Louise by his former hot trumpeter Harry James and most likely had been familiar with Louise's Dallas experience, singing with fellow Dallas music director Hyman Charninsky as well as her work with Hicks. Smith's orchestra recently added the versatile and entertaining Jimmy McManus, who had worked up a couple of novelty numbers with Louise during the Art Hicks tour. Hence, with Smith, Louise enjoyed the benefits of familiarity and experience, both of which she lacked with Charlie Davis, who was a seasoned bandleader and at the time was at the end of his ten-year commitment to his wife to quit the band business.[28] Perhaps Davis was expecting more of an act with Louise, more novelty. The Davis ensemble fundamentally was an entertainment show band more than a sweet-sounding orchestra. The ensemble's visible shtick may have been engaging for live audiences, but the music was arguably less aurally satisfying, as evidenced when radio broadcasts did not result in fan mail and future gigs.[29] In his autobiography, Davis concluded that, "stage band music just wasn't tailored for the airwaves. The smart money kept on telling Charlie's lads to quit worrying about stage excellence and concern themselves with what goes into that microphone—not what people out front were seeing and applauding; but the lads paid little attention to advice."[30]

Louise never worked with Davis again. Shortly after this engagement, Harry got a call from drummer and bandleader Ben Pollack, who invited him to Chicago for an extended engagement at Lincoln Gardens.

Pollack, "The Dean of Sophisticated Swing," had been developing a reputation for hiring talented white musicians who went on to make their own marks as bandleaders. Pollack hired Benny Goodman in August 1925, giving him his first significant professional job.[31] By 1928 arranger and trombonist Glenn Miller joined the band. Peter Levinson, in *Trumpet Blues*, writes that "by September of that year the Pollack band had become established, and, according to bandleader Charlie Barnet, was renowned among musicians as the only white big band playing real jazz.[32] The band broke up in late 1934, and Pollack was again looking for versatile players who were adept at both dance music and hot, improvisatory jazz.

Harry fit the bill and joined Pollack in November 1935, and, as Louise recalled, "that was his dream, because that was the swingin'-est band in the whole country, so he was just absolutely thrilled, because everybody on that band was a wonderful player, and Pollack was primarily a jazz musician."[33] Their first gig at the Lincoln Gardens earned James $75 a week.[34] Harry and Louise moved into the Carlos Hotel, where most of the band members were staying, and to the delight of baseball fan Harry, many of the ballplayers with the Chicago Cubs. It was a dive, but the young couple were living in Chicago, a city whose jazz scene was characterized by both the community of African American musicians in the South Side black-and-tan cabarets and white dance bands that had by the mid-1920s included what Chicago jazz historian William Howland Kenney described as "an inner circle of brash young whites . . . who strongly identified with Chicago's jazz scene and devoted themselves with a religious fervor to jazz music and the jazz life."[35] According to Kenney, "banjoist Eddie Condon, did a great deal to promote the notion of an inner circle of true believers, whom he labeled in 1927 'the Chicagoans,' and later 'the barefoot mob' or the Condon 'Gang.' They were jazz zealots who played a definable style called 'Chicago Jazz.'"[36]

Living and working in Chicago proved to be transformative for Louise both personally and professionally. She arrived in winter 1935 as the wife of Pollack's new trumpeter Harry James. By the end of the following year, Louise had become an experienced, self-reliant professional singer and entertainer. But these were tough money days, and while Harry had steady work with Pollack, Louise found it difficult to get singing gigs.

Chicago in the mid-1930s had all of the institutions of a thriving music scene: a multitude of nightclubs, hotels, movie theaters, dance halls, sheet music publishers, radio stations, automatic music machine manufacturers, record makers, and piano roll makers.[37] All of which provided opportunity as well as challenges for newcomers to the scene.

Musicians are faced with many challenges on arriving in a new city, and among them is penetrating the defining walls of the local music scene. Louise found that, despite her experience of the past fifteen months performing on the Interstate Theatre circuit and then with the orchestras of Art Hicks, Ligon Smith, and Charlie Davis, it was difficult to get work in such a thriving music scene as Chicago's. Participation in what can be labeled a translocal music scene did not translate into automatic acceptance in local music scenes.[38] "I did nightclub casuals when I could, but I wasn't very professional. I didn't know how to get jobs. I didn't work a lot. I worked as much as I could," Louise recalled. From her connections to "guys on the band and their wives," Louise worked a number of low-paying club dates shortly after the first of the year, 1936. "But it was good, because I don't think Harry was making much money, and I didn't make much money on those jobs, but it was the experience that I got that was so good for me at that time. I was learning a lot all the time."[39]

The first two weeks in January, Louise sang on the 7:30 p.m. radio broadcast featuring WGN orchestra leader and radio personality Harold Stokes.[40] A conductor, composer, and arranger, Stokes had worked with the Jean Goldkette Orchestra, the renowned ensemble of 1926–27 that had included Bix Beiderbecke, Frank Trumbauer, and arranger Bill Challis and had taken over the leadership of the WGN orchestra, a studio band, about which a *Down Beat* writer observed, "closely resembles that of Benny Goodman at times."[41] Asked about this experience, Louise recalled the radio date but did not remember anything about Stokes.[42]

On January 21, the *Daily Times*, Chicago, announced that "Louise Tobin, singer of popular ballads, joins [Leonard] Keller's orchestra for a week's personal appearances at Marbro Theater, opening Friday [Jan 24]."[43]

Leonard Keller was a young violinist, bandleader, composer, and arranger; he had dubbed himself "The Tone Poet" and was also known as "The Poet of the Violin." Keller had an academic background in classical music and had been getting favorable press in Chicago. In the summer of 1936, he hired the Andrews Sisters who first appeared with him at the Lowry Hotel in St. Paul, Minnesota.[44] Keller's dance band since the summer of 1934 had also regularly appeared in the Walnut Room of the Hotel Bismarck, perhaps suggesting the ensemble's second-tier status. Jim and Wynette Edwards's *Chicago Entertainment between the Wars, 1919–1939* includes a photograph of Keller's orchestra with the following caption:

> The dance bands that appeared in the Walnut Room of the Hotel Bismark [*sic*] were less renowned than the bands that appeared in the larger ballrooms. During the days of the tango's popularity, the Leonard Keller Orchestra mounted productions that featured a lead singer with a dance troupe of nine to get the diners in the mood for dancing [to] the sultry music.[45]

An announcement in the July 1934 *Down Beat* described his "exceptionally good band" as featuring "original romantic type of music built around strings and woodwinds, using only for brass one trumpet and one trombone. Keller himself is featured in violin solos which are rendered very artistically."[46]

Just as a few professional doors seemed to be opening for Louise in Chicago, she received what she later recalled as the first "punch in the gut" from Harry. During our first interview in July 2009, she described it this way:

> So, when the [Pollack] band decided to go on the road, Harry said, "I think you better stay here until we get on a location, and as soon as we get on a location, I'll send for you." That was my first big mistake. But it's ok. So, it was kind of frightening to me, because I'd always had my sister with me, and the gal's name who helped me so much was named Evelyn [Pollack's bass player's (Thurman Teague) wife]. But Evelyn was going to stay in town, and so I felt a little bit better about that, but I didn't feel very secure, but, you know, I was brought up in Texas, and you just did whatever your husband told you to do. It didn't matter. (I'm glad he didn't have any enemies he'd wanted me to go shoot, because I would have just done it. You know? I mean, it's just that simple.) So, he told me to stay there, so I stayed there. Harry was a lot older than his nineteen years, because of his experience. He'd been around a lot. So, anyway, I stayed. And I didn't work very much after they left. I don't remember exactly if it was because I was just frightened or just couldn't get the jobs. I don't remember why I didn't

work much, but I didn't. That was a long, hard period. [Visibly upset.] Can we stop here for a minute? [Interview stopped.][47]

Peter Levinson, about Pollack tours, writes that "the band was booked by MCA and was constantly on the road throughout the country—from the Cotton Club in Culver City (Los Angeles) to Hamid's 'Million Dollar Pier' in Atlantic City."[48] Harry told Louise that once the band got settled in a city for an extended engagement, he would send for her and that until that time, he would wire money to the Carlos Hotel in order to cover her room and board. Louise could eat her meals in the hotel café.

Louise soon found that her relationship with Evelyn grew from friendship to professional mentor. In addition, two musicians staying at the hotel were also wonderful to her. Pianist Charlie LaVere taught her "Truckin'," rehearsing her for free in a small room by the lobby, which had a piano.[49] A guitarist from the Horace Heidt band named Dick Morgan taught her "Stars Fell on Alabama" and "Deep Purple." But, for Louise it was a difficult, lonely time.

She continued to develop her singing, learning all of the new songs that she heard over the airwaves. Louise would soon learn that in order to be a successful singer, she had to learn the world of theater, that she had to do something more than just get up on the stage and sing. "I was not a professional. I became a professional in Chicago."[50]

Weeks passed with Harry still out on the road. "We talked and occasionally met. He'd write, and I'd write, and occasionally he'd send some money home. It was convenient for him. He could wear his wedding ring and stay out of trouble," she stated sarcastically.[51]

Then, one morning when Louise sat down in the café for her breakfast, the owner of the hotel who "was a big gangster, said 'You're not eating in the coffee shop anymore.' I was sixteen and a grownup said that to me. I just figured 'Well, I guess I'm not going to eat.'"[52] Harry had stopped sending money. Despite the occasional club date, Louise was not working, and she had little money of her own. She later admitted in an interview that no matter how bad it got in Chicago, she didn't want to go home.[53]

Louise learned about an opening in a large stage show that had been making headlines and was preparing for an extended tour heading east and ending in New York. *Bring on the Dames* was the brainchild of Mike Todd and featured the "Moth to a Flame" dance.

It had been raining when Louise arrived for her audition for Mike

Todd, and she was soaked and looked vulnerable. Louise overheard the star of the show, Eva Gardner, a.k.a. Muriel Page, speak openly to Todd: "Todd, you better hire her, or she's going to get killed."[54] Louise looked back on Muriel Page as "my guardian." "I learned everything on that show. Muriel took me under her wing. I will never forget her. She wasn't that much older than I was, but she seemed older," Louise recalled.[55]

Louise was hired and went on tour with Todd's *Bring on the Dames* and a company that ultimately included Flame Girl Muriel Page and her mother, eight showgirls and twenty-four chorus girls, Pete, the Personality Penguin, and comedian Harry Savoy.[56] "It was not a very good show. It was his [Mike Todd's] first show," Louise recalled.[57]

After touring with *Bring on the Dames*, in July 1936 Louise was back in Texas singing with Ligon Smith and His Orchestra for an engagement in Amarillo at "The Nat." The Amarillo Natatorium opened in July 1922 and initially featured a swimming pool, which in 1926 was covered and converted to a dance floor. In the early 1930s, under a new owner, the establishment was renamed The Nat Dine and Dance Palace and during the big band era featured such entertainers as Benny Goodman, Guy Lombardo, Duke Ellington, the Dorsey Brothers, and Harry James.[58]

In the following month, Louise was back in Dallas, singing with Carlos Shaw and His Orchestra at the Chez Maurice.[59]

In September and October of 1936 Louise joined Harry in New York, where he was making his recording debut. On September 1, he "recorded four tunes with The Rhythm Wreckers (the group, from Pollack's band, included Pollack himself on drums)," and two weeks later, September 15–16, he recorded with the full Pollack ensemble (Brunswick and Vocalion). On October 2, Harry recorded four tunes with Chuck Bullock and his Levee Loungers for Meltone Records.[60]

Louise had been strengthening and capitalizing on her own connections and experience. One job seemed to lead to another. Indeed, her work with Mike Todd served her well. Through that connection, she found work in New York City performing at the 3,500-seat Loew's State Theatre with former *Bring on the Dames* comedian Harry Savoy with whom she provided fill and "threw him a few lines."[61] George Hall and His Orchestra was the musical foundation of the show.

A review of a later version of Savoy's routine published in *Billboard* captures the spirit of Louise's experience with Savoy. In this instance, the person throwing Savoy a few lines was "a tall redhead (announced as Helen Holden)."

> Click of the bill is Harry Savoy. Lad's method of selling gags, even the oldies, is out of the top drawer. His sidewalks-of-New York accent, sentences left hanging in mid-air and stage manner wins him a terrific hand. Some of his stuff runs to blue but crowd laughed and could have taken more. For encore Savoy brought on a tall redhead (announced as Helen Holden) who played straight for a little more blue stuff. After three curtain calls comic begged off.[62]

Louise Tobin promotional photograph by Chicago-based celebrity photographer Maurice Seymour, ca. 1937. (Photo by Maurice Seymour. Courtesy of Ronald Seymour)

Pollack and His Orchestra had another recording date later that year, during which they recorded "Peckin," Harry's composition and arrangement, on December 18, 1936, for Variety Records.

According to Levinson, "Harry James's musical reputation was growing rapidly. On two separate occasions during 1936, Tommy Dorsey wired James offering him a job. Two bandleaders whose music was considerably more conservative, Henry Busse and Horace Heidt, also made him offers to join their respective bands during the same year. He turned them all down."[63]

The day after his recording of "Peckin," Benny Goodman listened to a broadcast from the Cotton Club in Culver City. He called the club, asked to speak with Harry, inviting him to join his band at the Madhattan Room of the Hotel Pennsylvania in New York and offering him $150 a week plus train transportation. Goodman confirmed the offer the next day by telegram."[64]

"We were more trying to establish Harry than we were trying to establish me," Louise recalled of the early years with Harry.[65] With Benny Goodman for 1937 and most of 1938, Harry found himself among the most notable trumpet players, performing and recording with Goodman and some of the top players, leading his own recordings on Brunswick, and was voted leading trumpet player in both *Down Beat* and *Metronome* magazine polls.[66]

When Harry began working with Goodman, he roomed with pianist Jess Stacy while in New York. Louise joined Harry there, and when the band went on the road,

> I lived with one of the wives. Her husband, Brownie [Vernon Brown?], was one of Benny's trombone players. Their apartment had two bedrooms, and Harry paid for me to stay in one of them. This woman was quite a bit older than I, and I liked her a lot. But they no sooner left town, then she came home with a guy. I was terrified, absolutely terrified. I didn't want Harry to think that I was playing the game, you know, which she was, no question. I told Harry about it. "I don't think I should stay here." And I told him about it, and he said, "Well, so long as you lock your door . . ." I was so young.[67]

Eventually, Harry and Louise moved to the Whitby Apartments, located on West Forty-Fifth Street between Eighth and Ninth Avenues in the heart of New York City's theater district.[68]

Harry James with Benny Goodman Orchestra. (Courtesy of the Louise
Tobin and Peanuts Hucko Jazz Collection)

There was not much work for Louise in 1937, although she accepted
an opportunity to return to Loew's State Theatre, performing again with
Savoy.[69] During these months, while Harry was working with Goodman
full time, rehearsing, performing, and recording, Louise was more of an
"orchestra wife" than professional singer. She and the other wives went
to movies and hung out together, keeping their distance from their boys
in the band. "Wives had hard lives, because they were not included in the
band life, per se. They would hang together, go out to movies, and they

would take me with them. They looked for things to do. Some became bad alcoholics. Most did not stay married."[70]

"Benny knew Harry was married, but he didn't know me, because I was never around the band," Louise recalled. "The only time I was around the band is when the guys—two or three of them lived in the same apartment house as we did—and we—and I got to know the wives, and it's kind of interesting. None of those wives were allowed around the band much."[71]

Louise recalled that "Harry had some funny little rules—fetishes, you might say—one of them was never let the wives around the band; they cause trouble. I didn't like that, but whatever he said, that's the way it was."[72] When I asked Louise about her experience witnessing Goodman's 1938 Carnegie Hall concert, she said that she and the other wives were not given tickets to see the performance. Nevertheless, she admitted that they had "snuck backstage" and heard the performance from the wings.

Photo taken by Harry James of Louise Tobin on the roof of the Paramount Hotel, New York City, 1938. (Courtesy of the Louise Tobin and Peanuts Hucko Jazz Collection)

Reflective of her distance from Goodman's band when Harry was leading the trumpet section, *Billboard* magazine reported on October 1, 1938, that

> the boys in Benny Goodman's Band are blaming trumpeter Harry James for holding out; the Goodman lads had been raving about the singing of Louise Tobin at Nick's Greenwich Village nitery—and when they advised James to go down there for an earful, he calmly informed them that Miss Tobin only happens to be Mrs. James.[73]

In 1938 Louise continued to pick up a few singing engagements, and by the end of the year had caught the attention of radio personality and columnist for the New York *Daily Mirror*, Nick Kenny.[74] Titled "Nick Kenny Speaking," Kenny's column combined verse, jokes with his commentary, and recommendations on current radio programs, one of which he hosted in the mid-1930s titled "The Nick Kenny Radio Hour." Kenny touted Louise as "the most promising girl singer we have heard in years," and the following week on December 29 Louise was featured on his radio program and headlined Kenny's "Road to Fame" column. "Louise Tobin, Texas thrush . . . hailed as a combination of Maxine Sullivan and Helen Morgan will sing 'Two Sleepy People' and 'Exactly Like You.'"[75] Indeed, her "road to fame" was about to take her to new heights under the direction of none other than the King of Swing.

Louise Tobin on the Nick Kenny Radio Show, 1938. (Courtesy of the Louise Tobin and Peanuts Hucko Jazz Collection)

3

Singing with the King of Swing, 1939

There'll be a change in the weather, a change in the sea.
Before long there'll be a change in me.
My walk will be different, my talk, and my name,
Ain't nothin' 'bout me gonna be the same.[1]

FOR BOTH Harry and Louise, 1939 was a transformative year on a grand scale. In January, Harry left the Benny Goodman Orchestra, following Gene Krupa in that great leap from sideman to bandleader. "I think that for both James and Krupa were the only two guys that Benny didn't inhibit," Louise recalled. Though it proved a difficult transition for both Harry and Gene Krupa, Harry's orchestra ultimately had more staying power. Louise remembered these early years, however, as "tough money days."[2] She continued to sing at odd jobs around New York to supplement their income.

Harry's time was filled with the numerous demands associated with starting a big band, from hiring personnel, designing music stands, and selecting uniforms, to developing the arrangements. In addition to dealing with these responsibilities, Harry was in the studio. One notable session centered on a recording of Sammy Lerner and Ben Oakland's "Everybody's Laughing" with Billie Holiday and Goodman pianist Teddy Wilson. While no doubt aesthetically satisfying, pragmatically and economically such sessions most often fell short; again, times were tough financially.[3] By the end of January, Harry was no longer earning the big salary of $350 a week playing with Goodman, and, until he was able to launch his own orchestra, he joined the 17.2 percent of unemployed Americans in 1939.[4] James biographer Peter Levinson quotes Harry as stating that, "When I started the band, I had $400—that was my bank account."[5] Supporting a big band was expensive, and Harry was only able to hire the musicians and start his tour with a loan from Goodman, ultimately costing him $43,000.[6] Through these hard times, Louise's freelancing became their primary source of income. Since her time in Chicago, the money she earned by singing in various bands and orchestras allowed her to become more financially independent from Harry. "Money was very scarce, so I was doing club dates and 'casuals' when I could . . . just to have a little extra cash, so we could eat. I went to work at Nick's in the Village with Bobby."[7]

Nick's in Greenwich Village, Frank Sinatra, and John Hammond

Trumpeter Bobby Hackett (1915–1976), who had performed with Goodman at the historic 1938 Carnegie Hall concert, was leading a small group at Nick's in Greenwich Village.[8] The owner of the club was Dixieland jazz enthusiast Nick Rongetti. Writing about Nick's, Warren Vaché Sr. noted that "among the customers on any given night would be stars of the stage, the movies, and radio; college students, writers, politicians, and especially musicians. To quite a few musicians it became a second home, the place to hang out on off nights, and maybe be invited to sit in. To others, and the growing coterie of jazz fans and record collectors, it was a landmark, a place to visit whenever they were in town."[9] Louise recalled how she began singing with Bobby Hackett: "Nick's was well known in New York. Of course, I knew who Bobby was, though at the time I didn't know him personally. There was a wonderful piano player that worked with him named Dave Bowman. I was friends with his wife and somehow or another I got word that Bobby liked my singing and that I should go down to Nick's and sing a couple of tunes. Bobby was from Rhode Island: [speaking slowly, sounding like Bobby] 'Well, if you don't have anything to do, and you don't want much money, we'd like to have ya.' It just took him forever to say anything. He was a darling, and that's how I came to go to work at Nick's."[10] That was in the fall of 1938.

One night, as Louise was getting ready to go to work in the Village, she heard WNEW's "Dance Parade" program. There was a young singer performing with Harold Arden's band at the Rustic Cabin in Englewood, New Jersey. As Louise recalled, "We were looking for a boy singer. We already had a girl singer, Bernice Byers. Harry was lying across the bed. He was thinking about his band; I'm sure. I was getting ready to go to work, and back in that day there were small speakers mounted on the walls of the room to broadcast the radio. I said, 'Honey, you might want to get up and hear this guy. He sounds like a pretty good singer.' I found out later that he and Claude Bowen went over to the Rustic Cabin that night."[11] According to George Simon, Harry asked the manager where he could find the singer and was told, "We don't have a singer. But we do have an emcee who sings a little bit."[12] Harry signed Frank Sinatra to his band that night.

"While all this was happening, John Hammond came down to Nick's," Louise continued. "He came in a lot. I didn't realize that he was coming in to hear me. I guess he wanted to be sure I was consistent. But he was very, very nice to me."[13] Hammond first wrote about hearing Louise with Hackett at Nick's in his column for *Down Beat* titled "J. Hammond Says," in October 1938. Likely thinking of Louise as a potential vocalist for Goodman, he wrote:

> When I returned to New York a most agreeable surprise awaited me at Nick's, where Bobby Hackett plays. Louise Tobin, who happens to be Mrs. Harry James, is singing there with taste, warmth, and a small but very attractive voice. And I know of a certain band leader who might well keep his eyes and ears open.[14]

Jazz enthusiast, critic, and impresario Hammond, through his interest and talent as a producer and music lover, was ultimately involved in the careers of such musicians as Billie Holiday, Pete Seeger, Aretha Franklin, Bob Dylan, Bruce Springsteen, Stevie Ray Vaughan, and Benny Goodman, among others.[15] Indeed, Hammond suggested that Louise would be a fine replacement for Martha Tilton (1915–2006), whom Goodman had fired on learning that she was having a relationship with the band's manager, Leonard Vannerson. Tilton was out; Vannerson kept his job.[16]

Louise recalled that while Goodman was out on the road, Hammond "called Benny, spoke to Benny about me. He told Benny, 'if you want to hear her, she's going to have to come to where you are.'"[17] Goodman agreed, and Louise caught the next plane to Cleveland, Ohio. When she arrived at the theater, Louise saw a man holding drumsticks, lounging just inside the stage door. She asked him if that was the place where Benny Goodman was rehearsing. He said, "I hope so, I'm the new drummer. But it's not a rehearsal, we are performing." This was drummer Nick Fatool, who had joined the band the same day as did Louise.[18] Goodman himself had yet to arrive.

"You don't need a rehearsal. You're just going to sing the blues."

Despite her marriage to his former trumpet star, Louise did not recall meeting Goodman more than perhaps by way of a casual introduction. "Benny had a rule," she stated during our first interview, "Wives were not allowed around the band; too distracting."[19] Louise remembered her exchange with Goodman when he first arrived at the theater for what she thought would be a rehearsal and her audition: "'Can you sing the blues?' and I said, 'I can sing the blues. So, he said, 'that's what you're going to do on the show [as] an audition,' . . . that was not a problem for me. So, he hired me. 'You don't need a rehearsal,' he said. 'You're just going to sing the blues.'"[20]

No rehearsal. Her audition would be a live performance, cold. Goodman had invited her to sing on Hammond's recommendation alone. "He hadn't heard me," Louise recalled, "and it was a good thing, for some reason I wasn't scared. I was never around the band very much when Harry was with the Goodman band, and I had only seen Benny from a distance, and I wasn't scared of him. I didn't know enough to be scared of him. And that was the only reason I sang well, I'm sure, because it was not a big thing to me. I just loved working with Bobby [Hackett], but I wanted to play with Benny. He had the top swing band in the world."[21]

Louise herself soon discovered that playing and singing the blues contrasted sharply with both singing the standard dance repertory and the rehearsal requirements necessary to tackle the intricate charts of Goodman's new arranger, Eddie Sauter (1914–1981).[22] Indeed, as blues scholar Paul Oliver has written, "In much of the white jazz of the 1930s . . . the inclusion in the repertory of blues was at best infrequent and was then generally incorporated as a token gesture."[23] Nevertheless, Goodman routinely asked Tobin to sing the blues in live performances.

When asked what blues she sang for her audition, Louise said, "just a southern blues."[24] Thanks to surviving "Air Check" recordings of several

Promotional photos for *Camel Caravan* radio show with Benny Goodman and Louise Tobin, 1939. (Photo by Tom Fitzsimmons)

broadcasts of the Goodman Orchestra performing on the May 16, 1939, *Camel Caravan* radio show, we can hear Louise sing a version of blues close to what she might have sung on that first performance about one week prior.[25]

As Louise had done before with Bobby Hackett and others, she made up her own words, and, in contrast to an unissued studio recording, later referred to as "Louise Tobin Blues," addressed in more detail below, her lyrics for her live performance were autobiographical and a fitting introduction to Goodman fans noting the missing Martha Tilton. Lyricist Johnny Mercer was emceeing the broadcast, and he with Goodman introduced Tobin, an introduction that reflects the emphasis on the visual aspects of swing era vocalists as well as the value placed on their ability to sing the blues.

> **Goodman:** "Under new business in tonight's meeting, we have a candidate for admission to our candlelight club. She's five foot two,"
>
> **Mercer:** "Eyes of blue?"
>
> Goodman: "No. Brown and black hair and very attractive."
>
> **Mercer:** "Never mind the details. Can she sing, too?" [laughs from audience]
>
> **Goodman:** "Listen, VP. We musicians have a way of finding out things like that. Whenever we want to get the lowdown on whether a person can really swing, we try them out on the blues."
>
> **Mercer:** "And, candidate, that's your cue. Step up to the mic, and state your qualifications."[26]

After this introduction, the orchestra does little more than set the tempo and key, and Louise starts singing:

> My last name's Tobin; my first name is Louise.
> My last name's Tobin; my first name is Louise.
> And my only aim, is that I aim to please.
>
> I was born in Texas; raised in Texas, too.
> I was born in Texas; raised in Texas, too.
> But I came up north to sing some blues for you.

One day while I was walking by a studio,
One day while I was walking by a studio,
John Hammond heard me swingin,' swingin' so soft and low.

So, Johnny told Benny, and that's how things began.
So, Johnny told Benny, and that's how things began.
Now, here I am on your Camel Caravan.

Now, in conclusion let me thank you all.
Now, in conclusion let me thank you all.
And, thank you Mr. Goodman for the use of the hall.

While her performance followed the standard harmonic and stanzaic structure of the blues, textually, in its autobiographical narrative, it deviates from what ethnomusicologist Jeff Todd Titon has described as the overarching theme in blues lyrics, namely, freedom from mistreatment.[27] Indeed, rather than singing about being a victim of mistreatment by her man, the men involved in this blues—Johnny Mercer (with his introduction), John Hammond (with his recommendation), and Goodman's use of the hall—all appear to be the primary agents involved in her evident professional success, singing with the Goodman orchestra on a live, nationally broadcast radio program.

Not mentioned in Louise's autobiographical blues lyric was Harry, her husband of four years who was on the road with his own band. After an initial one-week engagement at the Garden Terrace of the Benjamin Franklin Hotel in Philadelphia (February 1939), where they had coveted air time, Harry took his band on a grueling schedule of one-nighters. He had heard Louise's performance with Goodman and after the broadcast wired Louise, stating flatly: "If I hadn't heard it, I wouldn't have believed it."[28] Louise recalled her reaction to Harry's message:

> This telegram devastated me, because he seemed so skeptical about my talent. He didn't want me to sing. He always wanted to know where I was, though he may not have wanted me with him. He never said anything complimentary to me, and I remember someone quoted him in *Metronome* saying, "the reason Louise is singing with Benny is because I'm not making a lot of money, and we need the money." Despite this, one of the guys in his band told me he always listened to all of our broadcasts. Harry was an enigma, but this telegram really made me mad. He didn't want me to sing. [pause] I never knew why.[29]

In many ways, James signifies the stereotypical 1930s man. He wanted Louise to be dependent on him, and he also wanted his own freedoms and independence. Louise's professional achievements, actualized in her singing with Goodman, at the time among the most popular and financially successful orchestras in the land—"Everybody wanted to work with Benny," she recalled—were in no small part due to her talents and accumulated experience working in Texas, Chicago, and New York. In many ways, her tenure with the Goodman orchestra exemplifies the stereotypical 1930s female big band singer and allowed her to achieve a degree of independence from her husband, Harry—financial, professional, and personal—and singing the blues, in particular, provided her more creative and expressive control.

In addition to her blues, Louise also sang the chorus to a new Fletcher Henderson arrangement of "It's Never Too Late."

Louise received favorable reviews of her first performances with Goodman. Describing both the visual and vocal aspects of her performance and in a language typical of the era, the May 17, 1939, issue of *Variety* described her as "an eye-filler with good swing pipes."[30] Considering her replacement of Martha Tilton as Goodman's vocalist, Joseph F. Laredo wrote that "Tobin countered her predecessor's wholesome girl-next-door appeal with a sensual quality and an undeniably bluesy approach to her ballads."[31]

Louise was soon no longer "filling in for the ailing Martha Tilton"; she was Goodman's new vocalist. Indeed, shortly after Louise first sang with Goodman on the *Camel Caravan* radio show, newspapers announced that "Benny Goodman will introduce a new girl singer, Louise Tobin, a brunette Texan," and that "Miss Louise Tobin of Denton, a well-known singer in Denton, has been selected to sing with Benny Goodman's orchestra, and report has it that he said that she was the finest singer that he had ever had with his group. The Goodman orchestra is on tour now over the United States."[32] An article for *Tempo* magazine titled "Louise Remains" stated that, "Louise Tobin . . . will continue to hold the spot of featured vocalist."[33]

"Louise" and Other Changes in the Goodman Band

The vocal department was just one area of many that Goodman was changing in 1939. The May 24, 1939, issue of *Variety* noted additional changes to the Goodman orchestra expected on its return to New York on June 8: "Nick Fatool, formerly with Bobbie Hackett, has replaced Buddy Schutz on drums; George Rose is in place of Ben Heller on guitar; Toots Mondello is in Arthur Rollini's sax spot. Artie Bernstein recently took Harry Goodman's place on bass fiddle; Corky Cornelius, once with Les Brown, took Irving Goodman's trumpet chair several weeks ago, and a recent outright addition was Bruce Squires, trombone."[34] By this time, trombonist Red Ballard and pianist Jess Stacy were the only surviving members of the Palomar Ballroom band of August 1935. Goodman made additional changes in the studio.

In May, the band had made its last recording for Victor, following John Hammond to Columbia starting August 10, 1939, the first session to include recordings of Goodman's new arrangements by Eddie Sauter, who also joined the organization in May.[35] Sauter had worked with Red Norvo's Orchestra as both trumpet player and arranger earning about $60 per week. Goodman first called him in February 1939 and, according to his wife, offered him anywhere from $175 to $240 for two arrangements per week. Sauter first met the band in Columbus, Ohio, the location of the May 23 *Camel Caravan* broadcast.[36]

No doubt the most significant addition to Goodman's band, according to her family back home in Denton, was Louise. Her proud sisters had started a scrapbook of newspaper clippings, and they were tuning their radios to station KRLD-CBS Tuesday evenings for the *Camel Caravan* program, featuring Benny Goodman from 7:30 to 8:00 p.m. Louise phoned home to make certain that her mother was tuned in during that time on May 30 in particular, when she would be singing "Don't Worry 'bout Me" and a special song titled "Louise" with new words written by Johnny Mercer to the tune "Louise" by Richard A. Whiting (original words by Leo Robin).

Benny provided the introduction for "Louise":

> And now club members, we're going to call on you to lend a little sympathy to the proceedings. Our new member from Texas, Louise Tobin, tells me that sometimes she gets a little homesick. For all those who feel sorry about that, please sigh. [Band members and audience sigh]. That's not a very good sigh. You see, Louise? Everybody knows how it feels, so why don't you airmail that little letter to your mother?

The band's rhythm section set the tempo and key and Louise sang:

> Are you listening mom? It's your daughter, Louise,
> dropping a note on the etherized breeze.
> Just thought I'd say, things are okay,
> And tell you I miss you.
>
> Everything is swell; Cincinnati is fine,
> And how are the folks on the old party line?
> Say "howdy-do" and tell them that you've
> Just heard from Louise.
>
> Did you get my letter, written on the train?
> By the way, you better, write to me Ft. Wayne.
>
> We'll be playing there, starting on Friday this
> Now that's about all, so I'll close with a kiss.
> Oceans of love; I'm thinking of you.
> Always, Louise

Virtually from the moment she started singing with the Goodman orchestra, Louise began a grueling schedule of radio broadcasts, rehearsals, dance performances, and recording sessions. After the band's three weeks in Ohio, they flew to Fort Wayne, Indiana, for a June 6, *Camel Caravan* broadcast for which Louise sang two numbers: "The Lady's in Love with You" and a current hit first sung by Martha Tilton by Goodman trumpeter Ziggy Elman with lyrics by Johnny Mercer, titled "And the Angels Sing." Programmed also for this broadcast was the instrumental "Without a Song," which, according to Sauter biographer Alex Chilowicz, is the first recorded arrangement for the Goodman band by the twenty-five-year-old Sauter.[37]

Back in New York for a June 1, *Camel Caravan* broadcast, Louise sang two choruses of another Mercer lyric, "You and Your Love," with music by Johnny Green.[38]

For the following week, Louise was asked to sing two songs: "The Lamp Is Low"[39] and "There'll Be Some Changes Made." The music for "The Lamp Is Low" was written by Peter DeRose and Bert Shefter and was heavily inspired by French composer Maurice Ravel's *Pavane pour une infante défunte* (Pavane for a Dead Princess). The words were by Mitchell Parish (original French lyrics by Yvette Baruch). According to Tom Lord's

The Jazz Discography, the song was first recorded in New York, April 24, 1939, by Mildred Bailey and Her Orchestra. Prior to Louise's live performance of the tune on the June 20, *Camel Caravan*, the song was recorded by Tommy Dorsey, Glenn Miller, and Jimmy Dorsey. Sinatra sang "The Lamp Is Low" during the July 10, 1939, CBS radio broadcast from the Roseland Ballroom, New York, with Harry James and His Orchestra. Hence, the song was well known to radio listeners of this time.

Benny Goodman Band with Louise Tobin pose outside airplane, 1939.
(Courtesy of the Louise Tobin and Peanuts Hucko Jazz Collection)

Benny Goodman and Johnny Mercer introduce Louise and "The Lamp Is Low":

> **Goodman:** You know club members this year has been quite unusual in Tin Pan Alley. Many writers of big song hits have come right out and said that they got the tunes from the classics. From a Debussy melody, they gave us "My Reverie." Then there was "Our Love," written about a theme, or on a theme . . .
>
> **Mercer:** flub, flub; you owe me that one.
>
> **Goodman:** . . . on a theme by Tchaikovsky.
>
> **Mercer:** Yes, and any day now a scat song based on Beethoven's Fifth. Meanwhile, three of the boys have decided that you can't improve on Ravel, so basing their song on a phrase from Ravel's *Pavane*, Peter DeRose, Bert Shefter, and Mitchell Parish have turned out a new hit. Louise Tobin sings it, and it's called "The Lamp Is Low."

Louise and the Band Go West: In the Air, on the Air, and in the Studio

By the end of June, Louise and the Goodman orchestra were back on tour by air, heading toward the West Coast. Goodman had canceled a number of cities in the East in order to accept a lucrative date at the Golden Gate International Exposition, playing three outdoor concerts a day at Treasure Island, San Francisco, as part of the San Francisco World's Fair. *Variety* announced that Goodman and his band would net $10,000 a week. The first four weeks (starting on July 8 from 10 to 10:30 p.m.) would open a weekly series of WEAF radio broadcasts originating at the Exposition. Bert Parks was to be his new emcee, replacing Johnny Mercer who had gone with Bob Crosby's orchestra, to emcee their Tuesday night spot at 9:30 p.m.[40]

On July 2, 1939, the *Amarillo Sunday News Globe* announced that "Benny Goodman's blazing hot swing band will open a new *Camel Caravan* series on the NBC-Red network, July 8 to be broadcast Saturdays from 8 to 8:30 p.m . . . Louise Tobin, 20-year-old Dallas beauty recently discovered by Goodman in a Greenwich Village night spot, will be featured as a vocalist in the new series. Other principals include the Goodman Trio, composed of Benny himself with his famous clarinet; Lionel Hampton at the drums and Fletcher Henderson."[41]

Louise Tobin singing with Benny Goodman Band in San Francisco, 1939.
(Courtesy of the Louise Tobin and Peanuts Hucko Jazz Collection)

Mayor Rossi joined Louise Tobin and Benny Goodman on stage,
Treasure Island, San Francisco, July 8, 1939. "He thought he could sing!"
Louise recalled.[1] (Courtesy of the Louise Tobin and Peanuts Hucko Jazz
Collection)

1. Tobin interview, February 24, 2012.

Heard over the airwaves across the country each week during the *Camel Caravan* radio show, singing with the top band in the land, Louise's star was rising fast. Newspapers featured her in their "Interesting People" sections. Characteristic of the time, writers focused more on the visual attributes of Louise rather than the musical. An unidentified clipping in the scrapbook kept by her sisters titled "When Louise Tobin Swings the College Boys Swoon" presents one such example. Dated July 16, 1939, the article described her as new among that

> small but lively sisterhood of singing women known to the cats as ca-
> naries. . . . They can't sew and they aren't meek, but they're dynamite
> in front of a microphone . . . a career girl with convictions . . . [and]
> the cats will tell you that not only does she warble terrifically, but she
> possesses an exceptional ability for running away with the imagina-
> tions of college boys. College boys, fortunately, are Mr. Goodman's
> best customers. . . . Most sisters of swing have tended to be on the
> portly side. There was Bessie Smith, for instance, who arrived from
> New Orleans in the days of Bix Beiderbecke, the boy with the horn.
> Rhythm coursed through her 200 pounds. Mildred Bailey, still going
> strong, never was a sylph. Sophie Tucker, the original red hot mama,
> was and is generously upholstered. But Louise—Ah![42]

The article closed with a list of Louise's hobbies: "When she's not work-ing, she likes to dabble around with recipes, ride horses, and dream up a little esoteric poetry on the side. She is sort of a singing Sappho, you might say."[43]

In addition to such feature articles, Louise received fan mail. There were love poems, flowers, and requests for her to sing certain songs, most often sent from college students and soldiers with the hope that she would reciprocate with a letter, card, or photo. As a representative example, consider this letter sent from the USS *California* by E. H. McAdams and mailed on July 20, 1939:

On Board USS. California
Tacoma, Wash.
July 20, [19]39

Dearest Miss Tobin,
     I don't know just how to start this but I wanted you to know that more than one sailor thinks you are 4.0, the Navy way of saying you

are perfect. There is no mark more perfect in the Navy than 4.0, but I have reserved one for you, *especially for you.* 4.9. The picture you allowed me to take is swell just as it would naturally be with such a nice subject. When I take it out of my locker it is the subject of drawn out discussion. I asked you if you would autograph an enlargement of it for me and even though I was slightly? tight I remembered and had the enlargement made. It is in our photo shop now. I will send it soon. Please don't disappoint me. I overheard you tell another person you hated to write but even a note would make me happy. *Oh boy*! For your own information, I had 20 prints made of your picture for shipmates who asked and now they want enlargements but, no soap. I am sending you a picture of yourself in action. You were singing "The Blues" I have some swell shots of Benny and you, so thanks again and lots of luck. If you even like your national defense a little please answer.
"Can't say it"

E. H. McAdams
USS California
San Pedro, Cal
Box 37[44]

On Wednesday, August 2, Louise arrived in Los Angeles with the Goodman band for its Saturday performance at the Hollywood Bowl: a "Special Concert" titled "Symphony under the Stars," featuring pianist, composer, and improviser, Alec Templeton. Louise was programed to sing "a rendition of Southern Blues" for the second of three pieces during the second set.[45] It was her only song for this date, if we are to believe that there were no late changes to the program. Louise confirmed with the author that this was "Louise Tobin Blues." *Los Angeles Times* music critic Isabel Morse Jones noted that "Hollywood Bowl changed its tune Saturday night," given the mix of classical and jazz on the program. "Alec Templeton brought Bach and Mozart up to date and later led a jam session at the piano in which the crowd joined with cries and low moans of appreciation that made the Bowl reverberate with rhythm just like an old-time revival meeting." Then Jones favorably singled out Louise and other individual members of the band: "Pretty little Louise Tobin sang some sorrowful blues in a deep and throaty voice that was enough to make you weep and then Lionel Hampton had them in convulsions with his antics at the drum. Every member of the band is a soloist and can demonstrate both technique and personality."[46] The Goodman band had a two-week break before they were scheduled to return to the Hollywood Bowl for an August 19, *Camel Caravan* live radio broadcast. This was not a leisure break. The interim was spent mostly in rehearsals and three days recording in the studio, August 10, 11, and 16.

These were Louise's first recording sessions with Goodman. On August 10, she recorded two versions of "There'll Be Some Changes Made," two versions of "Comes Love," and one version of "Rendezvous Time in Paree." "Comes Love" and "Rendezvous Time in Paree" were Eddie Sauter arrangements.

Given the choice, Louise would have preferred to sing standards arranged by Fletcher Henderson, but, whether on stage or in the studio, she did not have a say in the selection of the songs she sang with Goodman. She recalled that "he was in the process of changing his whole concept of his band. I didn't know that at the time. I learned that later, because I kept wondering when I was going to get some good tunes, standards to do. I got all those funny tunes that nobody could sing, and it turned out that he got the idea. He wanted to modernize his band, and he hired Eddie Sauter, a wonderful arranger, but he put him out on the limb to do modern stuff, and he picked the tunes, and they were tunes, beautiful tunes, but nobody could sing them. I mean, that 'Rendezvous Time in Paree,' my goodness. I doubt that they ever played it twice. It wasn't a good dance tune; it wasn't a standard. It was just a blaagh. So, I was really [singing with Goodman] in that time, when he tried to do something different with his band."[47]

"I remember hearing someone say at a rehearsal, 'I don't think she can hear that change of key.' Sauter wrote beautiful parts, but all his tunes were hard to get into, but they were wonderful, if Stan Kenton had been doing them at that time. With Benny, they didn't do very well. Kids didn't like it. Kids that came to see us and hear us were very disappointed with those tunes. They would dance up to the dance band and kind of look at Benny like 'What are you doing?' And then they would yell, 'Satin Stockings' or something that really swung, and, to Benny's credit, he always played what they asked."[48]

A Closer Look at "Louise Tobin Blues"

On the August 11 session, Louise recorded two takes of "Blues," neither of which Benny ultimately wanted to release. While Louise loved singing, and would happily sing whatever tunes Benny called, her favorite was singing the blues. "All musicians like the blues," she recalled. They get to show off with the blues. Improvising, and you can never use up all the possibilities with the blues. Just however you are feeling. . . . You just make up lyrics as you go along. 'Louise Tobin Blues' had different words depending on who I was with and where I was. . . . I wound up doing blues with everybody. Blues is the basics; you just write your own story to it however you feel."[49]

Indeed, Louise had stated during numerous interviews that she would make up lyrics to the blues. Here is the text to the version she recorded during that session on August 11, 1939.

> I was born in Texas, raised in Tennessee.
> I was born in Texas, and raised in Tennessee;
> But it took a western man to make a fool out of me.
>
> Now, this man that I love, is as mean as he can be;
> This man that I love, is as mean as he can be;
> I never knew there'd be a man could be too mean for me.
>
> I'm gonna get me a shotgun, just as long as I am tall;
> I'll get me a shotgun, just as long as I am tall;
> I'm gonna shoot that man, to see him jump and fall.
>
> [Fletcher Henderson piano solo chorus]
>
> Now, if anybody asks ya, who it was that wrote this song,
> If anybody asks ya, who it was that wrote this song,
> You say it was a girl you know, but she done been here and gone.

Readers with some familiarity with blues may recognize a few phrases of Louise's lyrics. Closer examination reveals striking similarities to numerous blues phrases recorded between 1923 and 1939. Michael Taft's three-volume *Blues Lyric Poetry: A Concordance* (1984) facilitates identification of Louise's blues sources.[50] Consider the first line in stanza 1: "I was born in Texas, raised in Tennessee." Taft's concordance references this line to two sources: Daddy Stovepipe's "Stovepipe Blues," recorded

Table 3.1 Variants of "But it took a western man to make a fool out of me."

From the perspective of the woman:
Clara Smith, "Down South Blues," July 27, 1923
"Don't go north and let them men make a fool out of you."
Hannah Sylvester, "Down South Blues," September 21, 1923
"Don't go north and let them men make a fool out of you."
Hannah Sylvester, "I Want My Sweet Daddy," September 21, 1923
"That's the reason why: he makes a fool out of me."
Anna Bell, "Hopeless Blues," September 1928 (precise day unknown)
"Love sure have: made a fool out of me."
From the perspective of the man:
Robert Hicks, "California Blues," April 18, 1929
"Wild women and whiskey: can make a fool out of me."
Robert Hicks, "Me and My Whiskey," November 3, 1929
"Wild women and whiskey: can make a fool out of me."

March 10, 1924, and Blind Percy's "Fourteenth Street Blues," recorded in November 1927 (precise day unknown).[51]

The third line of stanza 1: "But it took a western man to make a fool out of me"—seems to be derived from similar examples, but I have only identified variants. From the perspective of the woman, see Clara Smith's "Down South Blues" recorded July 27, 1923; Hannah Sylvester's "I Want My Sweet Daddy," also recorded in 1923; and, Anna Bell's "Hopeless Blues," which includes the line "Love sure have: made a fool out of me" recorded in September 1928 (see table 3.1).

There is no direct reference to either phrase of the first line of stanza 2: "Now, this man that I love, is as mean as he can be." Two lines are close: Walter Vinson (Mississippi Sheiks), "Your Good Man Caught the Train and Gone," a song that includes the line "You can treat me mean: mean as you can be," recorded December 15, 1930; and, Peetie Wheatstraw's "Low Down Rascal," includes the line "You's a lowdown rascal: just as mean as you can be," recorded February 18, 1936. There were no hits for either phrase in the last line of stanza 2, "I never knew there'd be a man, could be too mean for me."

Two possible sources for the first line of Louise's stanza 3—"I'm going to get me a shotgun, just as long as I am tall"—are Lonnie Johnson's "Low Land Moan," which includes the line "I'm going to buy me a shotgun: long as I am tall; I'm going to shoot my woman, just to see her fall," recorded December 12, 1927, two months *before* Jimmie Rodgers's "Blue Yodel No. 1" was released, a song that included the same line,[52] and the other possible source is James Cole's "Mistreated the Only Friend You Had," which includes the line "Going to buy a shotgun: long as I am tall; I'm going to shoot my baby just to see her fall," recorded January 16, 1932.

Note that these examples are from the male perspective: "gonna shoot that woman." There are a couple of examples of women shooting their man: Texan Maggie Jones's "Undertaker's Blues" includes the line "Had to shoot him: because he was too smart," recorded April 16, 1925; Bessie Smith's "Black Mountain Blues" includes the line "I'm going to shoot him if he stands still and cut him if he run," recorded July 22, 1930; and, Rosetta Crawford's "My Man Jumped Salty on Me" includes the line perhaps taken from "Black Mountain Blues," "cut him if he stands still: shoot him if he runs," recorded February 1, 1939, just six months prior to Louise's August 11, 1939, recording date.

The final stanza, "Now, if anybody asks ya, who it was that wrote this song / You say it was a girl you know, but she done been here and gone," is a common or cliché last stanza in blues. See table 3.2 for a list of examples of blues songs that include the same or slight variant of Louise's last stanza.

Table 3.2

Ma Gertrude Rainey	"Last Minute Blues"	December 1923 (precise date unknown)
Julius Daniels	"My Mama Was a Sailor"	February 19, 1927
Lewis Black	"Corn Liquor Blues"	December 10, 1927
Ishman Bracey	"Trouble-Hearted Blues"	August 31, 1928
Black Bottom McPhail	"Down in Black Bottom"	March 17, 1932
Huddie Ledbetter	"Mr. Hughe's Town"	February 5, 1935

In all, I have been able to cite twenty-nine sources of lines and/or phrases from which Louise might have drawn her lyrics dating from July 27, 1923, to February 1, 1939. (See Appendix B for a complete list.) What is curious is that when asked, Louise only recognized one perhaps two names on this list: Bessie Smith and "perhaps" Lonnie Johnson.

Reminiscing on her recording of the blues, Louise recalled,

> "I was Born in Texas, Raised in Tennessee" is an old blues; everybody's sung it, and when Benny decided to do that, I'd been with him a few months. Benny had lost Jess Stacy playing piano, and to my knowledge, he didn't try any piano players for a while. All of a sudden, we had to go somewhere, and Benny had to have a piano player. He took Fletcher Henderson to the recording date. Fletcher was a great arranger but was not a Jess Stacy or Teddy Wilson on piano.[53] Benny never released the tune. Benny decided that he wanted to record the blues, but that tune did not work out. We recorded that day and left for a job in another state, and so I didn't think that it would ever come out. It's a collector's item, now, I understand. One of the trumpet players called me a couple of years ago, and he said, "I got your blues with Benny. You better be proud, it's selling for a hundred bucks."[54]

Goodman was not happy with Henderson's solo on this recording, according to Louise, and it was not released until 1993. He liked Louise's blues, and, indeed, she recalled a remark Benny had made to her: "'You remind me of Bessie Smith,' who at that time I had never heard of, 'and you're going to be a great blues singer!'"[55] Might there have been reasons other than his dissatisfaction with Fletcher Henderson's blues that prevented Goodman from releasing this recording?

Goodman biographer James Lincoln Collier rightly notes that Goodman "was always conscious of the fact that he was running first and foremost a dance band."[56] "Louise Tobin Blues" was not a dance number. Were the lyrics too confrontationally explicit for commercial late 1930s, mainstream music? "Louise Tobin Blues" arguably presents more than a raised fist against the mistreatment of women.[57] The protagonist responds with a shotgun, points, and shoots, responding to violence with violence. Jeff Todd Titon in *Early Downhome Blues* identified some common blues themes and noted that while "threats of reprisal for mistreatment are more common than acts," he cites a few examples where the threats were carried out. For example, in "Got the Blues, Can't Be Satisfied": "Took my gun, broke the barrel down / Put my baby, six feet under the ground." This and most of his examples are from the perspective of the man. In her book *Blues Legacies*, Angela Davis sites a number of examples where blues women "found ways to express themselves that were at variance with the prevailing standards of femininity."[58] She cites Bessie Smith's "Hateful Blues" where she sings of cutting up her husband who has been abusing her: "If I see him I'm gon' beat him, gon' kick and bite him, too / Gonna take my weddin' butcher, gonna cut him two in two." Daphne Duval Harrison, in her seminal book on blues women titled *Black Pearls*, cites Texan Victoria Spivey's "Bloodhound Blues," for another example of reciprocated violence in the extreme.[59]

Louise Tobin recorded such commercially successful songs with Goodman as "There'll Be Some Changes Made," "Scatterbrain," and "What's New?," but her favorite recording and the work for which she is most proud is "Louise Tobin Blues." Perhaps it's not too hard to imagine why. First, she was featured in a way that was unique from her other performances with the band. Typically, as was the style for swing era singers, the orchestra would play a chorus, then the singer would step up to the microphone and sing a chorus, and then sit down for solos and the final statement of the tune. The singer was an added feature rather than featured. With her blues, there is a short four-bar intro, and Louise begins the first of four stanzas. After her last stanza, following a brief piano solo, the orchestra states the final cadence, and that's it. Secondly, just as an instrumentalist personalizes his/her performance with improvisation, Louise's improvised lyrics empowered her in a forum that typically offered little power to women. "Louise Tobin Blues" stands in stark contrast with such mainstream popular songs and Eddie Sauter arrangements as "Rendezvous Time in Paree," "Comes Love," and "Love Never Went to College," citing a few more of the recordings voiced by Louise with Goodman in 1939.

Singing the blues provided Tobin a forum for a more significantly gendered form of self-expression that would not have been acceptable in mainstream discourse. Her absorption of African American blues was significant, and her performance of the blues challenged the contemporary image of women swing singers as songbirds, and ultimately provided her a means of empowerment that she did not have with the other songs that she sang with Goodman and others.

Another Day in the Studio, the Hollywood Bowl, and Charlie Christian

The last day of recording sessions in Los Angeles was on August 16, 1939, the third and final day of the band's first recordings for Columbia Records. Louise recorded two takes of "Blue Orchids" and two takes of "What's New?" Three days later the Goodman band was back at the Hollywood Bowl for what has become a historic *Camel Caravan* broadcast performance, one that featured a new addition to the Goodman Sextet, guitarist Charlie Christian, whose first recorded rendition of "Flying Home" with the Sextet has since become a classic in early electric jazz guitar recording history.

Goodman had broken many barriers. He added African American musicians to his band at a time when segregation was the norm. John Hammond was the catalyst for Benny adding Charlie Christian, who had experienced regional success in Oklahoma. The fact that Christian was African American wasn't the only issue for Goodman; he played electric guitar. According to Hammond, Benny at first said, "Who the hell wants to hear an electric guitar player?"[60] Though he doubted Hammond initially, after hearing Christian play "Rose Room," the Goodman Quintet became the Benny Goodman Sextet. Louise recalled working with Christian: "He was a great player and a polite, shy guy. We didn't really think about his being black. He played great guitar. I guess I was just so young, and I had played with a black piano player and guitarist in Texas as a child, so I didn't realize racial barriers were being broken in the band. These guys were just great players."[61]

Back to New York: Depart, Arrive, Rehearse, Perform, Repeat

After their Hollywood Bowl performances, Louise and the Goodman band chartered another plane, ultimately returning to New York City for another recording session in addition to daily performances at the New York World's Fair. They stopped in a number of cities along the way, performing in Wichita, Kansas; Atlantic City, New Jersey; and Detroit, Michigan. First, they had to refuel in Amarillo, Texas, and, as was typical with each of their stops, they were "greeted by thousands." "Word had somehow leaked that the Benny Goodman Orchestra would be stopping for gas," Louise recalled, "and when we landed, the tarmac was filled with thousands of people. They wanted us to come out and play for them. We did end up walking out on the steps, and Benny played a bit on his horn, but all we could hear was fans screaming and yelling. It was great."[62] As Louise scanned the crowd, a familiar face from her past caught her eye. "Right in front was Mr. Patterson. They wouldn't let me off the plane, but I waved to him. I don't know if he realized I recognized him, but there he was. When I was in the Palace Theatre [back in Dallas], he was very kind to me."[63]

Their schedule was tight. The band had only a short time to prepare for their performance later that night for a dance and CBS radio broadcast at the Blue Moon. After the dance, the band members boarded the plane again and headed to Atlantic City for a Monday night engagement. After their performance later that week at the "Steel Pier" (August 23), they were off to Detroit, Michigan, for a *Camel Caravan* broadcast from the Michigan State Fair. For that performance, Louise sang three songs: "Day in, Day Out," "The Jumpin' Jive," and "I've Been There Before."

Goodman still demanded rehearsal time during the exceptionally busy second week in September, which included daily (afternoon) performances at the World's Fair in New York City (September 6–12), a *Camel Caravan* broadcast back in Detroit (September 9), and a lengthy recording session back in New York on September 13, during which Louise recorded four takes of "One Sweet Letter from You," two takes of "I Didn't Know What Time It Was," three takes of "Love Never Went to College," two takes of "Scatterbrain," and two takes of "I've Been There Before."

Two days later, on September 15, the public heard Goodman's first Columbia recordings, those recorded in Los Angeles virtually one month prior, and the early reviews were in print. Victor Davis, music critic for the *Dallas Morning News*, praised the new release, singling out "Dallas songstress, Louise Tobin."

> Definite improvement in Benny Goodman's band as the result of recent changes is reflected in "Comes Love" and "Rendezvous Time in Paris [*sic*]," Columbia, as disced by that old master of the clarinet. Using a somewhat more commercial approach than previously, Goodman's treatment of these hit tunes is easy on the ear as well as luring to the feet. First-rate vocalizing is contributed by Louise Tobin, the Dallas songstress.[64]

Washington Post critic Bill Gottlieb praised the recording as well, particularly in the context of Goodman's move from Victor to Columbia with this latest release. Here is an excerpt:

> Benny christens the new label in fine style, too. I can't recall his band having played with more bite and dash during the past year than he does on "Jumpin' at the Woodside," written by Benny's own favorite bandleader, Count Basie. Most brilliant solo on the four Goodman sides is a tremendous alto sax introduction to "Comes Love" that, at times, sounds more like a clarinet played in the lower register. I wouldn't be surprised if it were Benny playing it rather than the regular altoist. Regardless of its author, it's something with more ideas than even a half dozen consecutive playings will entirely reveal. "Comes Love," together with "Rendezvous Time in Paree" and "There'll be Some Changes Made," also features the steadily improving voice of Louise Tobin (Mrs. Harry James).[65]

On October 6, the Goodman orchestra headlined a second Carnegie Hall concert.[66] Louise could not have known back in January 1938 when, unable to get a ticket, she snuck backstage with the other orchestra wives and listened to the historic event from the wings, that within the following year she would have an opportunity to be the featured vocalist with Goodman on that famous stage.

The enormous shadow of the first historic concert contributed to the second Carnegie Hall extravaganza falling a bit short. Despite guest appearances of Louis Armstrong, Cab Calloway, Paul Whiteman, and Glenn Miller, the event was not greeted with the enthusiasm from audiences and critics as was the historic 1938 concert. Louise recalled that "the first concert caught everyone by surprise, and Benny had Krupa and Harry at the time. There were problems with the second concert that were distracting, from lighting problems to problems with the microphones. We weren't that happy with the performances," Tobin recalled. Indeed, technical difficulties with her microphone prevented Louise from performing. It was inevitable that this second Carnegie concert be compared to the first, which had the advantage of being a performance that was not the usual classical music but rather the hot new swing music. The reviewer in November's *Metronome* wrote that "Paul Whiteman and Fred Waring also appeared but failed to satisfy. The affair was scheduled to be a Swing Concert. Pops pleased the older folks, but it wasn't swing."[67]

Leaving Benny

Louise did not sing with Goodman's band the following evening (October 7) for the *Camel Caravan* broadcast. Mildred Bailey was called in to sing "The Lamp Is Low." Louise returned for just two more weeks of *Camel Caravan* broadcasts from the Empire Room at the Waldorf Astoria hotel: on October 14, singing "I Didn't Know What Time It Was" and the following week, singing "Lilacs in the Rain" and "Make with the Kisses." Unfortunately, an accident not only prevented her from finishing the extended engagement at the Waldorf Astoria but also may have led to her leaving Goodman.[68] Coming down out of the main dining room of the grand hotel, Louise stepped on her long gown, tripped, and fell, badly spraining her ankle. "I missed a few gigs," she recalled. "It was really bad. They rushed the hotel doctor up there, and it was a big ruckus. A short time after that is when I had to tell Benny I was leaving. It was one of the hardest things I've ever had to do.[69] [Benny] was absolutely crushed. 'I can't believe it,' he said. 'You know you're going to sit in the apartment somewhere,' which is exactly what happened."[70] Benny likely suspected that Harry had played no small part in Louise's decision to leave.

Harry had been putting increasing pressure on Louise to leave Goodman's band and to join him in Hollywood. Louise recounts that Benny strongly advised her not to go. "He used to tell me to have Harry come to me and not fly out to see him every time we had a few days off. But I wanted to keep my marriage together. I think Benny knew some of the things that Harry had done and that the marriage more than likely wasn't going to work."[71] Benny was far more famous than Harry, and it may be that Harry was somewhat envious of his wife performing in a band that was more popular than his own. Regardless of Harry's motivation in pressuring Louise to leave Goodman, he did respect her musicianship. Indeed, both Benny and Harry sent telegrams praising her performances. This was uncharacteristic of Benny, who just expected every one of his band members to be excellent without praise. The guys in the band also valued Louise, and many of those friendships lasted for the rest of their lives. Ziggy Elman once said to Louise, "You sing like a good musician plays!"[72]

The articles mentioning Louise printed in the jazz magazines in November 1939 do not mention her fall at the Waldorf. Rather, they speculate on her possible departure from the Goodman band, suggesting that she would be leaving "because a little Harry or Louise is on the way" or that she was merely "retiring temporarily to bring an addition into the James family."[73] *Down Beat* reported that "Louise Tobin will leave the Benny Goodman band in November for a good reason—to become a mother," and further stated that "at press time she was preparing to give Benny her notice. She will go to California to join her husband, Harry James, whose band, after doing tremendous business at Chicago's Sherman Hotel, moves into the Victor Restaurant in Beverly Hills this month."[74]

Louise and Benny on the cover of Swing Magazine. November 1939. (Courtesy of the Louise Tobin and Peanuts Hucko Jazz Collection)

By mid-November, *Tempo* ran a story titled "Louise Tobin Leaves Benny," including her photo, under which read "Home for Rest" and "Louise Tobin; Tough luck brings momentary halt to career." Reporting from New York, the unidentified author wrote that

> Louise Tobin, the little girl from Texas who flashed into national prominence last spring when she replaced Martha Tilton as featured vocalist with Benny Goodman's band, has returned to her home for a rest following her recovery from a serious illness that forced her to withdraw from the band sooner than was expected. Miss Tobin, who expected to become a mother, planned to leave Goodman this month.[75]

At the same time, *Down Beat* reported: "Stop the Press." "Louise Tobin recovering from a critical illness."[76]

Jazz periodicals continued the following month to write about Louise's recuperation and speculate on her post-Goodman future. One announced that "the former Goodman vocalist will record with picked small bands when she returns to New York this spring."[77] *Down Beat* published a photo of Louise under the heading tellingly worded, reflecting her new identity: "*Mrs. Harry James* Recovers (author's emphasis)." The unidentified author wrote:

> Forced to give her notice a few weeks back to Benny Goodman because she expected soon to become a mother, Louise Tobin suddenly became ill and, according to friends, nearly died. The plucky Texas gal, whose blues singing got her the job with Benny, has since returned to her home to convalesce. She is reported out of danger now.[78]

Whether due to pregnancy, illness, a fall at the Waldorf, or primarily to follow Harry's wishes that she become Mrs. Harry James, Louise stopped singing with Goodman at the height of her tenure with the King of Swing and arguably at the height of a career that would last another fifty-plus years. End-of-the-year polls ranked Louise Tobin fourth behind Mildred Bailey, Bonnie Baker, and Billie Holiday, who took the first through third spots, respectively. Louise's vocal on "Scatterbrain" was the number one Record of the Month for December 1939.[79] Among "The Biggest News Stories of the Year" reported in *Down Beat* magazine for November was: "Louise Tobin left Goodman."[80] A large photo of Louise and Benny appeared on the cover of the November issue of *Swing: The Guide to Modern Music*, a magazine in which the following month reported with bitter enthusiasm that

> the lovely Louise Tobin surprised quite a few people by rounding into swell singing form the last few weeks that she was with Goodman. She gave out with a style that had several well-knowns booster her as the next great singing star of the country, and so you can look for her back in the bigtime (if only through records) as soon as she's had enough rest in her native Texas. Also there's a possibility she'll join husband Harry James.[81]

Louise harbored fond memories of working with Goodman. "Unlike most of the people that had worked with Benny," she recalled,

> I got along with him because I just never did cross him. I guess. I didn't understand it at the time, but my understanding is that he was exceptionally nice to me. The only bad thing he ever did that I was aware of was he took back all my beautiful wardrobe when I left, but he paid for it. I guess it was fair. I remember that designer's name: Elizabeth Hawes. She wrote a book called *Fashion is Spinach* [New York, 1938], and was a wonderful designer. I had the most gorgeous clothes in New York City. Opening night at the Waldorf-Astoria, I wore a fuchsia pink satin evening gown. It was off the shoulder and tight almost all the way to my ankles where is flared. This gorgeous dress had a bustle and a train. They lit me with a white spotlight and that dress was just beautiful. I hated to see that dress go, and I wondered who they gave it to.[82]

"I think that I was the only singer who really liked Benny," she also recalled. "I really liked him, and he really liked me. I got along with him. He kept saying to me, 'I'm going to make you the greatest blues singer who ever lived.' It might have been that he took an interest in trying to help me sing in the manner he thought I ought to. Or, I just really don't know why he liked me, but he did."[83]

4

From Louise Tobin to Mrs. Harry James, 1939–1960

From now on, she's going to be plain Mrs. Harry James.[1]

THE 1940S AND '50S included perhaps the most turbulent years in Louise's long life, decades that began with America's entry into its second world war on December 7, 1941, that included a recording ban at a time when a new jazz style, bebop, was emerging concurrently with the growing decline of swing music. The birth of a new musical style favored by a younger generation highly charged with the white-hot popularity of Elvis Presley and rock and roll also followed.

Louise felt the turbulence of these musical, political, and cultural changes both personally and professionally. Conceding to Harry's wishes, she left Goodman; nevertheless, she continued to find her spotlight, whether via Hollywood screen tests for potential film work, as a celebrity fashion model, or through her recordings and performances with Jack Jenney, Will Bradley, Ziggy Elman, Emil Coleman, Tommy Jones, and Stan Hasselgard. Still, any hope she might have had for lasting tenures with such ventures was complicated if not compromised with the birth of her sons in 1941 and '42. Then, in the summer of 1943 Harry filed for divorce, leaving Louise officially in charge of raising her boys Harry and Tim. Touring with an orchestra, for Louise, was now out of the question. Despite intermittent performances during these decades, she had essentially suspended her singing career, until publicist, author, and friend George T. Simon brought her out of retirement and arranged for her to sing at the 1962 Newport Jazz Festival, where she met her future husband and love of her life, Andrew "Peanuts" Hucko, but her second career and marriage will be covered in the next chapter.

After leaving Goodman, Louise first spent time resting with her family in Denton, and then, as often as she was able, she connected with Harry on the road or joined him in Los Angeles, which at the time was the closest thing for them to call home. Recalling Benny's prediction that if she left the band she'd be sitting alone in a hotel room waiting for Harry to come home, not long after she stopped singing with Goodman, Louise wanted to perform again. In March 1940, Harry invited her to sing with his band, which was scheduled to appear at the Madhattan Room at the Hotel Pennsylvania for a nationally broadcast performance. "I think it was the Chesterfield show. Benny had Camel [Caravan]; Harry got Chesterfield," Louise recalled.[2] It was the first and last time she ever sang with Harry's band, and she knew it. That night she improvised new lyrics to "Louise Tobin Blues." "I used to just make up lyrics to blues. There is a chorus I used to say, 'I was born in Texas, raised in Tennessee, but it took a northern man to make a fool out of me."[3] Louise recalled that "in the lyric [for my performance with Harry's band, I sang] 'from now on I just want to be plain Mrs. Harry James.'"[4]

Louise and Harry returned to Texas after the Madhattan Room engagement to visit their respective families. Their first stop was Beaumont to visit Harry's parents and then to Denton for the wedding of Louise's sister, Dora.[5] Louise sang at the wedding and to her surprise was nervous and found herself fighting stage fright. Entertainers know that a group of family and friends can often be a performer's most critical audience; nevertheless, it is not hard to imagine other reasons that Louise might have suffered from anxiety, singing at her sister's wedding. Consider the setting. In a church bathed in sunshine filtered through colorful stained glass, the smell of fresh flowers on the altar and lining the aisle, and a crowd of family and friends all gathered in celebration of the couple's ceremony. Dora's wedding could not have been more different than Harry and Louise's intimately recited vows away from home before a justice of the peace and alongside a couple of witnesses. Considering the circumstances, singing at Dora's wedding had to be emotional for her. "It's strange: I wasn't a bit scared at Carnegie Hall, but I nearly fainted before I got through that wedding," Louise recalled.[6]

With family commitments behind them, Harry and Louise left Denton to resume engagements in Boston, Pittsburgh, Chicago, and New York City, where they were living. Louise looked forward to spending more time with Harry, but she was enticed with performing opportunities. In addition to considering whether to accept a Hollywood offer to appear in the movie *Captain Caution*, Louise recounted to a *Denton Record-Chronicle* reporter that she was under contract to do recordings in New York City, most likely referring to a session with trombonist Jack Jenney.[7] Louise turned down the Hollywood offer. When asked why, she simply stated: "All I wanted to do was sing. I guess my heart was just a singer."[8]

Louise's first professional gig since leaving Goodman in October 1939 was a performance with trombonist and bandleader Jack Jenney, with whom she had had her first recording session on April 11, 1939, in New York about one month prior to singing with Benny Goodman.[9] Louise was invited to record "Got No Time."[10] The recording was primarily a demo for promotional purposes. She recalled the rehearsal but not the studio time. She learned many years later that Peanuts Hucko had played saxophone on that session, but they were not in the studio at the same time and did not have a chance to meet. In an interview on May 24, 2014, Louise remembered that "there were guys trying to book bands who needed recordings for promo purposes. Jack had been married to [singer] Kay Thompson and was terribly shy. He got on stage at one point and just froze. He was a great trombonist and famous, but [he] had stage fright. My session with Jenney was ultimately for agents."[11] Jenney, learning of Louise's availability, invited her to sing with his orchestra for an upcoming performance. An advertisement in the Pennsylvania *Chester Times* announced that Jack Jenney and His Orchestra, "featuring Louise Tobin (Lovely singer of songs)," would be part of a stage show performing the last Saturday in April.[12] Jenney disbanded his orchestra not long after this performance, and, leaving the responsibilities and pressures of leadership to someone else, he joined the Artie Shaw band. Jenney died on December 16, 1945, from complications following an appendectomy.

There is evidence to suggest that John Hammond continued to assist Louise with finding professional work. Leonard Feather wrote in *Down Beat* that "Louise Tobin is coming back—via records. Though she's still content to be just Mrs. Harry James, the former Goodman thrush expects to get into the swing again soon with a session John Hammond is arranging for her at Columbia. There's also a slight chance that she may take a band job again, in which case the Will Bradley combo stands first in line."[13] Indeed, the following month of this announcement and about two months after her performance with Jenney, on July 16, 1940, Louise was in a New York studio recording for Columbia Records with trombonist Will Bradley and his orchestra.[14] Her session resulted in two releases: "Deed I Do" arranged by Al Datz and "Don't Let It Get You Down." Datz (b. Alex V. Datzkenko) also arranged for Chicago-scene regular Muggsy Spanier.[15] Louise was called in for this recording date to replace Carlotta Dale (1915–1988), who with Ray McKinley and Jimmie Valentine had been taking care of the vocals since Bradley had formed his band back in July 1939. Louise's recollection was that because her recording session was her first day with the orchestra, there was not time to arrange anything for her, so she had to sing in McKinley's key (B♭ major) instead of hers (G major).[16] With confidence most likely developed after having performed and recorded such difficult charts as Goodman arranger Eddie Sauter's "Blue Orchids" (G major) and "Scatterbrain" (B♭ major), Louise's vocal on "Deed I Do" swings. The band opened at the State Ballroom in Boston followed by a tour of New England.[17] (Dale had performed with pianist Jess Stacy's band and also with fellow Philadelphian Jan Savitt and the Top Hatters.) Although Peanuts Hucko was a semiregular with Bradley at this time, performing on both tenor sax and clarinet, on this date with Louise, Peanuts was replaced by tenor sax player, clarinetist, and arranger Nick Caiazza.[18] Louise stated that Peanuts was fired for not playing clarinet. During a phone interview with Graham Pass of the BBC, Louise recalled that

> Peanuts was a name among musicians as a hot tenor player and [he] worked with Will Bradley. When Ray McKinley called me to work with Will Bradley in Boston where they would be for two weeks, Peanuts was with that band and had been fired *that* day for not being willing to play clarinet. They had certain arrangements and Peanuts was supposed to play certain notes on his clarinet, and he said he played them low on his tenor. He had issues with the alto sax player, and the guy went to Will and said Peanuts wasn't playing his clarinet part. They reprimanded him, and he got fired. He left the day I joined.[19]

Louise also sang with Bradley's orchestra at the Ritz Carlton in Boston. Her last performance with this ensemble was at the Merrimack Square theater in Lowell, Massachusetts, after which she traveled to Fayette-

Will Bradley and His Orchestra. (Courtesy of the Louise Tobin and Peanuts Hucko Jazz Collection)

ville, Arkansas, to stay with her sister.[20] Bradley and Tobin were getting favorable reviews in the jazz periodicals. Bob Bach for *Swing* wrote that "another new band that is worth your attention is Will Bradley's, and not the least of that band's assets is the recent acquisition of vocalist Louise Tobin, a swell singer."[21] Writing more specifically on Bradley's Columbia recording with Louise, Gordon Wright penned: "That Will Bradley band, paced by its stupendous rhythm section, lets loose more fine sides this month. . . . The leader plays more fine jazz on 'Deed I Do,' which Louise Tobin sings with much rhythmic gusto."[22] Despite such promising work with Bradley, by October 1940 the ninth-ranked "Girl Singer" left the band and public life in order to have her first child.[23] Indeed, about six months later she gave birth to Harry Jr. (b. March 3, 1941).

On January 1, 1941, Harry sent Louise a telegram: "Happy New Year darling. May the coming year be the happiest of your life. Love, Harry."[24] If professional achievement and acclaim resulted in happiness, then, yes, both Harry and Louise seemed from outside perspectives to have achieved much to be happy about. In February, Harry was voted the No. 1 white trumpeter, "the best since Bix Beiderbecke."[25] The following month they celebrated the birth of their first child, the same month during which Louise's 1939 recording of "There'll Be Some Changes Made" reached

No. 2 on Your Hit Parade. The recent success of the Goodman-Tobin version no doubt benefited from attention garnered by the RKO Radio Pictures film, *Playgirl*, staring Kay Francis, which included the song sung by another singer and which became a Billboard No. 1 hit for four weeks during April and May.[26] "There'll Be Some Changes Made" was, and would remain, Louise's biggest hit of her entire career. On May 20, Harry recorded what would become *his* most successful record, "You Made Me Love You."[27] Late that summer, July or August, Louise and Harry were already expecting their second child. Harry's band was booked for an extended run at the Hotel Lincoln, New York, which included air time. He had sublet a large apartment and invited Louise and baby, along with his father, Everett, as they were making plans to write a book, to all come and stay together. On her birthday, November 11, Louise received a lovely card and flowers from Harry: "Happy Birthday to the sweetest wife and mother in the world."[28] Louise was a famous celebrity with a famous husband whose band was hot and getting hotter. Late in 1941, Harry's recording "You Made Me Love You" and his orchestra were a national hit, and Louise was posing for pictures as a fashion representative mostly for clothes but also for such merchandise as a Bar-B-Que Pit.

At least this was the outside perspective, the public face of celebrity, achievements, and accolades. Privately, their relationship was becoming strained, ultimately to a point beyond repair. The separation between Harry and Louise, both physical and emotional, was growing greater and greater.

As the birth of their first child came nearer, Harry, typically, was on the road with the band, and Louise came home to Denton to be with her family and have the baby. Her doctor, not comfortable with Louise driving about forty miles of rough road to Dallas in order to see him, suggested that she find an apartment in Dallas. "I can't have the responsibility; you are liable to have that baby in Sanger!" she recalled him saying.[29] On March 3, 1941, Harry Jeffery James Jr. was born in Nightingale hospital, Dallas. The impact that parenthood had on each of their professional careers can be summed up in the newspaper announcement, which read: "The Harry Jameses (he's the great trumpet player, she was Louise Tobin, Benny Goodman's lark) are lullabying a baby."[30] He is; she was.

Shortly after mother and child returned home from the hospital, Harry's parents, Maybelle and Everett, arrived to see Louise and their first grandbaby. Unfortunately, tragedy fell on what should have been a joyous occasion. As they were heading out to lunch, Maybelle had just stepped outside and suffered a severe heart attack; she died instantly. "Then Harry had to come home," Louise recalled. He came back, picked up his father and Louise's sister, Virginia, and drove them to Beaumont for the funeral, immediately after which he took Virginia back to Louise in Dallas and left for a gig in Florida. About two months later on May 20, 1941, Harry recorded "You Made Me Love You."[31]

Harry was back in New York for a seventeen-week engagement, performing in Maria Kramer's Blue Room of the Hotel Lincoln, which included national CBS radio broadcasts. He had sublet a beautiful, five-bedroom apartment from a conductor at Carnegie Hall (Walter Damrosch?) with room enough for himself, Louise, Harry Jr., Everett, and Harry's bass player's wife, "because she didn't have any place to stay. Bands just did that," Louise recalled.[32] Everett, as noted above, was there, because he and Harry had planned to write a book together. "Harry was so busy getting the band together, he didn't have time to work on the book with his dad."[33]

"And one weekend [in July 1941]," Louise recalled, "I call it the 'fatal weekend,' Harry said, 'I'm just exhausted. I've got the whole weekend off. Let's run up to the Adirondacks. Dad will keep the baby.' And something happened then, when we were driving. And en route he heard Helen [Forrest] sing on the radio. She was singing 'Springtime in the Rockies,' which actually was the first record I ever heard. My dad brought that home. Anyway, we only stayed overnight, and we were supposed to stay three or four days. Harry said, 'I've got to get back.' So, we went back to New York, and, somehow, he got hold of Helen and made arrangements for her to come with the band. And then it wasn't very long after that till he wasn't coming home at night. He decided to stay at the hotel. That just got to be a deal. It wound up not being very good. I'd barely gotten there with the baby and got pregnant again. I remember my conversation. I called him on the phone. I said, 'You're not coming back, are you?' and he said, 'no.' 'What am I gonna do?' and he said, 'I don't give a damn.' And I said that's the end of that."[34]

"That *was* the end of that. Dad decided to go home, and he did. My bedroom was way at the back of this apartment. I woke up the next morning and three of my sisters were standing over me. From Texas, they came to take me home. I had called and told my younger sister and said, 'this thing has fallen apart.' I said, 'no matter what happens, don't let him get this baby.' That was what I was concerned about, and the next day there were three of my sisters. I thought I had died. I woke up and there [they were], so two of them flew back, and one stayed and packed me up. And she said, 'they are waiting for you in California. One of my sisters was there. She said they've got an apartment near her, and everything is going to be okay. So, we drove to Texas. Dad went home on the train. And then we went on out to California. That was the end of that."[35]

They did not officially divorce until July 1943; nevertheless, three undated poems that Louise wrote and typed up all on one page reveal her suffering over her separation as well as her feelings of rejection from Harry.

Any One for Tea?
The tea bag lies forlornly there
Squeezed of usefulness, brittle and dry
Forgotten after dinner
My heart, discarded by your love
Lies, too cowardly to rise again to life's balm
Of self-giving
And deteriorates in the yellow juice of Bitterness
Oozing from its grieving innards

Finality
What is so final to a boy renegade
As to come from breakfast
To find his bed made?

On Wings of Wind[36]
It's dusk . . . the moon rises thru the mist
To light my evening shroud
There . . . somewhere you are on a podium
Lost in the adoration of the crowd
The music fills the hall you're in
And drifts across the sea
They hear music . . . I hear sobs. . . .
You're not coming back to me.

Louise dated her poem, "Obliteration" November 1942.

Obliteration

A gaping hole torn in her heart for all the world to see
With mortal wound she gropes for self under
reeling waves of uncertainty
He's gone. The life-giving blood of love drained
She will arise a ghost at dawn
To move through nights and days of numb despair
The river of futility seems long
Spreading over the golden desert of joy
Black, Black and empty is the future of the deserted
When the sun is gone
The yawning abyss of self-destruction lies temptingly near
But truth pierces the curtain of tears
To say "all's not in vain,"
But life does not return until love comes back again.

Helen Forrest was Benny Goodman's "permanent" replacement for Louise; she sang for Goodman from December 1939 to mid-June 1941, during which time she recorded fifty-three sides.[37] In her autobiography, Forrest recalled that when she quit the band at the beginning of August 1941, Goodman made her fulfill her contract until the end of the month, during which time she "sat alongside Peggy [Lee] on the bandstand and didn't sing a note for four weeks. She'd get up and sing, but I never got up. When people would ask me why I wasn't singing, I'd say, 'Ask Benny.' They'd ask him, and he'd say, 'She's got laryngitis.' I was healthy as a horse."[38]

As recounted, Louise recalled that "somehow Harry got a hold of Helen and made arrangements for her to come with the band." Helen Forrest, no doubt, would have loved to have written in her autobiography that Harry had reached out to her, but it was in fact the other way around. According to Forrest, "When I heard Harry James was auditioning girl singers, I asked for an audition. I don't know what instinct drew me to Harry, but I loved the way he played, especially on ballads."[39] Sinatra had left Harry to sing with Tommy Dorsey, and Harry then had hired Dick Haymes. Harry auditioned Forrest "at the Lincoln Hotel in New York one night in November 1941,"[40] during the orchestra's seventeen-week run.

Back in Texas on her way to the West Coast, Louise explained her trip and move to California to a Denton reporter, not surprisingly making no mention of her row with Harry. A September 1941 article in the *Denton Record-Chronicle* announced that "Denton's Big-Time Band Singer" was leaving to join Harry in California making domestic life her number-one priority with "plans to do a little radio and recording work on the side."[41] Louise had declared that "singing engagements in stage, radio and record- ing work have taken second place in the Denton-reared blues singer's life. 'We're going to have a home for this baby to grow up in,' she said, explaining her trip to California while James plays an engagement in Boston and is scheduled for five or six weeks of one-night stands soon."[42]

Louise Tobin with Harry James, ca. 1942. (Courtesy of the Louise Tobin and Peanuts Hucko Jazz Collection)

Despite having left Goodman, taking care of a new baby, and publicly expressing a move toward domesticity, Louise still bore both the fruits and challenges of celebrity. In the summer after the birth of Harry Jr., Louise made more news as a fashion model than a jazz singer. While in California, CBS Radio hired Louise to pose in a variety of photos promoting mostly women's fashion but also such home items as a "Colorful, New Bar-B-Que Pit."

> Miss Louise Tobin, lovely former radio singing star and who will be best remembered as the star vocalist of Benny Goodman's band, is seen inspecting the new patio and Bar-B-que Pit especially designed and created for her by Basso-Riddell & Fisher. Miss Tobin's Bar-B-que Pit is constructed of Roman brick. The flooring is colorful Arizona flagstone.[43]

In newspaper clippings dated from November 1941 to September 1942, Louise can be seen advertising a "Bowcatcher Playsuit," a "striking three-piece playsuit worn by CBS songstress Louise Tobin,"[44] bowling shorts, worn by "pretty CBS songstress Louise Tobin,"[45] a "bandana cloth in bright red and yellow is fashioned into a three-piece playsuit for pert CBS singer Louise Tobin—Bloomer Girl 1942,"[46] and a "Chicly Matched Summer hat and bag ensemble worn by songstress Louise Tobin while in Palm Springs [which] points to a new trend in the accessories field which is to be played up this fall . . . Louise's hat is white straw with red, white and blue facing to match her huge underarm bag."[47]

Louise and Harry's second child, Jerin Timothyray James, was born on March 21, 1942. Despite the support that she continued to receive from her sisters, 1942 was another difficult year for her. Harry was consumed with leading his orchestra, leaving Louise to raise the boys on her own, a recording ban in the fall had essentially curtailed any potential studio dates Louise might have had, and America's entry into the second world war, all had to have significantly heightened Louise's anxieties.

One afternoon in May 1943, Louise picked up her mail and noticed a letter from *Down Beat*. A representative from the magazine had sent her a list of questions in preparation for an upcoming article addressing the question: "Does Marriage Mix with a Career?" Among the specific questions were the following: "Do you believe a girl singer should marry in or out of profession? Have you and your husband made any special arrangements in your mode of living to compensate for professional difficulties that might arise? Do you believe a singer should continue working after wed, or retire? Do you believe rearing children interferes with a singing career? Was this or any prior marriage wrecked for you by professional differences? What would be your advice, based on personal experience, to a girl singer who is contemplating matrimony? Any other facts about yourself, or opinions concerning the problems confronting a singer who weds?"[48]

Given the fact that Louise was literally in the middle of a divorce, it is not surprising that she did not reply. Indeed, about a week before opening this letter, Louise's lawyer, Robert Ford, received a call from Harry's attorney, "requesting that she go to Reno as soon as possible" for divorce proceedings.[49] Harry had plans to marry actress Betty Grable, with whom he had been having an affair, or, quoting the cheeky language of a 1943 gossip columnist, [Harry] "began turning the primitive rhythms of his golden trumpet into a romantic plea to Miss Grable some six or eight months ago."[50] Louise agreed to the divorce, but stated that "it will have to be here in Los Angeles."[51] She ultimately agreed to meet in El Paso, Texas, for a quick and official separation across the river at Juárez, Mexico. A piece in the *New York Times* stated that "their marriage had been openly turbulent for more than a year."[52] A statement from Louise's attorney quoted her as saying that "Betty Grable had not caused the separation more than a year ago. James' absences from home while filling orchestra engagements was a factor in their decision to part, Ford said."[53]

Her original divorce settlement awarded Louise a yearly income of $6,000 for herself and the raising of her two boys. Adjusted for inflation, $6,000 in 1944 is equal to $86,632.07 in 2019. In October 1944, an out-of-court property settlement made prior to her divorce awarded her an additional $13,994, which, again, adjusted for inflation, is equal to $202,054.86 in 2019.[54] Indeed, she had enough money to live comfortably, and in an interview noted that anytime her boys wanted anything beyond what she could provide, Harry would approve his lawyer to make it happen. When the boys wanted ponies; they got ponies, for example.

After the divorce, Louise was soon no longer in the news, and she essentially stopped performing for two or three years. No more modeling the latest trends in fashion. With the exception of an invitation to pose for a screen test for movie producer Howard Hawks, Hollywood stopped calling.[55] She remained in California, however, and on occasion Louise

Louise Tobin's screen test photo for Howard Hawks, 1943. (© Wallace Seawell / mptvimages.com)

was able to take advantage of a few opportunities to perform and record; "people would call me," she remembered.[56]

The first documentation of professional work since she recorded and performed with Will Bradley and His Orchestra in the fall of 1940 was recording four tracks with Tommy Jones and His Orchestra in late 1945 or more likely early 1946. She did not have any live dates with Jones, and, while she recalled that he was a very good trumpet player, Louise could not add further information about her only recording date with his

Tex Williams with Louise Tobin, Harry James Jr., and Tim James, ca. 1944. (Courtesy of the Louise Tobin and Peanuts Hucko Jazz Collection)

orchestra. The recording session was in New York on the Sterling Records label, and she sang "One-zy, Two-zy," "We'll Gather Lilacs," "Where Did You Learn to Love?" and "All through the Day" (Sterling 7001–02).

An advertisement in the April 20, 1946, issue of *Billboard*, probably issued by Sterling, describes Jones's music as "highly commercial" and sporting "highly listenable arrangements." The ad also noted that "Louise Tobin, former vocalist with Harry James during his early days in the business, turns in some good singing on all four sides. 'One-zy Two-zy' gets a standard interpretation but Louise comes back with a sock 'We'll Gather Lilacs' as a backer. She repeats her success with 'All through the Day,' the Kern-Hammerstein song from 'Centennial Summer,' and does some nice singing on 'Where'd You Learn to Love?'"[57]

Louise's singing with Jones received greater praise than the orchestra leader in a review in *Metronome*:

> This sounds like just another band, dull arrangements, plodding rhythm section and leader Jones featured on an averagely good trumpet. But then on each side along comes Louise Tobin, the former Mrs. Harry James and Goodman vocalist, with some fine singing. She sounds especially fine on the two B minus sides ["One-zy, Two-zy" and "Where Did You Learn to Love"], singing lovely verse on the first and making more out of the tune than anyone else has on records, and getting a fine beat on Where despite the tempo being too fast. The ballads are less to everyone's liking, including Louise's.[58]

Maurie Orodenker, writing for *Band Leaders and Record Review*, offered a more favorable review of the Jones/Tobin combination:

> Louise Tobin, former chanter with Harry James, scores a personal triumph on all four sides and gets some mighty fine assisting from the Jones crew. "One-zy, Two-zy" is treated in nice style and is backed with a sweet rendition of "We'll Gather Lilacs." "Where Did You Learn to Love" is given jump treatment, which Louise handles very nicely, and she does as well on "All through the Day."[59]

Trumpeter and bandleader Tommy Jones was advertised as "still a newcomer in the field," yet he had headed an earlier version of his orchestra in

Harry James and Louise Tobin's two sons, Harry Jr. (b. 1941) and Tim (b. 1942), playing outside with trumpets, 1945. (Courtesy of the Louise Tobin and Peanuts Hucko Jazz Collection)

New York in the 1930s.[60] He also had played trumpet for Kay Kyser until joining the Army in 1942.[61] Indeed, as with many of the swing musicians discharged from service at the end of World War II, Jones had to restart his career and at a time when big band swing orchestras were on the way out and small ensemble bebop music was emerging. Musical styles were changing and swing musicians had to either adapt or struggle to forge careers performing music that was becoming more and more for aging audiences seeking nostalgia.

Around the time that she recorded with Tommy Jones, Louise accepted an invitation to sing with Emil Coleman and His Orchestra. Coleman (1892–1965), Russian immigrant, pianist, conductor, and arranger, had a high-priced society orchestra with regular engagements at the Mocambo in Hollywood and, starting in early October 1945, at the Empire Room of the Waldorf Astoria.[62] In 1945 Louise recorded two soundies with Coleman and his orchestra that included strings: "Just One of Those Things" and "June Comes around Every Year."[63] The string section in Coleman's orchestra, lack of improvised solos, and smooth style resurrect pre-swing-era dance orchestras. Louise's singing on these soundies is at times just behind the beat, presenting a confident, sexy, and swinging style.

Louise Tobin promotional photograph by Chicago-based celebrity photographer, Maurice Seymour, ca. 1945. (Courtesy Ronald Seymour)

The big band era was essentially over by the end of World War II. By December 1946, eight top bandleaders announced that they were quitting: Woody Herman, Benny Goodman, Harry James, Les Brown, Jack Teagarden, Benny Carter, Ina Ray Hutton and Tommy Dorsey. Perhaps, then, it is not surprising that Louise began working with a couple of smaller groups.

In Los Angeles, Louise performed a few dates in the fall of 1946 with Skippy Anderson, who had "a new small combo . . . featuring Louise Tobin on vocals," and on December 9, 1947, for the Rhythm Note label, she recorded two sides with Swedish clarinetist Åke "Stan" Hasselgård: "Lullaby in Rhythm" and "A Cottage for Sale."[64] A friend from her Goodman days, drummer Nick Fatool, was on the session, as were Al Hendrickson on guitar, Lyman Gandee, piano, and Jud De Naut on bass. Louise met Hasselgård through her niece, Barbara Turner, who had come to Hollywood chasing a dream to become a star. "She was in Wallach's Record Shop [in Hollywood]," Louise recalled. "They had these little booths where you took records to play them. She was in there, and, she was a really good looking girl. Two guys tapped on the door, and in their broken English said, 'we are from Sweden. Can you tell me a little about jazz.' And she [said] 'of course.' When they found out her aunt had been with Benny Goodman, here she stands at my door with these two Swedish guys, and they were very hard to get rid of. I don't think I remember how I did it. He was a very nice guy. They were with no money. Stan was a good player. Benny took him under his wing and was going to make him a major star. They were en route to a date, and the lady driving fell asleep and killed them both. He had such potential."[65] Louise did not perform any live dates with Hasselgård. This session is significant in Louise's recording history, her first recording with a small ensemble. She did not perform with small ensembles again until she came out of retirement in 1960.

Louise first met trumpeter Ziggy Elman (1914–1968) in the late 1930s through Harry's and later her own work with Goodman. Ziggy's tenure with Benny lasted from 1935 until 1940.[66] After performing for a bit with Joe Venuti, he joined Tommy Dorsey's band until he was drafted into the US Army in 1944. After the war, Ziggy worked a bit with Dorsey again but was eager to start his own band, which, after an attempt in 1947, he succeeded doing in 1948. The band opened at the Golden Gate Theatre, San Francisco, in late June of that year.[67] Elman had made a name for himself with Goodman, both as part of the renowned three-piece horn section nicknamed "The Biting Brass"—Harry James, Ziggy Elman, and Chris Griffin—and, after Harry's departure, as a soloist and composer of the popular song "And the Angels Sing," which became his theme song.[68]

For Ziggy's engagement at the Hollywood Palladium in late August and early September of 1948, he called Louise to fill out the vocal department.[69] Also singing with Elman were Bob Allen and the Top Notchers. Allen had sung with Hal Kemp's band in the middle and late 1930s until Kemp's death in an automobile accident in 1940. He later sang with Tommy Dorsey, no doubt where he met Ziggy, before and after the war.[70] Arranger and trumpeter Neal Hefti was writing arrangements for Ziggy.[71] He was also playing and writing for Harry's band in 1948 and 1949.[72] Hefti had left Woody Herman's band in 1946, and he was freelancing for most of the late 1940s until he began arranging for Count Basie in 1950.

Louise's vocal numbers with the Ziggy Elman Orchestra at the Hollywood Palladium include "A Boy from Texas," "September Song," "You Turned the Tables on Me," and "If I Could Be with You."[73]

Louise Tobin on stage with Ziggy Elman and His Orchestra at the Hollywood Palladium, Los Angeles, CA, 1948. Singer Bob Allen on her right and Ziggy Elman with trumpet, standing behind her left. (Courtesy of the Louise Tobin and Peanuts Hucko Jazz Collection)

According to Ziggy Elman biographer Charles Garrod, the band was a regular on the ABC *Jo Stafford Show* in the fall of 1948. Louise was not with the band for these appearances. She did record Philip Charig and Ira Gershwin's "Sunny Disposish" on Ziggy Elman and His Orchestra's Mercury 1951 recording, *The Birth of the Blues* (11089).[74] This was her last recording with Elman. Singer Virginia Maxey (1923–2016) "replaces Tobin," by December 11, 1951, according to Garrod.[75]

Down Beat reviewer Jack Tracy considered the Elman band's performance of "Birth of the Blues" as "highly unswinging." The band and Louise's singing on "Sunny Disposish" garnered higher praise: "Louise Tobin . . . sounds just like she did 10 years ago. The band is crisper, cleaner, gives a better performance."[76]

Barry Ulanov's review of these two tracks for *Metronome* characterized both Ziggy and Louise as products of "the dear dead days with Benny." "One of the sunny dispositions of the past, Louise Tobin comes back to sing with ex-husband Harry James' sidekick of the dear dead days with Benny. Louise ain't what she used to be in voice, except for a half-note or crotchet now and then of the Mildred Baileyish hum which used to warm her work, but she's still very nice to have around and Ziggy, when he plays muted trumpet is a doll too."[77]

Louise continued to pick up the occasional odd job, although still focusing more on raising her boys than on a singing career. She was active enough in entertainment circles to make friends with Hollywood musicians and actors, drawn to several who shared strong, Christian beliefs. Early in the 1950s she was part of a group who regularly gathered together and listened to a Gospel preacher. A *Los Angeles Times* article dated February 6, 1950, shows a picture of such a group including Louise and cowboy singer Tim Spencer of the Sons of the Pioneers. Louise recalled that Marilyn Monroe was a regular among the group.

On November 27, 1954, *Billboard* reviewed two recordings that Louise had done for the MGM music label: "Hurry Home" and "Lonesome Road." The MGM film studio launched its record division as MGM Records in 1946. The reviewer praised Louise's performance on the recordings: "Louise Tobin, who sang with the Benny Goodman ork [*sic*] a few years ago, bows on the label with a warm reading of a pleasant new ballad over appropriate ork [*sic*] backing. Good late hours program wax. She has a chance with the right material."[78]

By the end of the decade, Louise's boys were off to college, and she began to work toward coming out of retirement. She had kept in touch through correspondence with many of her musical friends of the past. Jazz writer, critic, and editor of *Metronome* magazine, George T. Simon, took the time to forward fan mail with a penciled note at the bottom of one letter from himself: "Louise—Thought you'd like to see this. Will write more soon. How is everything? Love, George."[79]

Simon had long held a fondness for Louise as a person and continued to admire her abilities as a vocalist. Writing just a few months prior to her recordings for MGM in 1954, he included Louise in his list of predictions.

And finally I'd like to crawl out a bit more tentatively for a fine girl singer, Louise Tobin, who used to sing for Benny Goodman, who retired to be with her two sons, and who now, according to some acetates I received this month, is singing much better than ever. She combines a musical, jazz-tinged style with a commercial appeal that should make her a decided asset to a recording company and a very welcome talent to have back with us in this field that is suffering so from a dearth of singers as good and as honest-sounding as she is.[80]

The November 1, 1959, *Dallas Morning News* announced that "Nat Todora, who is personal manager for Dick & Kiz Harp, recently signed Louise Tobin to his list of clients."[81] Louise was officially coming out of retirement, and George Simon was not only instrumental in her return to the bandstand but also in introducing Louise to her professional partner and future husband, Peanuts Hucko.

5

"Can She Still Sing?" 1960–1970

Louise Tobin, ex-wife of Harry James,
will resume her career.[1]

IN A PHONE interview with BBC radio host Graham Pass on July 1, 2010, Louise recalled the circumstances that brought her out of retirement and led to her meeting Glenn Miller, Benny Goodman, and Louis Armstrong alum, clarinetist Peanuts Hucko.

> I had a dear friend who was very in to music, and she wanted to go to New Orleans to hear Al Hirt and Pete Fountain. My sons were gone, and I was just sitting on the hill by myself. We were two women, and when we went into Al's club, we kind of got in the corner, in the dark, and we thought we were isolated. The bartender kept looking at me kind of strangely. He came over and said, "Are you a singer? Is your name Tobin?" It turned out that he was an ex-musician who had been in a band in New York, and I had worked with him in New York. Al called me up to sing and was very nice to me. That little song was recorded by someone who sent it to George Simon. He was a friend of mine and a special friend of Harry's. He was a jazz critic, and he wrote *Simon Says* and the big band books.[2] A very nice man. I had known George in New York and was very fond of his wife Beverly. Bev's mother was my age, and we were very good friends. George called, and said "Louise, you have got to come to New York and sing again." He insisted, and I fumed around about that, and finally I said, "George, I haven't worked for years, and I don't think I should do

that." I did finally go, and I stayed with George and Bev. He wanted to do some records with me, and he contacted George Wein, and
they wanted to put me on the Newport Jazz Festival. "Oh, George, I
just can't do that. I'm so nervous, and I haven't worked in so long."
He said, "I'm doing a small jazz festival in Fairfield, Connecticut, and
how would you like to go up there and get your feet wet." "I would
like that," [I said,] "because I don't know if I can do Newport." I asked
him who was playing the festival, and he said Peanuts Hucko. I said,
"you mean the hot tenor player." George said, "Louise, you have been
gone a long time. He's now a fantastic clarinet player, and he has a
good little band, and you'll like it." I said, "Can he still play?" He called
Peanuts, and said, "I have a girl I want to put on the show up there,
and her name is Louise Tobin. She sang with Goodman." Peanuts said,
"I remember her. I used to listen to her records, when I was with the
Will Bradley band. We'd play Dallas, Texas, and I used to go downstairs and put money in the record machine to hear her records." He
said, "Can she still sing?" George told him I wanted to know if Peanuts could still play.[3]

Peanuts had been at the epicenter of swing and traditional jazz, having played during the 1940s with Glenn Miller, Benny Goodman, Ray
McKinley, and Eddie Condon among others, and, in the 1950s, as many
swing era musicians did after the war, he began doing more studio work,
in his case working at the CBS studios in New York City as a staff musician. Musicians who could get enough regular calls for studio work benefited by being able to stay off the road. Nevertheless, by the mid-1950s
and with the emergence of rock and roll, Peanuts found himself back
on the road, touring Japan with Goodman (1956) and in 1957 touring
the greater part of western Europe with Jack Teagarden and Earl Hines.
From 1958 to 1960 he performed regularly with Louis Armstrong's
All-Stars. When he met Louise in preparation for their festival gig in
Fairfield, he was back in New York, playing with Ralph Sutton's quartet
at Eddie Condon's.

Peanuts and Louise quickly began to forge a strong connection both
personally and musically. They were the same age, had both worked with
Goodman and McKinley and others, and they shared a musical preference
for the big band era, Dixieland, and traditional jazz, styles of music in
contrast to such modern jazz streams as hard bop, West Coast jazz, soul
jazz, modal jazz, Third Stream jazz, and free jazz.[4] Peanuts and Louise were

among what one contemporary *New York Times* contributor called "the faithful of jazz—those musicians . . . whose interest in non-contemporary jazz styles has never flagged," swing era veterans whose music that was once mainstream had become marginalized.[5] Bus tours with large orchestras traveling from city to city and ballroom to ballroom were no longer money-making ventures. A musician might find work as a studio musician or on television with one of the house orchestras, but for the most part, it was the era of the small combo, working in nightclubs, perhaps at festivals, or such house parties as Dick Gibson's Colorado Jazz Party and its model, the Odessa Jazz Party in West Texas.[6]

The first annual Connecticut Jazz Festival was associated with Fairfield University in July 1956 and featured Duke Ellington, who appeared with pianists Willie "The Lion" Smith and Hank Jones, trumpeter Buck Clayton, bassist Walter Page, and drummer Art Trappier.[7] Further information on Louise's (and Peanuts's) performance at this jazz festival in the early 1960s to supplement her mention of this in her interview with the BBC quoted above is minimal. More documentation, in contrast, is available regarding the Newport Jazz Festival, its history in general, and the 1962 event more specifically.

The Newport Jazz Festival was launched in the summer of 1954 by Boston jazz promoter George Wein (at the time owner of the city's Storyville Club [opened in 1950] and Mahogany Hall [opened in 1952]) and Newport jazz aficionados Elaine and Louis Lorillard, who had the capital to bankroll this venture.[8]

After a riotous incident in 1960 and despite the favorable advertisement the Festival received with the 1960 release of the film of the 1958 Festival titled *Jazz on a Summer's Day*,[9] the Newport city council canceled the Festival in 1961 but allowed it to resume the following year. Paul R. Laird in his "Newport Jazz Festival" entry in *Grove Music Online* notes that during the 1960s, the Festival "grew considerably, in part because popular music was added to its programs . . . and in part because of [corporate] sponsorship."[10] Though the 1962 festival contained no "fringe-jazz acts or out-and-out pop acts, which," according to critic David Bittan, "have often marred the artistic integrity of the festival during its nine-year history," programming did offer a mix of traditional and modern jazz, or perhaps rather than characterized as "a mix," programming might more accurately be described as representing two extremes reflective of a growing chasm between traditional (à la Louis Armstrong) and modern, more progressive jazz (à la Max Roach).[11]

Louise performed on Sunday evening, July 8, the second day of the three-day festival, at Freebody Park, Newport, Rhode Island. She sang three songs—"Should I," "I Got It Bad and That Ain't Good," and "Deed I Do"—each with the Newport All Stars, which included George Wein on piano, Ruby Braff on cornet, Marshall Brown on valve trombone, Pee Wee Russell on clarinet, John Neves on bass, and Buzzy Drootin on drums.[12] Also on the program were Duke Ellington and His Orchestra, with Thelonious Monk sitting in, and Monk's quartet, which accompanied Aretha Franklin on a couple of numbers.

Louise's performance has not been preserved on the film directed by Buddy Bregman, which was issued on DVD in 2004.[13] Two of the most detailed published reviews of Newport 1962 are Whitney Balliett's for the *New Yorker* and David B. Bittan's for *Variety*; both were favorable of her set overall, though neither mentioned Louise specifically.[14] Among the "other delights during the weekend," Balliett wrote the following:

> Sunday night, Wein, crowning his managerial functions, sat down at the piano and, in an engaging Jess Stacy–Fats Waller–Teddy Wilson fashion, led a group consisting of Ruby Braff, Pee Wee Russell, Marshall Brown, Bud Freeman, John Neves, and Buzzy Drootin through six numbers. These included a relaxed rendition of Waller's "Crazy 'Bout' My Baby"; a "Blue and Sentimental" notable for its tempo (molasses dripping) and for Braff's gorgeous playing; and a slow blues in which Russell tunneled through four lower-register choruses. Wein's group, which has worked together off and on for several years, represents a type of jazz that is rapidly disappearing. Relaxed, emotional, unpretentious, and of no school, it firms the heart and brightens the eye, and it will be a gloomy day when it is gone.[15]

Bittan's review noted the dominance of traditionalism over modernists with respect to programming, noting that "the riot of 1960 was all but obliterated by a wave of respectability, of dignity that pushed the 'jazzniks' and their antics into the background."[16] "This was the year for the jazz purists, and Wein didn't disappoint them," Bittan continued, "Ellington and Count Basie showed as usual that the big bands are the real essence of jazz."[17] He then lists Sunday night's features ending with a set by "the

Festival All Stars, featuring a group of veteran jazzmen including producer Wein on piano."[18]

Although neither critic mentioned Louise's specific performance at Newport 1962, Balliett did ultimately send her a personal letter, bestowing high praise. It is worth quoting in its entirety. On September 18, 1962, Balliett wrote, acknowledging Louise's launch on her new career:

> Dear Miss Tobin: You sang at Newport the way the young Billie Holiday, the young Ella Fitzgerald, and Mildred Bailey used to sing—with warmth and a total lack of calculation. May your new career top your first one. Sincerely, Whitney Balliett[19]

Louise Tobin photo by James L. Kriegsmann, 1965. (Courtesy of James J. Kriegsmann Jr)

After the Festival, Louise returned to New York and began to work with Peanuts around the city. Her younger sister was president of the Gramercy Park Hotel chain, and she gave Louise a reasonable rate on an apartment there, the Gramercy Park Hotel, Twenty-First Street and Lexington Avenue, New York City. She and Peanuts were initially doing a lot of club dates and some weddings. She was pleased to be singing regularly again, though she found navigating the new scene to be challenging. "We did a lot of casuals," she recalled. "I had not been in New York for a while, and things had really changed. I had to get arrangements made and figure out the new scene. We started playing in New York, New Jersey, Massachusetts, and other places."[20] "It was a difficult time for a lot of jazz musicians," she recalled. "Jazz was beginning to be overwhelmed by rock and roll. Peanuts worked on the NBC house band. He recorded with several people. Major name musicians stayed in New York, and their basic income was from the studios and [they] made their main money with recording, and their supplemental income from going out and doing dates."[21]

Louise's return to performing was not without its bumpy roads. Critics labeled her a nostalgia-invoking product of the big band era, singing, in the words of Balliett, "a type of jazz that is rapidly disappearing."[22] Nevertheless, she embraced her role, singing in a manner more evocative of a past era than experimentally modern. Her vocal style as well as her promotional material linked her directly to Goodman and the swing era. To at least one critic, she sounded "rusty." Writing on her singing with Peanuts and the Tommy Gwaltney Quartet with whom they joined for a two-week gig at Gwaltney's Blues Alley in Washington, DC, in the spring of 1965, John Pagones noted that "both Hucko and Miss Tobin are products of the big band era and in no way are they incompatible with the Gwaltney combo. Miss Tobin sounds rusty. She has been out of circulation for some years and it shows by her uneven performance. She does some ballads well and performs better in her duets with Hucko, but then there are some tunes in which she all but flounders. No doubt she'll be in fine fettle before the engagement is over. I must say, with that big open voice, she sounds startlingly like Martha Tilton. Remember her?"[23]

Pagones expressed a more favorable review of her return performance at Blues Alley about four months later: "Louise Tobin, Benny Goodman's onetime soloist who had been out of music for almost a decade, and Maxine Sullivan, a grandmother now, . . . they did fabulously well."[24]

Peanuts liked working with Louise, featuring her on vocal numbers. Back in New York at Eddie Condon's in late April, early May 1966, they continued to perform together and were falling in love.[25] In between engagements in New York and along the East Coast with Louise, Peanuts had been performing in Colorado for Dick Gibson's jazz parties. Gibson had invited Peanuts virtually every year since the first Jazz Party back in 1963.[26] Peanuts for a long time had been aware of the jazz scene in Denver and other cities in Colorado. In addition to Gibson's yearly jazz parties, the Trocadero Ballroom at Elitch Gardens was still featuring dance bands. Though mostly racially segregated at the time, Denver had been a hub for jazz musicians, particularly during the 1930s, '40s, and '50s, when such musicians as Duke Ellington and Ella Fitzgerald were among those who stopped to perform in some of the night clubs along Welton Street in the predominantly African American neighborhood of Five Points, referred to as "Harlem of the West."[27] Writing in 1976, Robert H. Byler Jr. noted that the "magnet for preservationists," however, is across town at "Larimer Square, and for jazz fans, The Basin Street lounge at Zeno's in Larimer Square, where the Queen City Jazz Band performs. The band, led by Alan Frederickson, was formed in 1957. Zeno's is named for Henry Zeno, a pioneer New Orleans jazz drummer."[28] For Peanuts, the draw to Denver was a business venture that would set him up as headliner of his own jazz club and restaurant.

As Louise recalled, "over a period of time people in Denver (a lawyer, oil man, and two doctors) wanted to open a jazz club. They wanted [Peanuts] to go to Denver and open a club, use his name and open a posh club. Peanuts would have a third. He asked me to go to Denver to open the club. Peanuts and many of the better musicians who had been pushed out by rock and roll were going to Europe to play. He opened the club in 1967. Peanuts said: 'I want to get married in June, and I want you to marry me, and if you don't want that, then I want you to leave.' I said, yes!" [29]

Both Peanuts and Louise looked forward to starting a new chapter in their lives. Working from a home base where they had steady work would allow them more financial security as well as reduce their time on the road. Indeed, they opened Peanuts Hucko's Navarre restaurant and jazz club in light of such appealing prospects.

Louise arrived in Denver alone. Peanuts had sent her on to make sure all of the preparations were in order at the Navarre; he had to fulfill a

Peanuts Hucko and Louise Tobin outside their newly opened club and restaurant, Club Navarre, 1967. (Photo by Fred Moldenhauer, The Louise Tobin and Peanuts Hucko Jazz Collection)

Promotional photograph of Louise Tobin and Peanuts Hucko inside Club Navarre, 1967. (Courtesy of the Louise Tobin and Peanuts Hucko Jazz Collection)

Louise Tobin and Peanuts Hucko at their wedding. (Courtesy of the Louise Tobin and Peanuts Hucko Jazz Collection)

brief solo tour of the United Kingdom. He would complete the tour and return to Louise in Denver just prior to the opening of the club and their nuptials. Louise was immediately busy, overseeing the club renovations and preparations and also planning their wedding.

The grand opening of the Navarre at 1727 Tremont Place, Denver, Colorado, was on Wednesday, May 31, 1967. Peanuts and Louise were married about four weeks later on June 25 in a Presbyterian Church in Littleton, Colorado.[30]

They performed most nights at the Navarre as part of a house band that backed such invited guests as pianists Dave McKenna, Ralph Sutton, and Teddy Wilson, trumpeter Bobby Hackett, banjoist-singer Clancy Hayes, drummer Morey "The Greyhound" Feld, and clarinetist and bandleader Woody Herman, to name only a few of such musicians from the big band era.[31] James D. Shacter, author of Sutton's biography, interviewed Peanuts, who recounted their association and work at the Navarre.

> Hucko, who regarded Sutton as a brother, thoroughly enjoyed having Ralph at the Navarre: "He plays magnificently. He's got such beautiful time, and he knows how to complement me. He always plays the right thing behind me, and he's just sensational as a soloist."[32]

Sutton was also living in Colorado, having met and married Sunnie Anderson, owner of an Aspen supper club called Sunnie's Rendezvous. They met during Dick Gibson's second Jazz Party in September 1964. Peanuts had known Sutton for many years, having worked with his sextet at the Famous Door in New York back in 1947 and more recently (1960) with Sutton's quartet at Eddie Condon's.

Local reviews of the Navarre restaurant and club were favorable, one describing Louise in these words: "The ribbon on the package was pert and petite Louise Tobin (Mrs. Hucko since June 26 [*sic*]) who has to be the happiest jazz singer around. She charmed the crowd with her warmth and tremendous range on everything from 'It Had to Be You' to 'Have I Stayed Too Long at the Fair?'"[33]

The Navarre had a checkered past, and Peanuts and his investors played it up in the *Navarre Times*, a single-issue "newspaper" given to Navarre guests, combining fact and fiction in creatively written narratives (by unattributed author[s]) about Louise, Peanuts, the establishment, restaurant, chef, menu, artwork on the walls, and musicians who had joined Peanuts and Louise as guest artists for the nightly music. Nevertheless, the history of the establishment recounted in this paper is rather accurate:

> Now featuring some of the finest swinging jazz and French cuisine in the country, the Navarre began as the Brinker Collegiate Institute in 1879. The institute taught "fineries" to proper young Denver ladies for about ten years.
>
> When the institute closed its discreet doors about 1889, it fell into the hands of two gambling kings, who ran it as the Richelieu, a questionable but classy hotel.
>
> Legend says that the gamblers lost the hotel to two other gamblers. These gay dogs changed its name to the Navarre, after Henry of Navarre who was reputed to have been a lover of wine, women, and song.
>
> The Navarre became a famed gambling house and brothel. Underneath the building, the two owners built a railroad which still exists, so that wild and whoopin' Denver's gentlemen of leisure could come and go without their wives or the Ladies' Sewing Circle seeing them. The tracks ran underground across the street and into the basement of a nearby building.
>
> In 1904, all this fancy sin came to an end when a crusading mayor lowered the boom on gambling and prostitution. The fabulous Navarre became the dully respectable Navarre Café.

PEANUTS HUCKO and LOUISE TOBIN

"Peanuts" Hucko. . . First Class Clarinetist
- Bob Sylvester, N.Y. Daily News

▼

"Louise Tobin sings like the young Ella Fitzgerald."
The New Yorker (at Newport Festival)

Louise Tobin and Peanuts Hucko promotional flyer, late 1960s. (Courtesy of the Louise Tobin and Peanuts Hucko Jazz Collection; photo insert by James L. Kriegsman)

From 1914 until 1946, it was operated as a club for the Republicans or Democrats, depending on the way the votes went. From 1946 until 1967, the Navarre was acquired by various owners as a fine restaurant or private club.

In the spring of 1967, one of the great jazz clarinetists, Michael "Peanuts" Hucko, took over the Navarre with a formidable team of "greats" in the field of cuisine.

On the night of June 2, 1967, the "beautiful people" of Denver society turned out in Victorian costume to celebrate the opening of the new Navarre.[34]

Louise recalled that her marriage, and the opening of the Navarre, "was the beginning of Peanuts and I really working together. It had been intermittent before. We had a wonderful life. I was just thrilled to go hear him play every night. Besides the new experience of our being married, the club was a new adventure."[35]

Peanuts drew on his connections to musicians from the 1940s and '50s and offered them work as guest artists at his club, not only performing for audiences at the Navarre but also Saturday evening live broadcasts over radio KOA. Musically, the club was a success, at least evidenced by the numerous letters of praise and appreciation in the Louise Tobin and Peanuts Hucko Jazz Collection, expressing thanks for the music and hospitality that Peanuts and Louise provided at the Navarre. Sounding like an A&R man from Memphis, fan Michael Kelly wrote to Peanuts:

> Dear Sir: For me it's very good listening when your combo has its Saturday evening broadcast over KOA. If you would ever be interested in doing some 45 rpm records, I think I would be greatly interested in having two 3-minute recordings of your combo on tape for use in Memphis and do a search for a local recording company that would be interested in selling yours [sic] records.[36]

In addition to performing at his club, Peanuts continued to play for Gibson's and Odessa's annual jazz parties, and at various venues in Denver including Elitch Gardens' Trocadero and Pinehurst Country Club to name a few.[37] Louise did not always perform with Peanuts, particularly if he was not the leader for the gig.

After about three years managing and performing at the Navarre, Louise and Peanuts discovered that, despite consistently large crowds

Louise Tobin and Peanuts Hucko performing together, late 1960s–early 1970s.
(Courtesy of the Louise Tobin and Peanuts Hucko Jazz Collection)

and positive press, it was difficult for them to turn much of a profit from this venture. Investors took their monthly cut. Vendors were notorious for selling eight- and ten-ounce steaks that in actuality were not eight and ten ounces. It was difficult keeping kitchen staff from stealing food. Then there was a change in the partnership.

"We had the club for three years, and it was great," Louise recalled, "until a new partner wanted to put rock and roll in one of the downstairs rooms. Peanuts was not interested in that, and we went to California and got a big band."[38]

What first drew them to California in the late 1960s was a performance on September 19, 1969, for a set at the Monterey Jazz Festival, featuring the Peanuts Hucko–Red Norvo Quintet, including Morey Feld on drums, David McKenna on piano, Bill Bastien on bass, and Louise singing the vocal numbers.[39] A nonprofit music event, the Monterey Jazz Festival was in its twelfth year in 1969. An estimated 33,600 attended the five concerts that weekend, including such artists as the Modern

Jazz Quartet, Cannonball Adderley Quintet, the Buddy Rich Band, Buddy Guy, Thelonious Monk, the Fourth Way, the Tony Williams Trio, Sly and the Family Stone, Miles Davis, and Sarah Vaughan. The Peanuts Hucko–Red Norvo Quintet, "known for its performances in traditional jazz forms,"[40] opened a session that reportedly "went over with a resounding bang. . . . The sounds got under way Friday night with Red Norvo Quintet featuring vocalist Louise Tobin and Morey Feld on drums. Following them came The Modern Jazz Quartet, Tony Williams Trio and the fantastically popular Sly and the Family Stone."[41]

Louise noted how the audiences had changed. As she stepped on the stage, she witnessed a guy lying in front of the stage smoking a joint. The crowd was noticeably unenthusiastic. Joe Pass and Peanuts played a fabulous number to very little response. "For the first time, it wasn't hard to get off of the stage," Louise recalled. They were accustomed to encores and wildly enthusiastic crowds. "Even Arthur Fiedler got a cool reception." He was guest conductor of the San Francisco Symphony, and they played at the Monterey Jazz Festival. "He was marvelous," Louise recalled. She and Peanuts were "okay, but no screaming for more."[42] Edith Austin penned a critical review of the festival: "I don't know what Jimmy Lyons was trying to prove down in Monterey this past weekend other than the fact that you can sell the American public anything, anytime and at any price—but to call it JAZZ, is an affront to one's intelligence. *Chronicle* jazz critic Ralph Gleason called it a carnival. . . . Had it not been for Sly and the Family Stones [*sic*], Sarah Vaughan, Little Esther Phillips, Mr. Cannonball Adderley and Buddy Guy, you could have racked this one up as another NO, NO!"[43]

Melvin Maddocks's review for the *Christian Science Monitor* was titled "Monterey Jazz: The Annual Identity Crisis; Self Renewing Barbaric Honk"[44] and reflected the turbulent musical times. According to Maddocks, "The 12th Monterey Jazz Festival last weekend staged what is becoming an annual identity crisis for this sort of event. What is jazz? What is rock? What is jazz-rock?" Referencing the Hucko-Norvo Quintet set, Maddocks emphasized the extremes: "The hushed, superbly inventive Modern Jazz Quartet, conservatively immaculate in their British suits, shared the stage with Sly and the Family Stone and other musical neo-primitives wearing headbands, flapping leather vests, cowboy boots, and plugged-in guitars whose daintiest diminuendo would swamp 10 of

Louise Tobin with Louis Armstrong in his home, ca. 1969. (Courtesy of the Louise Tobin and Peanuts Hucko Jazz Collection)

Peanuts Hucko with Louis Armstrong in his home, ca. 1969. (Courtesy of the Louise Tobin and Peanuts Hucko Jazz Collection)

the loudest crescendos the MJQ [Modern Jazz Quartet] ever produced. Nuances vs. the pile-driver. And guess who won?" Maddocks continued: "On one side: MJQ; Miles Davis, playing with biting subtlety—and now and then just wandering off; Thelonious Monk, in form but not especially on; Red Norvo, with a Peanuts Hucko quintet, representing tradition at its most self-renewing. On the other side: Sly etc., Sons of Champlin, and the Lighthouse, the best of the rock groups."[45] Undeterred, Louise and Peanuts continued to represent "tradition as its most self-renewing" throughout the final decades of the twentieth century.

Peanuts had hoped to fulfill Louis Armstrong's invitation to join him and help to organize another tour, but Armstrong's declining health prevented that from happening.

6

Swinging through the Changes, 1970s–1990s and Beyond

LOUISE AND PEANUTS found themselves faced with new challenges while trying to navigate and sustain a career in the jazz industry of the 1970s, '80s and '90s, as had most of the swing era musicians who struggled to survive during the musical and cultural developments of the 1950s and '60s. Their audiences were aging, and despite a renewed interest in traditional jazz that emerged in the 1980s, they were still competing with the amplified "rock kids" as they had been doing for about the past twenty-five years. Not interested in the avant-garde, fusion, or any other progressive strain of jazz, they were traditionalists and old traditionalists at that. For them, their music was, as described by Peanuts, "jazz done in good taste—very listenable."[1] Louise and Peanuts and their contemporaries from the swing era, both musicians and audiences, viewed themselves as the torchbearers, keeping the music, *their* music, alive and well.

Jazz writers and critics whose sentiments leaned more toward traditional than progressive jazz looked for evidence of hope for the survival of a musical style that seemed to be on life support in the later decades of the twentieth century. Hollie I. West, writing a 1972 essay on several recently published books on jazz, reviewed the *New Yorker* jazz critic Whitney Balliett's new book *Ecstasy at the Onion: Thirty-One Pieces on Jazz* and noted that "he sees the music as being in a 'dwindling, defenseless state,' unable to 'bear much critical weight—if, indeed, it ever could.'" West continues: "It is easy to sympathize with this viewpoint. The enfeebled state of jazz would drive the most committed optimist to despair."[2] Linda Dahl, in her seminal book on women in jazz titled *Stormy Weather*, characterizes big-band singing in the later part of the twentieth century as "a dying art," and wrote that "in the 1970s, with the rekindling of interest in the big bands, some of the 'girl singers' of the thirties and forties began to appear publicly and record after a long hiatus; many—like Rosemary Clooney, Chris Connor, Helen Humes and Helen Ward—sounded better than ever. But by and large, big-band singing, with all its abuses, limitations and charms, is a vanished art, and the 'canaries,' in their high heels, low-cut gowns and gaudy makeup, are a set piece of the romanticized past."[3]

Peanuts and Louise were nostalgic memorialists of such a romanticized past reflected in their work in tribute bands—Glenn Miller and Benny Goodman—and tribute albums to Goodman and Louis Armstrong. Indeed, their performances contributed greatly toward the preservation of and nostalgia for swing and traditional jazz. But they struggled to reach larger and younger audiences, despite the renewed attention young artists—the "new traditionalists"—such as Terrence Blanchard, Harry Connick Jr., and, of course, Wynton Marsalis were bringing to traditional jazz during much of the last two decades of the twentieth century.[4] While jazz education was gaining importance and relevance, with the availability of recordings of and by the original artists that were reissued by Smithsonian and other labels, students of contemporary jazz of the later twentieth century were more interested in either listening and studying the original recordings, or, if more progressive leaning, would eschew such traditional music for the more progressive fusion.

Despite being out of step with mainstream music, Peanuts and Louise still found opportunities for live performances, artistic and economic lifelines as well as sites in which musicians and audiences gathered to celebrate "jazz done in good taste."

Consider, as examples, jazz parties, the two most significant being Dick Gibson's Colorado Jazz Party and Dr. O. A. Fulcher's West Texas Jazz Party, and festivals, such as the Concord Summer Festival. Steadier work for a few of the maturing musicians from the swing era might be found in the television studio with such bands as Lawrence Welk (in addition to the *Tonight Show* and *Merv Griffin Show*, both of which employed studio orchestras). Tribute orchestras, such as Bob Crosby's Big Band Cavalcade and Glenn Miller's Band, provided additional opportunities for steady work. Club dates and recordings or session gigs provided work in between engagements.

This chapter covers both Louise and Peanuts as they navigated the last three decades of the twentieth century, essentially the last three decades of their performing careers, years that were professionally challenging as well as personally fulfilling. Louise had "married the boss," as she liked to state, and as such she performed on most gigs for which Peanuts was the leader. Both nationally and internationally, they were keeping the torch alive for big band music and traditional jazz, and they were doing it together.

Most people legalize their relationship with marriage and hope that their love will grow into a more profound emotional connection with each passing year. When the couple is also in the same business, working together day after day, love and companionship can potentially have a positive effect on a professional partnership. Such was the relationship between Louise and Peanuts. Louise had the relationship she had expected and hoped to have had with Harry, and, for Peanuts, after speaking with an interviewer about his life's work and the international success of his career, he concluded that "meeting his wife Louise, has been the high point of it all."[5]

Jazz Parties

In the spring of 1970, jazz critic Nat Hentoff wrote a piece for the *New York Times* on the challenges that faced veteran musicians, concluding that

> jazz is an exceedingly hard vocation to grow old in on anything resembling your own terms. Duke Ellington, Count Basie, their sidemen, and a few others are able to continue more or less as in the past. But as time goes on, more and more jazzmen over 70 slide into a kind of limbo. Some wander as best they can. The more economically fortunate, though expressively attenuated, are those who find refuge in network or pit bands and in recording studios. Others take day jobs and play weekends, or they leave jazz entirely. A few can never really adjust to the disappearance of what was for so long the natural nocturnal order of free-wheeling improvisers and the audiences that honored them. "Do you know why he died?" Edmond Hall's widow said to me a couple of years ago. "He died of no one wanting him."[6]

Among Hentoff's evidence "that an audience does exist for autumnal jazz" is Dick Gibson's Colorado jazz parties as well as his role in booking the Yank Lawson–Bob Haggart World's Greatest Jazz Band at the Grill Room of the Roosevelt Hotel in New York, among other venues. "Going into the Grill Room on a recent night was like taking a half-step back into time," Hentoff recalled.[7] Before he ventured into forming and managing his hubristically named World's Greatest Jazz Band, the musicians themselves hated the name, Gibson had been hosting his annual jazz parties, forging a model for other enthusiasts to follow.[8]

The jazz parties were the result of a bankrolled individual who had the financial means and initiative to hire the particular musicians whose style aligned with said host and attract enough like-minded audience members who could afford the price of the ticket and offset the costs of renting hotel rooms and the performance space as well as the food and drinks for the musicians. Gibson hosted his first jazz party in 1963. Al White, photographer, jazz enthusiast, and author of *Jazz Party: A Photo Gallery of Great Jazz Musicians*, recounted that event in the preface to his pictorial history.

> Gibson and his family had moved to Denver from New York in 1960. He missed New York's jazz scene greatly and decided to do something about it. In 1963, during the three-day Labor Day weekend, Gibson put on his first jazz party, in Aspen, Colorado. It featured a band from Eddie Condon's club in New York. Wild Bill Davison fronted the group, which also included Cutty Cutshall, Edmond Hall, Ralph Sutton, Jack Lesberg, and Cliff Leeman. Alternating with the band was a trio led by Teddy Wilson, with Major Holley and Bert Dahlander.[9]

Gibson's jazz parties became a model for such imitators as Dr. O. A. "Jim" Fulcher in Odessa, Texas, and Dr. William MacPhearson in California, to name just two.[10] In all, the musicians tended to be mostly white and had begun their careers during the swing era, although there were a few selected young musicians who were viewed by the hosts as exhibiting enough traditionalism and maturity in their playing and demeanor to be seen as potential receptors of the torch being passed down from the veterans. There was a preference for instrumentalists, and the musical style generally leaned toward Dixieland. The audiences were mostly middle-aged, white, and of the means to afford the price of the ticket.

Peanuts soon became a regular performer at Gibson's jazz parties. After their marriage in 1967, Louise attended each year as well. Music critic Leonard Feather was press guest for most of Gibson's jazz parties, and as such he was the events' most prolific reviewer, primarily emphasizing the role such events played in preserving what he considered to be the best in jazz. Again, the musicians were selected by Gibson and reflected his more traditionalist taste. According to Feather,

> The music, in essence, was generally down the middle, always using a melody as a point of departure and never losing sight of the Ellington dictum that it don't mean a thing, if it ain't got that swing. If anyone had shown up with a Fender bass, he would have been tossed out on his amplifier. Pianist Victor Feldman was advised not to bring his vibraphone; Gibson doesn't generally dig electrified sounds.[11]

Feather concluded that, "The Great Jazz Party of 1971 was a vibrant reminder of the scope and durability of jazz, its repertoire, its exponents and its audience."[12]

Louise noted in interviews that Gibson preferred instrumentalists to singers and that vocalists were not typically part of his roster.[13] Hence, she participated in the jazz party as wife rather than as hired musician. As had happened each year, after the 1972 jazz party, she and Peanuts received a nice, handwritten invitation from Gibson to return the following year: "Dear Louise and Peanuts, Splendid . . . Having both of you at our Jazz party adds enormously to our own and our guests' pleasure. You are herewith invited back. . . . The consensus is that this Jazz party [1972] was the best one yet."[14]

Gibson was not involved in this to make money. Indeed, if the price of admission at least came close to covering his expenses, then he would continue the following year. On Gibson, jazz critic Hentoff wrote that "a large, enthusiastic man in his early forties, [Gibson] does not appear to have lost any of his missionary zeal. As a result of his successful involvement with the company that developed the Water Pik and was later sold to a large corporation, Gibson has more than sufficient capital to be a full-time proselytizer for the kind of jazz he likes."[15] Feather broke down the economics of Gibson's eleventh annual jazz party:

> Gibson, unique among major jazz promoters by virtue of the fact that he is in it only for the music, spent $43,000 to bring 50 musicians to

the ballroom of the hotel, where 500 guests (mostly well-to-do, white and middle-aged) paid $165 a couple (i.e., $41,250) to hear five marathon sessions . . . ranging from two to a dozen in size, were handpicked by Gibson according to his idea of their suitability to each other's styles. He was right 95% of the time. . . . [They played forty-five half-hour sets].[16]

Feather often emphasized the maturity of the musicians to distinguish them from the younger, more progressive, performers. In a section of his article titled "Definition of Maturity," he wrote that "the youngest were in their early 30s—Howard Johnson, 32 (tuba and baritone sax) and Roger Kellaway, 33 (piano). The oldest were in their 60s, 'topped by trombonist Vic Dickenson, 67.' The quality and vitality of the music demonstrated handily that you do not measure ability or wisdom by the calendar."[17] In order to get a sense of the dialectic between such veteran musicians as Peanuts and Louise of the swing era and what it must have been like working with younger musicians more readily influenced by amplified music of the more popular or progressive vein, it's worth quoting Feather at length.

[To Feather maturity is] the ability to play compatibly with musicians old enough to be your father or young enough to be your son. Maturity is saying it succinctly and knowing when to stop—a rarity nowadays. Maturity is the ability not to feel paralyzed should a power failure strike. (Amplified instruments were kept to a minimum; saxophonist Phil Woods, dispensing with his electronic equipment, was back in prime form.) Maturity is knowing how far your technique lies short of infinity, and what to do within that self-acknowledged range. It is remembering that technique is your servant, never a master. Maturity is the urge to maintain your level of accomplishment or to drive beyond it as far as the spirit dictates. Maturity is recognition of the inevitability of change, and knowing how to adapt to it (or, if necessary, to avoid being entrapped by it and to be willing to listen inquisitively from the sidelines). Maturity is the faculty for submerging the ego, a willingness never to try to dominate in a group of one's peers. (Though the trumpet player was usually appointed nominal leader in most of the Gibson-built groups, a cooperative sense was pervasive.) Maturity is a faculty for relating to the past, the present and the future in the selection and interpretation of works performed.[18]

Indeed, for Feather, the divisions in jazz about which he addresses in this article extend beyond the generational and include musical style, performance practice, and race. Any question Feather's readers might have had about his agenda here is answered in his next section titled "At Peak of Power," which begins with an overflow of additional definitions of maturity.

> Maturity is concerning yourself not with whether the men around you are black or white, geniuses or incompetents, traditionalists or modernists; it is the talent required for playing at your optimum level regardless of these varying contexts.
>
> It is odd, even sad, that in some of the lively arts today, a performer mature in years may be dismissed as "an old man" regardless of the quality and duration of his contribution. A passport bearing a birth-date before 1950 may render the owner suspect. This has never been the case with classical music or with painting; a Picasso, a Casals, a Segovia has been respected at every stage of his life. This should be no less applicable to jazz, as Gibson parties make dazzlingly clear.[19]

Feather then lists several examples including a duet by Peanuts Hucko and Benny Carter, "among countless instances of great artistry, products of a long period of maturation and now at a peak of creative power." And finally: "The Colorado Springs convocation, by and large, was an enriching experience, untainted by any hint of one-upmanship, precocity or intramural animosity. It gave one hope for the continuation of jazz as a common ground and unifying force, at a time when such values are in desperately short supply."[20]

Feather's writings on Gibson's jazz parties often concluded with such optimism for traditional jazz. In his review of the 1974 Colorado Jazz Party, his enthusiasm for the future of jazz was in the context of his criticisms of such progressive strains as fusion jazz.

> At the Broadmoor [hotel] there were no huge batteries of percussion, no organs, no wah-wahs or echoplex, no electronics except for nor-mal amplification on the stringed instruments, no ego trips, no racial hostility or separatism (almost all the groups were integrated); noth-ing but jazz in its most undatable state. All it will take to keep things this way is the survival of great musicians like those who played at the party (most are young enough to be Venuti's sons, so their future is in

no immediate danger), along with the arrival of enough newcomers like Watrous, Wilkins, Faddis, Duffy Jackson et al who will eventually supplement or replace them. . . . Jazz simply has to mean something more than Herbie Hancock's or Herbie Mann's latest chart hit. If that were all we could look forward to, I would pack it in right now.[21]

The jazz party, described by Feather as "an event far more esoteric and exclusive than the conventional festival," had been spreading around the United States, "thanks to the initiative of a series of well-heeled patrons."[22] Such was Dr. O. A. "Jim" Fulcher, who attended Gibson's first jazz party back in 1963 and had become close friends with Gibson.[23] Fulcher modeled his jazz parties, which he began in 1967, after Gibson's. Indeed, many of the same musicians who were invited by Gibson for his Colorado parties were also brought to Texas, Peanuts among them. Like Gibson, Fulcher had traditional tastes in jazz and a preference for instrumentalists over vocalists. Hence, Louise was not invited to sing at the Odessa jazz parties.[24]

In the fall of 1970, Peanuts performed with Red Norvo at Dr. William MacPherson's third annual jazz party at the University Club of Pasadena, California. MacPherson, an obstetrician and jazz fan in Altadena, California, followed the examples set by Gibson in Colorado and Fulcher in Texas. MacPherson had applied experience in jazz, having worked his way through medical school playing sax and clarinet. Highlighting the role he and other jazz party hosts were playing in providing opportunities to satisfy the traditional tastes of both the patrons and invited guests, Feather quoted MacPherson as stating, "People who love traditional jazz—and I don't mean just Dixieland—have so few places left to go."[25] In his review of MacPherson's jazz party, Feather also noted that "Hucko, whose clarinet lately has lent a rare hip touch to Lawrence Welk's TV program, drew a standing ovation when he and Norvo teamed on 'Avalon.'"[26]

The Grill (Roosevelt Hotel)

In an effort to expand his reach and influence beyond the limited scope of the jazz party, in late 1969 Gibson organized and managed a group of musicians he had regularly hired for his events, naming the group the World's Greatest Jazz Band (WGJB), and in order to give them a home base and performance space he reopened the Grill Room in New York's

Roosevelt Hotel, where he also planned to present jazz festivals from time to time as well as other prominent bands and groups.[27] Critics welcomed the reopening of the Roosevelt Grill, recognizing that traditional jazz was in need of more places for such musicians to perform and sustain their careers and preserve the music. Jazz writer Stanley Dance noted that "the re-opening of the Roosevelt Grill in New York on November 25th [1969] with The World's Greatest Jazz Band was an unexpected and welcome event. The room had long been the haunt of Guy Lombardo's band, and the change of musical policy was the kind of boost jazz sorely needs at this time."[28]

Gibson booked two groups most nights. For example, in addition to the WGJB or Eddie Condon's All Stars, Peanuts would lead an alternating quartet.[29] The Peanuts Hucko Quartet was considered an "auxiliary out-fit," essentially an intermission group, headed by Peanuts, with backing by pianist Dave McKenna, drummer Cliff Leeman, and bassist Jack Lesberg, all described as "top tooters who continue that jazzy and joyous atmosphere for excellent listenability."[30] Louise sang with Peanuts's quartet at the Roosevelt Grill in January until February 7, 1970.

The opening of the Roosevelt Grill was viewed, at least by *Billboard* writer Ian Dove, to be a "sign of the rebirth of this kind of jazz—essentially from the thirties and forties," and another such sign "is the opening of Sunday night sessions at Uncle John's Straw Hat, mining the rich vein of jazz musicians who play in either recording sessions or pit bands."[31]

Unfortunately, Gibson's Roosevelt Grill struggled to draw enough late night business to break even after expenses. Gibson, "in a survey of his own spot," found that crowds were larger during cocktail hour, so he offered a "no-cover-no-minimum" until 7:30 p.m., when cover charges started. An April 29, 1970, article in *Variety* reported that "the late business which has virtually disappeared except for weekends is causing café operators to consider moving up schedules to take advantage of the more productive cocktail hours." Such a move at the Roosevelt Grill "is therefore one of great interest in the industry. It is conceded that the Roosevelt is probably one of the best areas in the world for the start of such a policy. If it fails here, its future is severely in doubt, and the cafés would simply have to adjust to the curtailed grosses of one show nightly."[32]

In addition to the circuit of jazz parties, Peanuts and Louise participated in the growing number of annual jazz festivals emerging around the country and in Europe. Peanuts was typically among the headliners, with Louise invited to sing a couple of numbers.

Festivals

What Dick Gibson was for the jazz party, George Wein was for the jazz festival. Jazz festivals had been spreading since Wein's involvement with the first Newport Jazz Festival in 1954, though often not without controversy, as mentioned above in chapter 5. While all festivals serve as potential sites of both community and contention, it is the prospect of the former that has been the driving force behind those that became annual events. Indeed, festivals, like jazz parties, "really flourish when a community of mutual appreciation forms among the attendees, artists and organizers," according to Mike Griffith, writing on the jazz festivals of Newport and New Orleans more specifically, but his words are equally applicable here.[33]

On August 21, 1970, Peanuts and Louise performed at the second annual Concord Summer Festival, an event initially spearheaded by automobile dealer and jazz enthusiast Carl Jefferson, performing on opening night for "nearly 2,000" attendees.[34] Peanuts headlined with the Red Norvo All Stars. (Red Norvo and his wife Eve were particularly close friends to Peanuts and Louise.)[35] Other performers on that night included the Earl Hines Quartet, Oscar Peterson, Errol Garner, Dave Brubeck, and the San Francisco Symphony conducted by Arthur Fiedler."[36] Reviewer Irving Kolodin favorably characterized the Hucko-Norvo set as prelude to

> one of those evenings when things happen. No sooner had Hucko glided his clarinet effortlessly into the opening measures of "Avalon," echoed at the piano by the long-practiced Johnny Guarneri, than Norvo fell in with a dazzling vibes passage soundly backed by Nick Fatool on drums. From then on it was one felicity after another, whether the agenda called for "The Sheik of Araby," Fats Waller's "Stealin' Apples," or "A Closer Walk with Thee." Ray Leatherwood held up the bass end well. When this group dashed off to a plane headed, doubtless, to Denver, where Hucko-Norvo now have their home base, Hines took his place at the piano and quickly put the order of music it yielded beyond comparison.[37]

Louise Tobin and Peanuts Hucko with conductor, Arthur Fiedler, Concord
Summer Festival. (Courtesy of the Louise Tobin and Peanuts Hucko Jazz
Collection)

Louise Tobin and Peanuts Hucko on stage at the Sacramento Jazz Festival.
Ed Lawless photograph. (Courtesy of the Louise Tobin and Peanuts Hucko
Jazz Collection)

Kolodin concluded: Concord "happens to be a place where people like music, and where people from around the Bay Area who like music are welcome. This was immediately evident in the response to the Hucko-Norvo group, even more so in the avid attention to Hines's order of pianistic magic."[38] Kolodin did not mention Louise's performance.

Peanuts was asked to return for the Third Annual Concord Summer Festival, where he performed with the Concord Summer Festival All-Stars, including Harry "Sweets" Edison, George Auld, Kai Winding, Joe Pass, Ray Brown, Jimmy Rowles, and Nick Fatool. Louise is not mentioned in the program.[39]

Festivals continued to spread nationally and internationally in the 1980s. Feather's end-of-the year piece, reflecting on the state of jazz in 1981, stated that "among the most notable happenings of the past 12 months was the festival phenomenon." He mentioned such sold-out festivals as the Playboy at the Hollywood Bowl, the Monterey Festival, the Newport Jazz Festival, and noted that "other festivals flourished around the world."[40]

In July 1981 Louise sang with Peanuts's group in Reno, Nevada, for the Second Annual Dixieland Jazz Festival at the Eldorado Hotel and Casino. Several years later, in May 1986, Louise sang with Peanuts at the thirteenth annual Memorial Day Dixieland Jubilee, which at the time, according to Feather, was "the world's largest jazz festival, involving 40 locations indoors and out, close to 800 musicians, 100,000 patrons and bands from 14 countries."[41] In his review, Feather criticized the "almost total exclusion of black musicians, a policy unaltered since the jubilee began."[42] He praised Peanuts, who "offered the most sophisticated music of all, aided by the incredibly virtuosic pianist Dick Hyman, a vibraphonist from Canada named Peter Appleyard, the bassist Bob Haggart and Gene Estes on drums." Unfortunately, Louise did not illicit the same praise: "One set fell apart when the singer, Louise Tobin, after a pleasant ballad, duetted [*sic*] with Hucko on the seemingly mandatory 'Bill Bailey.'"[43] The audience for the Dixieland Festivals, according to Feather, "is a breed apart, primarily a white, middle-aged, middle-class, middle-American crowd, addressed for the most part by senior performers."[44] Feather's description could apply equally to the faithful audience of television's most visible bandleader, Lawrence Welk, an aging audience eager for a nostalgia trip down memory lane of big band dance music.

Lawrence Welk

Musicians who were invited to the jazz parties welcomed the work and attentive treatment by their hosts and audiences; nevertheless, they could not live solely on jazz parties, even with the addition of a few annual jazz festivals. Musicians who lived mostly on the road welcomed opportunities for extended gigs either away or better still in their hometowns. Peanuts had retained the hope of someday opening his own club, where he had sole control of the entire establishment, despite his experience with the Navarre as well as a brief attempt at another club in Denver, which, according to Louise, also didn't work out.[45] In an interview with BBC's Graham Pass in July 2010, Louise recalled Peanuts's work with Lawrence Welk, an opportunity they had hoped would boost Peanuts's career and also provide them with greater financial stability and more of a home life.

> Peanuts got an invitation to join the Lawrence Welk Show. Welk was an accordion player and primarily a showman, and musically he had some of the best players on the coast in his band. They had a home, and they got a check every week. Very good family show, and he had made a big star out of Pete Fountain who was one of the nicest men you would ever meet. Peanuts was reluctant at first but thought maybe the exposure would help him like it did Pete. So, he took that job, and we moved to California.[46]

Welk featured Peanuts on several numbers, which did increase his visibility. Audiences praised Peanuts's performances in letters forwarded by Welk: "I shall certainly pass your compliments along to him, and we will be happy to keep your requests in mind for him to play "The World is Waiting for the Sunrise," Stealin' Apples," "Closer Walk with Thee" and "Rose Room" when planning future shows."[47] Pianist Teddy Wilson sent a letter to Peanuts, complimenting him on his performance on Welk's show: "You got the whole gang, including Welk, swinging."[48]

There is evidence that Peanuts was able to capitalize on his association with Lawrence Welk, at least regionally. In both 1971 and 1972 Peanuts performed for the Lakeside Golf Club, Installation Dinner Dance, sponsored by the Sherman Oaks Chamber of Commerce, where the program listed "Music by 'King of the Clarinet,' Peanuts Hucko featured on the Lawrence Welk Show."[49] He and Louise connected with such other Hollywood residents as Steve Allen, Sandra Dee, Rose Marie, and Jerry

Louise Tobin, Peanuts Hucko, and Lawrence Welk, 1972, preparing to board airplane. (Courtesy of the Louise Tobin and Peanuts Hucko Jazz Collection)

Van Dyke. Louise's sister, Lucille, was outgoing and had a good business sense. Louise recalled that she had arranged for her and Peanuts to be at ribbon cuttings and other public events associated with Sherman Oaks. "She made Peanuts ambassador of goodwill for Sherman Oaks, and so we had to attend lots of events." Lucille was very active in social and political circles where she had been recognized as "mother of the year." She won the Hourglass Award, "which was very prestigious out there," and, "she was head of the local Republican Party," Louise recalled.[50]

Welk's show was filmed in Studio City, California. Louise at first regularly attended the broadcasts, but she quit going because every time Welk would see her, he would say, "Come on up and sing a number."

"You just don't do that," Louise recalled. "He didn't offer me a spot on the show. [He] just picked me out of the audience. I quit going. I never went up there. I wasn't prepared to do that. I had on blue jeans. I didn't go on stage. You just don't do that. I only went to see the taping, primarily to hear Peanuts play."[51]

Peanuts joined Welk's band in late 1970 and was with him for about three years, a period of time during which Louise sang little beyond "some single club dates."[52] Despite having the opportunity to play with such fine players as Welk had in his band, Peanuts found the autocratic bandleader to be difficult to satisfy and requiring too many restrictions on what he could play. Louise recalled that "Welk was a strange man. He was a tremendous showman. But he expected people to bow and scrape, and they did. He owned Santa Monica. After Peanuts left, he said he would never have another star [as part of his band]." Louise recalled that Welk had told Peanuts that "he would send him around the world with a big band to raise money for cancer, and the thought was [that] it would boost Peanuts's career and increase his earning power. Unfortunately, Welk did not get around to doing some of these things. As time went on Peanuts played less and less, and he and Welk had different ideas about what he should play. When the time came to play 'When the Saints Go Marching In,' Welk wanted him to play melody on all three choruses. As a jazz player, he didn't want to play melody on all three choruses, so they had a dispute over that, and Peanuts decided to leave. Welk didn't believe it. The next day they were leaving for Hawaii, and on the plane Welk kept saying, 'Where's Peanuts? Where's Peanuts?' The band had to remind him that Peanuts had quit."[53]

Glenn Miller Band

Shortly after leaving Welk, in the fall of 1973 Peanuts joined bandleader Bob Crosby's Big Band Cavalcade as "Guest Star."[54] The tour with Crosby was grueling for Peanuts and the other band members, but it was nothing compared to his schedule leading the Glenn Miller Band from January through September 1974. Peanuts was back as bandleader, and Louise was singing more regularly, performing on both American and European tours.

Louise had not performed much during the early 1970s. That changed when Peanuts accepted an offer to lead the Glenn Miller Band, an invitation that officially included Louise singing with the band.[55] Peanuts was an alumnus with the Miller Band, having played with Miller during World War II. Despite Miller being in the air force and Peanuts in the army, on the recommendation of drummer and vocalist Ray McKinley, Miller succeeded in getting Peanuts in his band. Louise recalled Peanuts stating that Miller's "was the best band ever assembled."[56] "Peanuts loved Glenn," Louise recalled. "He thought he was a wonderful man and a great musician. He wouldn't let the guys wear GI shoes. He made them buy their shoes."[57] Peanuts recounted Miller's death in interviews, particularly his experience as he and fellow band members waited for, and ultimately received, word that Miller's plane had not arrived as scheduled.

Glenn Miller Orchestra led by Peanuts Hucko, 1974. (The Louise Tobin and Peanuts Hucko Jazz Collection)

The Miller estate owned the band and had been actively protecting the Miller name since his death on December 15, 1944. Ray McKinley led the band for nine years and then Buddy DeFranco took over for eight. Peanuts replaced DeFranco as leader. Despite other changes in the band's personnel, the band attempted to retain the sound of the original Miller arrangements.[58] Peanuts, shortly after accepting the invitation to lead the Glenn Miller Band, received numerous letters and telegrams of well wishes and congratulations. His former boss, Lawrence Welk, wrote: "Dear Peanuts, Lois just told me the good news that you are going to be taking over the Glenn Miller Band, and I just wanted to pass along my congratulations. This is a great opportunity and I wish you a lot of success. Best regards to you and Louise. Sincerely, Lawrence."[59]

Not everyone was on board with Peanuts leading the Miller band. Some of the buyers expressed some skepticism regarding the changes in the band, including its new leader, Peanuts. In a letter to Louise, former Goodman agent and current agent for the Glenn Miller Band, Willard Alexander, wrote:

> Dear Louise: Thanks for the clippings,—I'm glad you sent them. From everything we have heard on the first few days that Peanuts has been with the band, he is doing an excellent job, which doesn't surprise me. I figured he would. We are having a few problems with some of the people the band will be playing for, but this is a natural reaction. I have advised them as to what has happened with other buyers, and I have told them they should wait and hear the band. So far, the responses have been good, and I hope this will continue. Insofar as I am concerned, I feel Peanuts is the best leader we have had for the band just from the brief experience we have had with his performance. Best. Fondly, Willard Alexander.[60]

If letters of praise sent to David McKay, attorney and representative of the Glenn Miller Band, are any indication, Peanuts, the band, and Louise were soon garnering rave reviews.

> The same kind remarks, and comments, do certainly apply to that fine vocalizing talent of Louise Tobin, and that nice young male vocalist appearing with the orchestra. All in all, the crowd of Saturday evening last, did really have some fine evening of dancing, nostalgia, and listening pleasures.[61]

In his *New York Times* review titled "Miller Band Given a Broader Scope by Peanuts Hucko," critic John S. Wilson wrote on how the band had changed under the leadership of Peanuts.

> With Louise Tobin, who was singing with Benny Goodman during the original Miller era (and who is now Mrs. Hucko), bringing experienced, band singer's authority to the vocals, this version of the Miller band is making its straight dance sets (it does not do a formal show) entertaining, listenable and, as the crowded floor shows, very danceable.[62]

Both Louise and Peanuts loved performing for such enthusiastic crowds, but they did not like the grueling tour schedule. Ultimately, they could not sustain the intense performance itinerary. "The band worked every night," Louise recalled. "They would have these long 500-mile trips in between, and it was excruciating. Play, jump on the bus, drive 400–500 miles, get two-hours sleep, play get on the bus."[63] After about eight months, Peanuts became ill and had to resign his post as leader of the orchestra.[64]

An itinerary in the Louise Tobin and Peanuts Hucko Jazz Collection at Texas A&M University–Commerce for July 8 through August 25 reveals only one "travel day" and one day off for which the band did not perform. The orchestra played twenty-two cities in fourteen states in thirty-four days. "Louise and I had three days off in eight months," Peanuts later recalled.[65]

Peanuts and Louise returned to Denver after their stint with the Glenn Miller Band. For the rest of the year (1974) and into much of 1975, Peanuts worked with Ralph Sutton in a jazz quartet in Denver. He also played at Dick Gibson's jazz party. Leonard Feather wrote that

> for Peanuts Hucko the party was a particularly meaningful release. The veteran clarinetist had just quit as the front man for the Glenn Miller orchestra after a grueling tour on road duty, playing mostly one-night stands (he wound up in the hospital). "I don't know how Buddy DeFranco stood it for eight years," said Hucko. "It was more than I could handle to take it for eight months."[66]

Air Force Museum Concert (1986), Glenn Miller Tribute. (Courtesy of the
Louise Tobin and Peanuts Hucko Jazz Collection)

Both Peanuts and Louise rejoined the Glenn Miller Orchestra for
tribute concerts as they did in 1986, performing for a large, enthusiastic
crowd at the Air Force Museum Concert near Dayton, Ohio.

Recordings

Louise's first time in the studio since her 1951 recording of "Sunny
Disposish" with Ziggy Elman for MGM, Hollywood, was with Peanuts
Hucko and His Orchestra in 1966, recording four tracks on the Avant
Garde Records label, a Division of Lincoln Square Productions Inc. The
purpose of the session was most likely to record demos for their own
promotional purposes. The result was four sides on two 7-inch, 45 rpm
discs: "Peanuts Popcorn & Crackerjazz" and "Filibuster," both written
by Hucko and Tobin, and on the second disc she sang "Wonderful One"
and "Scatterbrain." Louise's voice did not appear on record again until
1977 when in San Diego, California, on March 7 she sang two numbers

that were included on Peanuts's album, *The San Diego Jazz Club Plays the Sound of Jazz*: "I Left My Sugar Standing in the Rain" and "There'll Be Some Changes Made," both Bill May arrangements. Reviewer Geoff Millerman wrote that "this has got to be one of the tightest and best groups to come forth in the swing-trad area since the World's Greatest Jazz Band. Even vocalist, Louise Tobin, shows traces of Maxine Sullivan in her classic blues tinged style. . . . Peanuts Hucko does some beautiful clean work on "Stealin' Apples," nicely swung along by the rhythm which is excellent throughout the whole album. A near perfect album, what one would expect, but has not always received, from the caliber of the artists involved. Look for it."[67]

During a couple of European tours in the 1980s, Peanuts and Louise recorded multiple tracks that were issued on a number of tribute albums from two studio dates, October 24, 1983, and July 8, 1986, and a live recording from "Nick Vollebregt's Jazzcafe," Laren, The Netherlands, January 22, 1987. On the 1983 session, Louise sang "Georgia on My Mind," "Deed I Do," "The Man I Love," "Am I Blue," and "There'll Be Some Changes Made," "all excellent," according to reviewer Shirley Klett, "despite the fact that 'Man I Love' is taken so slowly you expect it to fall off the beat any moment."[68] In 1986, she recorded "Rockin' Chair," "After You've Gone," "He's Funny That Way," and "Goodnight My Love," of which, overall, reviewer Shirley Klett preferred this set over the 1983 issue, writing that "Peanuts is most compelling on 'Seven Come Eleven,' but everyone plays well throughout with Louise Tobin's vocals adding interest to this portion of the program. . . . While plowing no new ground, this is a solid set."[69]

Louise can be heard on three more live performance recordings with Peanuts. On *Swing That Music*, released in 1992, she sang "There'll Be Some Changes Made" and a duet with Peanuts that they often sung to close a show or as an encore: "When You're Smiling." These tracks were recorded live at Burgerzentrum in Waiblingen, Germany, on October 21, 1988.

On *Peanuts Hucko and the Anglo American All Stars Live in Britain*, recorded November 1–15, 1991, she sang "Deed I Do," "Hard Hearted Hannah," and with an ensemble of voices, "Sweet and Lovely," "I Can't Give You Anything but Love," and "Nobody Else but Me." Her last issued recording, a live performance at Rems-Murr-Jazztage," Schorndorf, Germany, October 27, 1992, was of "Loch Lomond."

In all, these recordings did not result in "hits" that would alone financially sustain Peanuts and Louise. Evidence suggests that this situation was not unusual for many such jazz artists. As another example, consider singer Joe Williams during an interview with Leonard Feather in the mid-1970s. Feather asks: "How . . . does one fight the system, retain one's self-respect and remain solvent? 'I don't need to rely on record sales,' Joe Williams replies. 'I'm on the Tonight Show, Merv Griffin, Mike Douglas and the rest often enough to reach audiences of millions. There are always night clubs that want me. Last year I worked 15 weeks in Las Vegas alone. Then there are occasional college dates and every year or two an overseas tour.' "His explanation: 'The artists at the top are promoted by the recording companies. The ones I've been with haven't done anything to help support me or increase the public's awareness. . . . As a result, the general public doesn't have a chance to get my records.' . . . To my [Leonard Feather's] suggestion that heavy promotion might be a consequence rather than a cause of an artist's original success, he answered: 'I don't think so. The record companies try to dictate what the public will like.'"[70]

In short, Williams's argument is that the studios do not promote jazz artists in the same way they promote popular music artists. Feather counters that this situation is symptomatic of a studio that responds more to public demand than their ability to shape demand. Certainly the specifics of the two sides can be argued; nevertheless, Feather concludes this piece, stating that "Far from reflecting a bitter, bad-at-the-world attitude, Williams' grievances are lodged in a most temperate manner. . . . He enjoys the respect of every fellow singer, wins a poll here and there as the greatest of all male vocalists (most recently the *Down Beat* International Critics' Poll) and is held in perpetual esteem by an international circle of admirers become personal friends. I would think that he embodies as much as any artist in today's irrational music scene, the living proof that limitless wealth and vast record sales are essential neither to success nor happiness."[71]

～

Considering Louise and Peanuts, they certainly did not acquire limitless wealth and vast record sales during their thirty-plus years of marriage and professional work, nor did they find them to be essential to success or happiness. Together, they were always able to secure work,

Louise Tobin performing with the alumni of the Benny Goodman Orchestra at Disneyland, 1988. (Courtesy of the Louise Tobin and Peanuts Hucko Jazz Collection)

Louise Tobin performing alongside Peanuts Hucko and alumni of the Benny Goodman Orchestra, 1988. (Courtesy of the Louise Tobin and Peanuts Hucko Jazz Collection)

whether in nightclubs, annual concerts, jazz parties, or festivals and tours throughout the United States, Europe, Japan, and Australia. Willing to travel, they followed the music, and often that meant heading overseas. Indeed, according to Peanuts in one interview in 1989, 70 percent of their touring time was spent abroad. Louise, concluding that same interview, stated that "it is so difficult to get dates here in our own country, because so many promoters push rock 'n' roll essentially. Few are interested in efforts to keep jazz music alive."[72]

Among those few were the folks at Disneyland in Anaheim, California, who had been keeping big band jazz alive with their annual summer concerts there since the early 1960s. In 1988 Louise was featured with the Peanuts-directed Benny Goodman Alumni Orchestra. The Goodman Estate had allowed Peanuts to obtain copies of the original Goodman arrangements from the Yale University archives. Louise proudly recalled their weeks at Disneyland "a thrilling success!!"

During the 1990s Peanuts and Louise began to slow down. They moved from Palm Desert, California, to Louise's musical and familial roots, Denton, Texas. Both lived long enough to enjoy deserved honors of a long life contributing to both to the preservation of swing, specifically, and the history of jazz more broadly. In 1995 Peanuts was inducted into the Syracuse Walk of Stars with his name memorialized with a two-foot bronze star that was embedded into the sidewalk adjacent to the Landmark Theatre of his hometown. In April 1998, then governor George W. Bush declared the first Texas Big Band Jazz Festival in honor of Peanuts's eightieth birthday. This two-day festival began on June 19, just five years to the day prior to Peanuts's death in 2003.

On August 13, 2011, Louise received an honorary doctorate from Texas A&M University–Commerce, where she had donated hers and Peanuts's archives to preserve their documents and to assist future generations in their studies of jazz history and thus sustaining her and Peanuts's ongoing efforts to keep jazz alive. Deborah Porter helped Louise edit her speech at the commencement ceremony, "but these are her thoughts."[73]

> In the field of music, swing and jazz have made a tremendous impact on the fabric of American culture and around the world. This music has expanded well beyond what any of us who were involved in it could ever have imagined. When we were learning, writing or playing those songs or making those great arrangements, some of us

were traveling around the world and performing live on the radio. In that era, radio was the TV or Internet of today, and it was critical to get your music on the air. Sponsors were the toothpaste companies, automobile companies and tobacco companies. I've always felt a little guilty about selling all those Camel cigarettes. None of us could have ever imagined that there would be whole college courses and degrees based on our music. To be a part of something that will live beyond our lifetimes is truly the highest of honors.

Sometimes I just have to pinch myself to realize that I was part of that. After all, I was just a young girl from rural Texas who loved to sing. I learned at an early age that it got me attention in a large family. It also got me out of many classes, and best of all it got me out of doing stacks of dishes when I got home from school every afternoon. And eventually it got me a measure of success. I had the pleasure of working with many of the most creative musicians, writers, and singers of that era, some of whom I've had the privilege of calling my friends. We were passionate about our music.

Because to us music was much more than just notes and words. It was emotional and it came from deep in our innermost beings. It was divinely inspired. The Bible even talks about music. It talks about trumpets, stringed instruments and singers, of course. But one thing that bothered me, back in Biblical days they consulted God when they went to war and he told them to put the singers in the front lines.

But we were truly passionate about the music and always trying to make it better, to communicate to our listeners what we were feeling.

If there is one thought I would like to tuck into your memory today it might be this. That no matter what you choose to do, whether you are going to be a teacher, a chemist, a farmer . . . that you do it with passion. From what I know, if you are passionate about it, it will spill over into other areas of your life. Your work becomes an adventure of joy.

I have had 93 years of all sorts of days but being here with you today will surely go down as one of the most shining and treasured days of my life.

And so, from the bottom of my heart I thank you for this high honor and I wish all of you, your families, the faculty and staff of this wonderful university . . . I wish you God Speed and joy in all your pursuits.

I would like to close with a couple of lines from a poem that has been meaningful to me written by Dr. Hartsill Wilson. His poem is

"A New Day," and this is what he said: "This is the beginning of a new day that God has given me to do with as I wish. I can waste it or I can use it for good. But what I do today is important because I will have exchanged a day of my life for it."

Thank you, again.[74]

Louise's artistry lasted nearly a century, and her life has extended even beyond that. At the time of this writing, she is 101 years old. The first two loves of her life are her sons; the second two were her husbands, Harry James and Peanuts Hucko. While Harry ultimately caused her heartbreak and disappointment, Peanuts not only viewed Louise as both a wife and a professional partner, but he also provided her with an opportunity to sustain her professional singing career throughout the remaining years of the twentieth century. Louise often said that she fell out of the crib singing, and that all she ever wanted to do was sing. And sing, she did, through the good times and the bad.

In one of our first interviews, Louise, her elder son Harry Jr., Deborah Porter, Mike Kubiak, and I were all together looking through her scrap-

Louise in Judy Garland's dressing room, Hollywood Palladium, ca. 1990. Photo by Peanuts Hucko. (Courtesy of the Louise Tobin and Peanuts Hucko Jazz Collection)

book. "What happened to my hair?" Louise asked after looking at an old, faded photo from her freshman year in high school. Then, the memories: "I won the friendliest girl contest. I remember the dress, which was a hand-me-down from one of my siblings. . . . We weren't allowed to wear makeup, and so this is with no makeup." Asked what she would say to that little girl now: "You wouldn't be smiling if you knew what was ahead of you. No, not really . . . I would say: Keep smiling; everything has a good ending."

Appendix A

Louise Tobin *Camel Caravan* Broadcast Performances with Benny Goodman 1939[1]

Compiled by Karl Wingruber

May 16, 1939
The Palace Theater, Cleveland, Ohio (Camel Caravan [CC] #86)

MC: Harry Holcomb   Network: CBS

Songs: Let's Dance (Theme), Don't Be That Way, **Blues** (vocal: Louise Tobin [LT]), Anything Can Swing/Make Believe, The Sheik (BG Quartet), Alexander's Ragtime Band (vocal: Johnny Mercer), **It's Never Too Late** (vocal: LT), Sent For You Yesterday, Goodbye

May 23, 1939
The Palace Theater, Columbus, Ohio (CC #87)

MC: Harry Holcomb   Network: CBS

Songs: Let's Dance (Theme), Blue Skies, **If You Ever Change Your Mind** (vocal: LT), Anything Can Swing / Russian Lullaby, Boy Meets Horn (feat. Chris Griffin), I Got Rhythm (BG Quintet), Three Little Fishes (J. Mercer vocal and special lyrics), Sugar Foot Stomp, Goodbye

May 30, 1939
The Albee Theater, Cincinnati, Ohio (CC #88)

MC: Harry Holcomb   Network: CBS

Songs: Let's Dance (Theme), Three Little Words, **Don't Worry 'Bout Me** (vocal: LT), Anything Can Swing / In A Little Spanish Town (J. Mercer vocal), Tea For Two (Benny and Arturo Bernstein duet), Indiana Speedway Race (J. Mercer—vocal and special lyrics), Stompin at The Savoy (BG Quintet), **Louise Parody** (vocal: LT; J. Mercer—special lyrics), Bugle Call Rag, Goodbye

June 6, 1939
The Paramount Theater, Ft. Wayne, Indiana (CC #89)

MC: Harry Holcomb   Network: CBS

Songs: Let's Dance (Theme), Love Me or Leave Me, **The Lady's in Love with You** (vocal: LT), Anything Can Swing / Without a Song (J. Mercer vocal), Memories of You (BG Quintet), The King and Queen Visit (J. Mercer-vocal and special lyrics), **And the Angels Sing** (vocal: LT), King Porter Stomp, Goodbye

June 13, 1939
New York City (CC #90)

MC: Harry Holcomb   Network: CBS

Songs: Let's Dance (Theme), Sweet Sue, **You and Your Love** (vocal: LT), Wishing (BG quintet), Old Fashioned Love (J. Mercer—vocal and special lyrics), Mozart Matriculates, One O'Clock Jump, Goodbye

June 20, 1939
The Ritz-Carlton, Boston, Massachusetts (CC #91)

MC: Harry Holcomb   Network: CBS

Songs: Let's Dance (Theme), Russian Lullaby, **The Lamp Is Low** (vocal: LT), Anything Can Swing / Down By The Old Mill Stream, **There'll Be Some Changes Made** (vocal: LT), China Boy (BG Quintet), Old Fashioned Love
(J. Mercer—vocal and special lyrics), Wrappin' It Up, Goodbye

*Note: This was Mercer's last broadcast with Goodman. He started the next week with Bob Crosby Orchestra on the CBS CC broadcasts while Benny went to Saturday night CC broadcasts on NBC.

July 8, 1939
Treasure Island, Golden Gate Expo, San Francisco, California (CC #92)

MC: Bert Parks   Network: NBC

Songs: Let's Dance (Theme), St. Louis Blues, Sunrise Serenade, Stealin' Apples (excerpt), Stealin' Apples, **If I Didn't Care** (vocal: LT), Wait Til the Sun Shines Nellie (Bert Parks, vocal), Opus ½ (BG Quintet), Honeysuckle Rose, Goodbye

July 15, 1939
Treasure Island, Golden Gate Expo, San Francisco, California (CC #93)

MC: Bert Parks   Network: NBC

Songs: Let's Dance (Theme), Sugar Foot Stomp, **Wishing** (vocal: LT), Night and Day, Boy Meets Horn (feat. Chris Griffin), **Well Alright** (Benny and Louise, vocal), I Surrender Dear (BG Quartet), Roll 'Em, Goodbye

July 22, 1939
Treasure Island, Golden Gate Expo, San Francisco, California (CC #94)

MC: Bert Parks   Network: NBC

Songs: Let's Dance (Theme), Minnie the Moocher's Wedding Day, **Rendezvous Time in Paree** (vocal: LT), When My Baby Smiles at Me (feat. Toots Mondello), Undecided, Limehouse Blues (BG Quartet), Sunrise Serenade, King Porter Stomp, Goodbye

July 29, 1939
Treasure Island, Golden Gate Expo, San Francisco, California (CC #95)

MC: Bert Parks   Network: NBC

Songs: Let's Dance (Theme), Down Home in Indiana, **The Lamp Is Low** (vocal: LT), I'd Do Most Anything for You, Stardust (BG Quartet), Alexander's Ragtime Band (feat. Toots Mondello), Bach Goes to Town, **After You've Gone** (Louise and Band, vocal), Jumpin at the Woodside, Goodbye

August 5, 1939
Radio City, Hollywood, California (CC #96)

MC: Bert Parks   Network: NBC

Songs: Let's Dance (Theme), Sweet Sue, **Comes Love** (vocal: LT), Stealin' Apples, Dinah (BG Quartet), **One Sweet Letter from You** (vocal: LT), Bolero, Goodbye

August 12, 1939
Radio City, Hollywood, California (CC #97)

MC: Bert Parks   Network: NBC

Songs: Let's Dance (Theme), Down South Camp Meeting, Sunrise Serenade, Henerson Stomp (BG Trio), **And The Angels Sing** (vocal: LT), Steal America First, **Rendezvous Time in Paree** (vocal: LT), Sing Sing Sing, Goodbye

August 19, 1939
Radio City, Hollywood, California (CC #98)

MC: Bert Parks   Network: NBC

Songs: Let's Dance (Theme), Night and Day, **What's New** (vocal: LT), Spring Song, Flying Home (BG Sextet feat. Charlie Christian), T'Ain't What You Do (Benny—vocal), **Oh You Crazy Moon** (vocal: LT), Jumpin at the Woodside, Goodbye

NOTE: This was Charlie Christian's first broadcast appearance with the band.

August 26, 1939
The Steel Pier, Atlantic City, New Jersey (CC #99)

MC: Bert Parks   Network: NBC

Songs: Let's Dance (Theme), Down by the Old Mill Stream, **Comes Love** (vocal: LT), Bublitchke (feat. Ziggy Elman), Flying Back (BG Sextet), Adios Muchachos (Arnold Corrubias, vocal), **Blue Orchids** (vocal: LT), Roll 'Em, Goodbye

September 2, 1939
Michigan State Fair, Detroit, Michigan (CC #100)

MC: Bert Parks   Network: NBC

Songs: Let's Dance (Theme), If I Could Be With You One Hour Tonight, **Day In Day Out** (vocal: LT), Stardust (BG Sextet), **The Jumpin' Jive** (vocal: LT), Sent for You Yesterday (feat. Toots and Ziggy), Boy Meets Horn (feat. Chris Griffin), **I've Been There Before** (vocal: LT), Pick-a-Rib, Goodbye

September 9, 1939
Radio City, New York (CC #101)

MC: Bert Parks   Network: NBC

Songs: Let's Dance (Theme), Spring Song, **Over the Rainbow** (vocal: LT), Jumpin at the Woodside, Moonlight Serenade, Flyin Home (BG Sextet), **Put That Down in Writing** (vocal: LT), Mozart Matriculates, Stealin' Apples (feat. Benny, Fletcher and Chris Griffin), Goodbye

September 16, 1939
Shea's Buffalo Theater, Buffalo, New York (CC #102)

MC: Bert Parks   Network: NBC

Songs: Let's Dance (Theme), Blue Skies, **Scatterbrain** (vocal: LT), The Jumpin Jive (Benny on vocal?), Hour of Parting (feat. Toots), Opus Local 802 (BG Sextet), **Blue Orchids** (vocal: LT), Bolero, Goodbye

September 23, 1939
Orpheum Theater, St. Paul, Minnesota (CC #103)

MC: Bert Parks   Network: NBC

Songs: Let's Dance (Theme), After You've Gone, **I Didn't Know What Time It Was** (vocal: LT), Clarence Meek, It Had to Be You (feat. Toots and Benny), Mendelsohn I'll Mow You Down, Opus ½ (BG Sextet), **What's New** (Louise—vocal), Bugle Call Rag (feat. Ziggy), Goodbye

September 30, 1939
Chicago, Illinois (CC #104)

MC: Bert Parks   Network: NBC

Songs: Let's Dance (Theme), **Love Never Went To College** (vocal: LT), Melancholy Mood, Steal American First (Benny and Bert Parks, vocal), 18th Century Drawing Room, Ciribiribin (feat. Harry James), Stardust (BG Sextet), **The Little Man Who Wasn't There** (vocal: LT), Jumpin at the Woodside, Goodbye

NOTE: Louise didn't perform on the October 7, 1939, CC #105 broadcast. Mildred Bailey filled in and took over after October 21, 1939.

October 14, 1939
New York City (CC #106)

MC: Ted Pearson   Network: NBC

Songs: Let's Dance (Theme), Pick-a-Rib, **I Didn't Know What Time It Was** (vocal: LT), Ain't Misbehavin (feat. Louis Armstrong with BG Sextet), Moonlight Serenade, AC DC Current (BG Sextet), Shadrach (feat. Louis Armstrong and the Lyn Murray Choir), King Porter Stomp, Goodbye

October 21, 1939
New York City (CC #107)

MC: Ted Pearson   Network: NBC

Songs: Let's Dance (Theme), Devil and the Deep Blue Sea, **Lilacs in the Rain** (vocal: LT), Opus Local 802 (feat. Ziggy, Arthur Berstein, Benny), Effervescent Blues (feat. Casper Reardon, harp), Chicken Reel (feat. Reardon), Soft Wind (BG Sextet), **Make with the Kisses** (vocal: LT), Swingtime in the Rockies (feat. Benny and Ziggy), Goodbye

NOTE: At the conclusion of this broadcast Pearson announces that Mildred Bailey is taking over the vocal spot with the band.

Appendix B

"Louise Tobin Blues"

Chronological List of Lyric Sources[1]
July 27, 1923, to February 1, 1939

Date (recorded)	Title	Singer
July 27, 1923	"Down South Blues"	Clara Smith
September 21, 1923	"I Want My Sweet Daddy"	Hannah Sylvester
September 21, 1923	"Down South Blues"	Hannah Sylvester
December [?], 1923	"Last Minute Blues"	Ma Gertrude Rainey
March 10, 1924	"Stovepipe Blues"	Daddy Stovepipe
August 19, 1924	"Texas Moaner Blues"	Clara Smith
April 16, 1925	"Undertaker's Blues"	Maggie Jones
February 19, 1927	"My Mama Was a Sailor"	Julius Daniels
November [?], 1927	"Fourteenth Street Blues"	Blind Percy
December 10, 1927	"Corn Liquor Blues"	Lewis Black
December 12, 1927	"Low Land Moan"	Lonnie Johnson
August 31, 1928	"Trouble-Hearted Blues"	Ishman Bracey
September [?], 1928	"Hopeless Blues"	Anna Bell
October 26, 1928	"No No Blues"	Curley Weaver

April 18, 1929	"California Blues"	Robert Hicks
November 3, 1929	"Me and My Whiskey"	Robert Hicks
July 22, 1930	"Black Mountain Blues"	Bessie Smith
November 26, 1930	"New Minglewood Blues"	Noah Lewis
December 15, 1930	"Your Good Man Caught the Train and Gone"	Walter Vinson (and Mississippi Sheiks)
November 24, 1931	"Blue Day Blues"	Francis "Scrapper" Blackwell
January 16, 1932	"Mistreated the Only Friend You Had"	James Cole
February 22, 1932	"Lonesome Day Blues"	Ruby Glaze (with Blind Willie McTell)
March 17, 1932	"Down in Black Bottom"	Black Bottom McPhail
August [?], 1932	"She Can Love So Good"	Frankie Half Pint Jaxon (with Tampa Red)
July 17, 1933	"T N and O Blues"	Lucille Bogan
February 5, 1935	"Mr. Hughe's Town"	Huddie Ledbetter
February 18, 1936	"Low Down Rascal"	Peetie Wheatstraw
May 12, 1936	"Pigmeat Blues"	Georgia White
February 1, 1939	"My Man Jumped Salty On Me"	Rosetta Crawford

Discography

The sources for this discography are Tom Lord's *The Jazz Discography Online*; D. Russell Connor's and Warren W. Hick's *BG-On the Record: A Bio-Discography of Benny Goodman*, Discogs.com; and Brian Rust's, *Jazz Records: 1897–1942*. See also Christopher Popa, "Collector's Checklists: Benny Goodman 33s," bigbandlibrary.com (2004), http://www.bigbandlibrary.com/collectorschecklists33s-goodmanbenny.html. This list includes only the tracks with Louise Tobin vocal or writing credit. Each entry includes such available information related to the recording as date and location of its source, leader, ensemble, song title and label, and notes. This list does not include reel to reel, cassette, and VHS personal recordings of both Louise and Peanuts in the LTPHJC. See the collection's inventory for a listing of those recordings.

New York, April 11, 1939

Jack Jenney

Jack Jenney and His Orchestra (including Peanuts Hucko on tenor sax)

24237-A   Got No Time   Voc 4803, BBA LP1218

Camel Caravan broadcast, Cleveland, Ohio, May 16, 1939

Benny Goodman

Benny Goodman And His Orchestra (**Louise Tobin replaces Martha Tilton**)

Louise Tobin Blues   Aircheck 32

It's Never too Late

Camel Caravan broadcast, Columbus, Ohio, May 23, 1939

Benny Goodman

Nick Fatool (d) added.

If You Ever Change Your Mind Aircheck 32

Camel Caravan broadcast, Cincinnati, Ohio, May 30, 1939

Benny Goodman

Don't Worry 'Bout Me Aircheck 32

Louise (parody)　Aircheck 34

Camel Caravan broadcast, Fort Wayne, Ind., June 6, 1939

Benny Goodman

Eddie Sauter (arr) added

The Lady's in Love with You　Aircheck 34

And the Angels Sing

Camel Caravan broadcast, New York, June 13, 1939

Benny Goodman

Toots Mondello (as) replaces Noni Bernardi

You and Your Love

**Sustaining Broadcast (unknown radio network),
Ritz-Carlton Hotel, Boston, June 16, 1939**

Benny Goodman Air Checks, Reel No. 1938-3/1939-1

If You Ever Change Your Mind, (n/c—first half missing, according to
Connor, p. 3)

Camel Caravan broadcast, Ritz-Carlton Hotel, Boston, June 20, 1939

Benny Goodman

Lamp Is Low

There'll Be Some Changes Made　Aircheck 34

Los Angeles, August 10, 1939 (recording session)

Benny Goodman

Benny Goodman and His Orchestra: Ziggy Elman, Chris Griffin, Corky
Cornelius (tp) Red Ballard, Vernon Brown, Bruce Squires (tb) Benny
Goodman (cl) Toots Mondello, Buff Estes (as) Jerry Jerome, Bus Bassey
(ts) Fletcher Henderson (p, arr) Arnold Covey (g) Artie Bernstein (b) Nick
Fatool (d) Louise Tobin (vcl) Eddie Sauter (arr)

LA-1947-A　There'll Be Some Changes Made
Col 35210, Tax (Swd)m-8021, Col CK40588 [CD], CK66198 [CD],
Classics (F)1025 [CD]

LA-1947-B　There'll Be Some Changes Made
Phontastic (Swd)NOST7606, NCD8821 [CD]

LA-1949-A   Rendezvous Time in Paree (Sauter, arr)
Col 35201, Tax (Swd)m-8021, Classics (F)1025 [CD], Collectors'
Choice Music CCM485-2 [CD]

LA-1950-A   Comes Love (Sauter, arr)
Col 35201, Tax (Swd)m-8021, Classics (F)1025 [CD]

LA-1950-B   Comes Love (Sauter, arr)
Phontastic (Swd)NOST7606, NCD8821 [CD]

Note: Columbia CL534 titled "Benny Goodman and His Orchestra."

Phontastic (Swd)NCD8821 [CD] titled "Benny Goodman—The Different
Version, vol. 1."

Mosaic MD7-240 [CD] titled "Classic Columbia and Okeh Benny
Goodman
Orchestra Sessions (1939–1958)."

Los Angeles, August 11, 1939 (recording session)

Benny Goodman

LA-1954-A   Blues
Phontastic (Swd)NOST7606, NCD8821 [CD], Classics
(F)1025 [CD]

LA-1954-B   Blues
Blu-Disc T1004, Neatwork (Au)RP2067 [CD]

LA-1954-S   Blues (spliced take) (Henderson, arr)
Collectors' Choice Music CCM485-2 [CD]

Los Angeles, August 16, 1939 (recording session)

Benny Goodman

LA-1963-A   Blue Orchids
Col 35211, Tax (Swd)m-8021, Classics (F)1025 [CD],
Collectors' Choice Music CCM485-2 [CD]

LA-1963-B   Blue Orchids
Phontastic NOST7606, NCD8821 [CD]

LA-1965-A   What's New?
Col 35211, Tax (Swd)8021, Col CK45338 [CD],
Classics (F)1025 [CD], Hep (E)CD1059 [CD]

LA-1965-B   What's New?
Phontastic (Swd)NOST7606, NCD8821 [CD]

Note: Phontastic (Swd)LV50 was distributed as a private release.

Phontastic (Swd) CD7660 [CD] titled "The Permanent Goodman, vol. 2
(1939–45)."

Columbia CK45338 [CD] titled "Best of the Big Bands—Benny Goodman."

Camel Caravan broadcast from Michigan State Fair, Detroit, September 2, 1939

Benny Goodman

(same orchestra and sextet)

Day In, Day Out   Jazum 54

The Jumpin' Jive (Tobin and ensemble, vocal)

I've Been There Before

Note: All above titles also on Phontastic (Swd)NCD8845/8846 [CD]. The complete broadcast is on this CD.

New Dance Pavilion, Canadian National Exhibition, Toronto, September 4, 1939

Benny Goodman Air Checks, Reel No. 1938-3/1939-1

What's New?

Camel Caravan broadcast, Detroit, September 9, 1939

Benny Goodman

(same orchestra and sextet)

Put That Down in Writing
Phontastic (Swd)NCD8845/8846 [CD]

New York, September 13, 1939 (recording session)

Benny Goodman

Benny Goodman and His Orchestra: Ziggy Elman, Jimmy Maxwell, Johnny Martell (tp) Red Ballard, Vernon Brown, Ted Vesely (tb) Benny Goodman (cl) Toots Mondello, Buff Estes (as) Jerry Jerome, Bus Bassey (ts) Fletcher Henderson (p, arr) Arnold Covey (g) Artie Bernstein (b) Nick Fatool (d) **Louise Tobin (vcl)** Eddie Sauter (arr)

25350-bk   One Sweet Letter from You (Henderson, arr)
Phontastic (Swd)NOST7606, NCD8821 [CD]

25350   One Sweet Letter from You (Henderson, arr)
Phontastic (Swd)NOST7606, NCD8821 [CD]

25350   One Sweet Letter from You (Henderson, arr)
Blu-Disc T1004, Neatwork (Au)RP2067 [CD]

25350-1   One Sweet Letter from You (Henderson, arr)
Col 35241, Jazum 35, Tax (Swd)m-8021, Col CK40588 [CD], Classics (F)1025 [CD], Hep (E)CD1059 [CD]

25352-1   I Didn't Know What Time It Was (Sauter, arr)
Col 35230, Tax (Swd)m-8021, Classics (F)1064 [CD]

25352-2   I Didn't Know What Time It Was (Sauter, arr)
Phontastic (Swd)NOST7606, NCD8821 [CD]

25353-1   Love Never Went to College (Sauter, arr)
Col 35230, Tax (Swd)m-8021, Hep (E)CD1053 [CD],
Classics (F)1064 [CD], Collectors' Choice Music CCM485-2 [CD]

25353-2   Love Never Went to College (Sauter, arr)
Blu-Disc T1004, Neatwork (Au)RP2067 [CD]

25353-4   Love Never Went to College (Sauter, arr)
Phontastic (Swd)NOST7606, NCD8821 [CD]

25354-1   Scatterbrain (Sauter, arr)
Col 35241, GL501, CL534, Tax (Swd)m-8021,
Classics   (F)1064 [CD], Collectors' Choice Music CCM485-2 [CD]

25354-2   Scatterbrain (Sauter, arr)
Phontastic (Swd)NOST7606, NCD8821 [CD]

25355-1   I've Been There Before
Phont (Swd)NOST7610, NCD8821 [CD], Col CK40588
[CD], Classics (F)1064 [CD]

25355-2   I've Been There Before
Blu-Disc T1006, Neatwork (Au)RP2067 [CD]

Note: The above session reflects the discovery in the Columbia vaults of a series of backup 16" 33-1/3 rpm direct cut acetates known as safeties, which were recorded simultaneously with the 78 rpm masters. These "safeties" also include performances additional to the master takes and occasionally completely unissued and unknown titles. None of these "extras" have official take numbers. However, take numbers have now been assigned per Dave Jessup. Further sessions involving "safeties" begin November 7, 1940 and continue until Goodman leaves the Columbia label in 1946.

The designation "bk" above indicates a breakdown or incomplete performance.

Phontastic (Swd)XM79 was distributed as a private release.

Hep (E)CD1053 [CD] titled "Benny Goodman Plays Eddie Sauter."

Classics (F)1064 [CD] titled "Benny Goodman and His Orchestra 1939 Vol. 2."

Waldorf Astoria, New York, October 4, 1939 (opening night)

Benny Goodman Air Checks, Reel No. 1938-3/1939-1 (See Connor, p. 5)

Oh, You Crazy Moon

New York, July 16, 1940

Will Bradley

Will Bradley and His Orchestra, Louise Tobin (vcl) added

28022-A   'Deed I Do (Alex Datz, arr)
Col 35629, Ajax 119, Bandstand BS7101, BS1,
Aerospace 7101 [CD], Hep (E)CD1071 [CD]

28023-A   Don't Let It Get You Down
Col 35629, Ajax 119,-

Los Angeles, 1945

Tommy "Madman" Jones

Tommy "Madman" Jones (ts) **Louise Tobin** + others unknown

One-zy, Two-zy
Sterling 7001

We'll Gather Lilacs

Where Did You Learn to Love?
Sterling 7002

All through the Day

Los Angeles (?), c. December 9, 1947

Stan Hasselgard

The Permanent Hasselgard: Stan Hasselgard Quintet: Åke "Stan"
Hasselgård (cl) Lyman Gandee (p) Al Hendrickson (g) Jud DeNaut (b)
prob Nick Fatool (d) **Louise Tobin (vcl)**

R518A   Lullaby in Rhythm
Phontastic (Swd)NCD8802 [CD]

R517B   A Cottage for Sale

**AFRS One Night Stand 1759, Hollywood Palladium,
Hollywood, CA, August 31, 1948**

Ziggy Elman

One Night Stand at the Hollywood Palladium: Ziggy Elman and His
Orchestra: Ziggy Elman, Neal Hefti (tp, arr) Claude Bowen, Everett
McDonald, Ray Horak (tp) Red Ballard, Moe Schneider, Norris Hurley,
Neil Reid (tb) Jack Dumont, Kenny Olsen (as) Roy Parkinson, Everett
McLaughlin (ts) Joe Koch (bar) Shelton Smith (p) Jimmy Stutz (b) Roy
Harte (d) Bob Allen, **Louise Tobin**, Top Notchers (vcl)

A Boy from Texas
Joyce 1059

You Turned the Tables on Me

AFRS One Night Stand 1793, September 7, 1948

Ziggy Elman

If I Could Be with You

You Turned the Tables on Me

Hollywood, CA, May 14, 1951

Ziggy Elman

Ziggy Elman (tp, ldr) with 3 tp, 3 tb, 5 saxes, cl, p, g, b, d, **Louise Tobin**, The Jud Conlon Rhythmaires (vcl) Heinie Beau (arr)

51-S-3078-2   Sunny Disposish (Heinie Beau, arr)
MGM 11089, Ajaz 442

51-S-3079-4   The Birth of the Blues (Heinie Beau, arr)
MGM 11089, 30672, K30672, E163, (E)488, (G)1055, Ajaz 442, Swing Era LP1015

Hollywood, CA, November 1954

Louise Tobin

54-XY-425   Hurry Home   MGM K11881

54-XY-427   Lonesome Road
(Vinyl. 7", 45 RPM. Released November **1954**)

54-XY-426   Goodnight My Love   MGM K12294

54-XY-428   I Thought about You
(Vinyl. 7", 45 RPM. Released November **1954**)

New York City, NY, 1964

Peanuts Hucko and Louise Tobin

LR 3220   Falling Tears (M. Hucko-L. Tobin)

LR 3220   Buck Dance (K. Stone, J. Schuster, W. Spencer, J. Val)
Peanuts Hucko, Laurie Records Inc., New York, Sunset Music Publishers Inc. Vinyl. 7", 45 RPM. Released 1964.

New York City, NY, 1966

Peanuts Hucko and His Orchestra

103   Popcorn & Crackerjazz

103   Filibuster
Avant Garde Records. Vinyl. 7", 45 RPM. Released 1966. (Both tracks list Hucko-Tobin as writers. Discogs.com dates this single 1961 without reference. Avant Garde Records, Ltd. was active 1966–1972 according to Discogs.com. Avant Garde Records, 250 W. 57, NYC., was a Division of Lincoln Square Productions, Inc.)

New York City, NY, 1966

Louise Tobin, Peanuts Hucko

104   Wonderful One

104   Scatterbrain

Avant Garde Records. Vinyl. 7", 45 RPM. US. Released 1966 (Louise Tobin listed on record "with orch. cond. By Peanuts Hucko" [Discogs.com].)

San Diego, CA, March 7, 1977

San Diego Jazz Club

The San Diego Jazz Club Plays the Sound of Jazz: John Best (tp) Carl Fontana (tb) Peanuts Hucko (cl) Eddie Miller (ts) Johnny Guarnieri (p) Ray Leatherwood (b) Nick Fatool (d) **Louise Tobin (vcl)**

I Left My Sugar Standing in the Rain
San Diego Jazz Club SDJC22477

There'll Be Some Changes Made

Note: All above titles also on Jazz Connoisseur (E)JCC54 [Cass] titled "The Sound of Jazz All Stars 1977."

All above titles also on NOJE KM11968.

Wageningen, Holland, October 24, 1983

Peanuts Hucko

Tribute to Louis Armstrong-Benny Goodman: Tribute to Louis Armstrong: Billy Butterfield (tp) Trummy Young (tb, vcl) Peanuts Hucko (cl,vcl) Marty Napoleon (p) Jack Lesberg (b) Gus Johnson (d) **Louise Tobin (vcl)**

Georgia on My Mind
Timeless (Du)TTD512/13, CDTTD512 [CD]

Note: Timeless CDTTD512 [CD] titled "Tribute to Louis Armstrong"; see July 8, 1986 for the rest of this CD.

All above titles also on Timeless (Jap)RJL-8094.

Monster, The Netherlands, October 24, 1983

Peanuts Hucko

Tribute to Benny Goodman: Peanuts Hucko (cl) Lars Erstrand (vib) Marty Napoleon (p) Jack Lesberg (b) Gus Johnson (d) **Louise Tobin (vcl)**

'Deed I Do
Timeless (Du)TTD512/513, CDTTD513 [CD]

The Man I Love

Am I Blue?

There'll Be Some Changes Made

Note: Timeless (Du)CDTTD513 [CD] titled "Tribute to Benny Goodman"; see July 8, 1986 for the rest of this CD.

Monster, The Netherlands, July 8, 1986

Peanuts Hucko

Tribute to Benny Goodman: Peanuts Hucko (cl) Frits Landesbergen (vib) John Bunch (p) Jack Lesberg (b) Jake Hanna (d) **Louise Tobin (vcl)**

Rockin' Chair
Timeless (Du)TTD541/542, CDTTD513 [CD]

After You've Gone

He's Funny That Way

Goodnight My Love

Note: Timeless (Du)CDTTD513 [CD] titled "Tribute to Benny Goodman"; see October 24, 1983 for the rest of this CD.

Live, "Nick Vollebregt's Jazzcafe," Laren, Netherlands, January 22, 1987

Tribute to Louis Armstrong

Tribute to Louis Armstrong and Benny Goodman: Randy Sandke (tp) Roy Williams (tb) Peanuts Hucko (cl) Danny Moss (ts) Lars Erstrand (vib-1) Johnny Varro (p) Colin Geig (b) Butch Miles (d) **Louise Tobin (vcl)**

The Man I Love
GB Private (Du)GBAJ-20 [CD]

There'll Be Some Changes Made

Live "Burgerzentrum," Waiblingen, Germany, October 21, 1988

Peanuts Hucko

Swing That Music: Peanuts Hucko and His All Stars Featuring **Louise Tobin**: Randy Sandke (tp) Roy Williams (tb) Peanuts Hucko (cl, vcl, ldr) Danny Moss (ts) Lars Erstrand (vib-1) Johnny Varro (p) Colin Gieg (b) Butch Miles (d) **Louise Tobin (vcl)**

There'll Be Some Changes Made   Star Line SLCD9005 [CD]

When You're Smiling (Hucko, Tobin vcl)

United Kingdom, November 1–15, 1991

Peanuts Hucko

Peanuts Hucko and the Anglo American All Stars Live in Britain: Peanuts Hucko and the 1991 Anglo American All Stars: Glenn Zottola (tp) Roy

Williams (tb) Danny Moss (ts) Peanuts Hucko (cl) Mark Shane (p) James Chirillo (g) Len Skeat (b) Mark Maniatt (d) **Louise Tobin (vcl)**

'Deed I Do
York (E)YCC19193

Hard Hearted Hannah

Sweet and Lovely

I Can't Give You Anything but Love

Nobody Else but Me

Live "Rems-Murr-Jazztage," Schorndorf, Germany, October 27, 1992

The Young Generation of Swing

In Concert at the Rems-Murr-Jazztage, Volume 2: The Young Generation of Swing Featuring Peanuts Hucko: Randy Sandke, Jon-Erik Kellso, Ralf Hesse (tp) Dan Barrett, John Allred (tb) Chuck Wilson (as) Rainer Heute (as, bar) Harry Allen, Christian Plattner (ts) Peanuts Hucko (cl) Mike Goetz (p) Howard Alden (g) Alec Dankworth (b) Gregor Beck (d) **Louise Tobin (vcl)**

Loch Lomond
Downtown (Swi)DR9206 [CD]

2010 (Compilation)

Louise Tobin—Changes: A Rediscovered Voice in Jazz. Produced by Mike Kubiak, 2010. (Compilation, including previously released as well as unreleased live recordings from the LTPHJC. Limited issue. All vocals by Louise Tobin. [CD]

There'll Be Some Changes Made, Benny Goodman recording

I've Been There Before, Benny Goodman recording

What's New, Benny Goodman recording

Rendezvous Time in Paree, Benny Goodman recording

S'Wonderful, Recorded at the Navarre, Denver, CO, Maury Feld (d) Freddy Hosteller (b) Dave McKenna (p) Peanuts Hucko (cl).

I Left My Sugar Standing in the Rain, recorded in San Diego. Arranged by Billy May. Nick Fatool (d), Roy Leatherwood (b) Peanuts Hucko (cl) Johnny Guarnari (p) Johnny Best (tp) Eddie Miller (ts) Carl Fontana (tb).

In My Honey's Lovin' Arms, recorded at the Navarre, Denver, CO, Maury Feld (d) Freddy Hosteller (b) Dave McKenna (p) Peanuts Hucko (cl).

It Had to Be You, recorded at the Navarre, Denver, CO, Maury Feld (d) Freddy Hosteller (b) Dave McKenna (p) Peanuts Hucko (cl).

Deed I Do, recorded at Birch Hall, England, Gus Johnson (d) Len Skeats (b) Mark Shane (p) Peantus Hucko (cl) Danny Moss (ts) Roy Williams (tb) Randy Sandke (tp).

It's Not That Easy Being Green, Recorded at Tulio's in Palm Desert, Arnold Fishkin (b) Sid Horowitz (p).

Bye Bye Blackbird, recorded at the Navarre, Denver, CO, Maury Feld (d) Freddy Hosteller (b) Dave McKenna (p) Peanuts Hucko (cl).

God Bless the Child, recorded at Birch Hall, England, Gus Johnson (d) Len Skeats (b) Mark Shane (p) Peanuts Hucko (cl) Danny Moss (ts) Roy Williams (tb) Randy Sandke (tp).

Notes

Introduction

1. Interview, July 16, 2009. Louise Tobin and Peanuts Hucko Jazz Collection, Texas A&M University–Commerce.

2. Kevin Mooney, "As Big as All of Texas: An Overview of Music in the Lone Star State," unpublished keynote address, Texas Music Conference, Dallas Public Library, Dallas, Texas, May 31, 2009.

3. The Louise Tobin and Peanuts Hucko Jazz Collection, housed at Texas A&M University–Commerce, has been inventoried and archived primarily by Andrea Weddle, and it includes recorded and sheet music, set lists, music arrangements, vinyl and acetate albums, reel-to-reel and cassette tapes, DAT recordings, photographs, negatives and slides, video recordings, television broadcasts, home movies, posters, concert programs and performance costumes, newspaper and magazine articles, ephemera, and memorabilia. The finding aid for the physical collection is available in the Special Collections, Waters Library, Texas A&M University–Commerce, https://archives.tamuc.edu/repositories/2/resources/17.

4. *Remembering Benny*: *A Tribute by Peanuts Hucko & Other Benny Goodman Alumni*, Swingband Records, SB1001. Originally released as *A Tribute to Benny Goodman*, produced by George T. Simon.

5. Louise Tobin and Peanuts Hucko Jazz Collection, J. DVDs: Tobin Louise; oral history interview conducted by Kevin Mooney in Garland, Texas; unedited version, Drawer 6, disk: DVD 22–25, July 16, 2009; edited version, Drawer 6, disk: DVD 26–28.

Chapter 1

1. Tobin interview with Deborah Porter, September 8, 2013.

2. Molly Billings, "The Influenza Pandemic of 1918," June 1997; last modified February 2005, https://virus.stanford.edu/uda/.

3. Hobby's term ran August 25, 1917–January 18, 1921. www.tsl.state.tx.us/ref/abouttx/governors.html. William P. Hobby Jr., "Hobby, William Pettus," *Handbook of Texas Online*, www.tshaonline.org/handbook/online/articles/fh004, accessed July 27, 2012, published by the Texas State Historical Association.

4. "In June 1919, Texas became the ninth state to ratify the Nineteenth Amendment to the United States Constitution, which took effect on August 26, 1920, and

fully enfranchised American women." See Elizabeth York Enstam, "Women and the Law," *Handbook of Texas Online*, https://tshaonline.org/handbook/online/articles/jsw02, accessed July 27, 2012, published by the Texas State Historical Association.

5. See *History of Aubrey, Texas*, compiled by The Aubrey Historical Society, 2nd printing, December 2012.

6. Tobin interview, July 16, 2009. See *History of Aubrey, Texas* (p. 137) for the date (1867) of their arrival in Texas from Alabama.

7. See *History of Aubrey, Texas*, for information regarding Laura Edwards's marriage to Rhoades, daughter Bertha's education in Chicago, at Baylor University, and at Texas State College for Women, and her marriage to A. Q. Mustain.

8. Tobin interview, July 16, 2012.

9. Louise's grandparents had eleven children; their firstborn, L. N. Edwards Jr., died in infancy.

10. Tobin interview, July 16, 2012.

11. *History of Aubrey, Texas*, 137.

12. Jackie Balthrop Fuller, "Aubrey, TX," *Handbook of Texas Online*, http://www.tshaonline.org/handbook/online/articles/hla28, accessed July 27, 2012, published by the Texas State Historical Association.

13. Fuller, "Aubrey, TX," *Handbook of Texas Online*.

14. See *History of Aubrey, Texas*.

15. Aubrey, Denton County, Texas, accessed July 27, 2012, www.usacitiesonline.com/txcountyaubrey.htm.

16. Aubrey, Denton County, Texas.

17. Tobin interview, July 19, 2011.

18. With the 1930s Depression and a growing migration to larger metropolitan areas, the population in Aubrey began to decline. See Aubrey, Denton County, Texas, accessed July 27, 2012, www.usacitiesonline.com/txcountyaubrey.htm.

19. Tobin interview, July 16, 2012.

20. Tobin interview, March 2016.

21. Tobin interview, July 16, 2009. See Rick Storm, "Business @marillo Globe-News: WDAG Made First Broadcast with 10 Watts of Power," *Amarillo Globe News*, May 18, 1997, http://amarillo.com/stories/051897/first.html#.Wb0VHzlukfE. Metzger's Dairies was founded by Jacob Metzger, Swiss immigrant to Texas. The company was purchased by Borden (Dairy) in 1984. The Metzger family also owned and operated Mr. M Food Stores until son David Metzger (1935–2009) retired and sold the business in 1995. See *Legacies: A History Journal for Dallas and North Central Texas*, Volume 21, Number 2 (Fall 2009), Dallas, Texas. texashistory.unt.edu/ark:/67531/metapth66965/m1/26/, accessed September 16, 2017, University of North Texas Libraries, The Portal to Texas History, texashistory.unt.edu, crediting Dallas Historical Society; "David Metzger-Obituary," published in *Dallas Morning News*, September 12, 2009, accessed September 16, 2017, www.legacy.com/obituaries/dallasmorningnews/obituary.aspx?pid=132684781; and, William T. Field, "Swiss," *Handbook of Texas Online*, www.tshaonline.org/handbook/online/articles/pns01, accessed September 16, 2017.

22. *Amarillo Sunday News Globe*, March 9, 1930, 2.

23. Undated clipping, Louise Tobin and Peanuts Hucko Jazz Collection, Texas A&M University–Commerce [LTPHJC]; *Denton Record-Chronicle*, June 10, 1930, 6.

24. Johnny King, *Campus Chat* (Denton, TX), Vol. 15, No. 18, Ed. 1, Saturday, February 28, 1931, newspaper, February 28, 1931; Denton, TX. texashistory.unt. edu/ark:/67531/metapth314075/, accessed September 17, 2017, University of North Texas Libraries, The Portal to Texas History, texashistory.unt.edu, crediting UNT Libraries Special Collections. The Mary Arden Lodge was the meeting place for the Mary Arden Club and a site for student teas and other social activities on the college campus. See James L. Rogers, *The Story of North Texas* (Denton: North Texas State University, 1965), 225 and 230.

25. The *Denton Record-Chronicle* announced that, "Miss Mary Louise Tobin has returned to her home in Denton after spending several months in Amarillo," October 24, 1931.

26. *Denton Record-Chronicle*, April 28, 1931, and November 7, 1931, respectively. The later article, "Mary L. Tobin Is Crowned Queen of Junior High School," includes the earliest evidence of Louise labeled a blues singer. I will address this designation in greater detail below. See also *Denton Record-Chronicle*, Tuesday, May 5, 1931, "$27.25 Realized in Pay Assembly": "The sum of $27.25 was realized at a pay assembly held at junior High School Tuesday morning. A musical program headed by 'Scottie and his Kilties' was presented. Catherine Coleman, Mary Louise Tobin, Reed Gosney and Dudley King sang several numbers and a style show was presented."

27. Tobin interview, August 30, 2012. Louise was neither able to recall specific experiences with this group nor specific circumstances of their performance occasions.

28. Tobin interview, July 16, 2009.

29. Tobin interview, August 30, 2012. Asked if she ever listened to Bessie Smith, Louise said that she had not until she went with Benny Goodman. "John Hammond said to me one day, 'You sound like Bessie Smith,' and I didn't want him to know I didn't know who Bessie was, and I didn't know for a long time who she was."

30. *Denton Record-Chronicle*, April 28, 1931.

31. "Assembly in Senior High School Friday morning was sponsored by the low senior class, opening with a quartet singing, composed of Leoland Edwards, Hamlett Harmon, H. M. Pitner and T. B. Stovall, accompanied on the guitar by J. W. Woods. Miss Mary Louise Tobin sang and F. C. Moore gave some harmonica numbers"; see "Special Program at Senior High," *Denton Record-Chronicle*, April 8, 1932.

32. *Campus Chat*, Vol. 16, No. 24, Ed. 1, Thursday, April 14, 1932. The *Campus Chat* was founded in 1916 and was renamed the *North Texas Daily* in 1971. North Texas State Teachers College was established in 1890 as the Texas Normal College and Teachers Training Institute. The college became a state institution in 1899, and, after a number of other changes, as of 1988 has been named the University of North Texas. See Rogers, *The Story of North Texas*.

33. "The Froggies Recreational Club entertained with a dance Friday evening in the home of Whitney Crow Wright. Music was furnished by Albert Allen's negro band, and punch and cakes were served. Messrs, and Mmes. Deats Headlee and

James Knox and Mrs. Cecil Bell Monroe were chaperones. Members and friends present were: Misses Ruth Martin, Herbertine Morrison, Billy Risenger, Lorraine Skinner, Louise Hubbard, Dorothy Hart, Mary Louise Tobin, Catherine Collier, Jerry Ashworth." *Denton Record-Chronicle*, April 16, 1932.

34. *Denton Record-Chronicle*, May 4, 1932, 5; the article also states that "Mrs. Clara Calmbach and Miss Verna Tobin led in the group singing, accompanied by Mrs. Oober Wright."

35. *Denton Record-Chronicle*, June 1, 1932.

36. On the Justimere Club, see *Denton Record-Chronicle*, January 29, 1934; on the Hi-Yi Club, see *Denton Record-Chronicle*, March 15, 1934.

37. *Denton Record-Chronicle*, March 15, 1934.

38. *Denton Record-Chronicle*, February 13, 1934.

39. *Campus Chat*, Denton, Texas, Vol. 18, No. 37, Ed. 1, Thursday, July 26, 1934.

40. A precursor to Graham's ensemble was an orchestra directed by mathematics professor James Willis Smith (1875–1937). Floyd Freeman Graham (a.k.a. 'Fessor) (1902–1974) took over after Smith's departure in 1927. The 1940 school yearbook includes two photos of Graham with the following caption: "Floyd Graham, assistant professor of music, holds the Bachelor of Music degree from the Chicago Musical College and the Master of Music degree from the American Conservatory of Music. He has been a pupil of Herbert Butler, Leo Swerby, Max Fischel, Wesley LaViolette, Fritz Mohler, Carl Venth, and Ferde Grofé. Mr. Graham organized the Aces of Collegeland in 1927 and has directed it into its present superior position. He also directs the College Symphony Orchestra and teaches instrumental conducting, orchestration, and string concentration." North Texas State Teacher's College, *The Yucca, Yearbook of North Texas State Teacher's College* (1940), Arthur Evans, editor; digital images, http://texashistory.unt.edu/ark:/67531/metapth61014, accessed May 17, 2010, University of North Texas Libraries, The Portal to Texas History, http://texashistory.unt.edu. See also, "One O'Clock Jazz Band," Wikipedia: https://en.wikipedia.org/wiki/One_O%27Clock_Lab_Band.

41. Rogers, *The Story of North Texas*, 223.

42. On "feature attraction," see North Texas State Teachers College. *The Yucca, Yearbook of North Texas State Teachers College*, 1940. See also, "One O'Clock Lab Band," Wikipedia: https://en.wikipedia.org/wiki/One_O%27Clock_Lab_Band. The Aces was a "stage band" and not a jazz ensemble, notably. The former was more of a dance orchestra of sweet music. The later establishment and development of the One O'Clock Lab Band and jazz program at the Denton College reflected the emergence of improvisation, "hot" jazz, indeed, *jazz*, as a legitimate, academic area of study.

43. Tobin interview, September 11, 2014.

44. *Campus Chat*, Denton, Texas, Vol. 19, No. 10, Ed. 1, Tuesday, November 27, 1934.

45. The Miss America Pageant added an optional talent competition in the 1930s. "The History of Pageants: 1930–1939," (1998) PageantCenter.com, accessed August 23, 2010, http://pageantcenter.com/history-30s.html.

46. See YouTube: http://www.youtube.com/watch?v=4BM50_elYnU.

47. See "The History of Pageants: 1930–1939" (1998), PageantCenter.com, accessed August 23, 2010, http://pageantcenter.com/history-30s.html.

48. "A group of Denton High School students went to Fort Worth Friday to enter the Interscholastic League district contest to be held in T.C.U. Four students are to present the one act play, 'The Last of the Loweries,' the cast including Mary Louise White, Marylillian Harshaw, Martha Ann Regan and Hugh Gentry. Miss Sara Wheat of C.I.A., their coach, accompanied them. For declamation contests Mary Louise Tobin and Jack Hubbard went, accompanied by their coach, Miss Eva Cain Hamilton of C.I.A." "Denton Students to League Contests," *Denton Record-Chronicle*, April 13, 1934.

49. "Rotarians Hear Local Declaimers," *Denton Record-Chronicle*, April 6, 1934.

50. Ada Jones and Billy Murray recorded "Emmaline" for Victor [5761] in 1910.

51. Tobin interview, August 30, 2012. For more information on the Texas Interstate Theatre circuit, see the Hoblitzelle & Interstate Theater Collection—Harry Ransom Center, The University of Texas at Austin, www.hrc.utexas.edu/collections/film/holdings/interstate. See also, Interstate Theatre Collection, Texas Archival Resources Online, https://legacy.lib.utexas.edu/taro/dalpub/07701/dpub-07701p1.html.

52. Tobin interview, August 30, 2012.

53. Tobin interview, August 30, 2012.

54. Tobin interview, August 30, 2012.

55. "Palace Engages Louise Tobin for Pit Program," undated clipping, scrapbook, LTPHJC.

56. "Donivee Perky, 10-year-old singer from Henderson, Texas, was the new Palace hit personality introduced Saturday. She did creditable work for a child singer in her numbers, "Out for No Good," "You Nasty Man" and "Kissin' Games." "Perky Introduced on Palace Musical," *Dallas Morning News*, August 19,1934.

57. Linda Dahl, *Stormy Weather: The Music and Lives of a Century of Jazzwomen* (New York: Pantheon Books, 1984), 128.

58. *Dallas Morning News*, August 2, 1934.

59. In October 1956, Charninsky and His Orchestra backed opening acts for Elvis Presley's State Fair performance at the Cotton Bowl. Sherry Davis, Howard and Wanda Bell, Rex Marlowe, Hubert Castle and The Jordanaires led the first hour, the last thirty-five minutes of the KLIF-Radio sponsored event was all Elvis and his band. See James V. Roy, "Scotty Moore—Official Website: Cotton Bowl," February 10, 2008, accessed September 12, 2009, www.scottymoore.net/CottonBowl.html. See also "Bandleader H. Charninsky dies at age 78," *Dallas Morning News*, July 12, 1977.

60. "Palace Engages Louise Tobin for Pit Program," undated clipping, scrapbook, LTPHJC, clippings 1930s.

61. *Dallas Morning News*, August 2, 1934.

62. "Pardon My Southern Accent," words by Johnny Mercer; music by Matt Malneck. See Robert Kimball et al., eds., *The Complete Lyrics of Johnny Mercer*, the Johnny Mercer Foundation (New York: Alfred A. Knopf, 2009) as well as the Johnny Mercer Foundation website, www.johnnymercerjoundation.org.

63. This is likely either the 1924 "I Never Knew What Love Could Do," music

by Harold Arlen and words by Hyman Cheiffetz, or it is "I Never Knew What a Moonlight Could Do" (1926), recorded by Oreste and His Queensland Orchestra in 1926. Johnny Mercer's "I Never Knew" was not written until 1956. A tune search of "I Never Knew" using Tom Lord's *The Jazz Discography* yields 369 hits and about twenty-five different extensions of the phrase.

64. "Louise Tobin, Denton blues singer, will be held over from the current program," *Dallas Morning News*, August 6, 1934.

65. C.I.A. is College of Industrial Arts, a successful, regional women's finishing school, first established and later renamed Texas Woman's University, Denton, Texas. Louise did not have an opportunity to enroll, since she ultimately followed her rising professional career. *Dallas Morning News*, August 6, 1934.

66. *Denton Record-Chronicle*, August 7, 1934.

67. "Former Plainview Girl Singing on Palace Circuit," undated clipping, scrapbook, LTPHJC, clippings 1930s.

68. W. Royal Stokes, *The Jazz Scene: An Informal History from New Orleans to 1990* (New York: Oxford University Press, 1991), 70.

69. Stokes, *Jazz Scene*, 80.

70. Tobin interview, July 16, 2009.

71. Tobin interview, July 16, 2009.

72. Tobin interview with Deborah Porter, September 8, 2013.

73. *Dallas Morning News*, August 15, 1934.

74. *Dallas Morning News*, August 15, 1934. *Houston Chronicle*, August 23, 1934. For more on the Metropolitan Theater, Houston, see www.houstondeco.org/1920s/metro.html, accessed September 15, 2009. Lloyd Finlay and His Orchestra was based in Houston and has the distinction of making the first recording in Texas for Victor on March 17, 1925. This information as well as two recordings by Finlay for Victor recording March 18 and 19, 1925, are available at www.oldtimeblues.net/2015/06/05/victor-19644-lloyd-finlay-and-his-orchestra-1925/. Finlay and His Orchestra performed and recorded dance music mostly of the 1920s and '30s.

75. Bess Whitehead Scott, "Tipping You Off," *Houston Post*, August 26, 1934, 11.

76. David W. Stowe, *Swing Changes: Big Band Jazz in New Deal America* (Cambridge, MA: Harvard University Press, 1996), 173. Quoted in Katherine Baber, "'Manhattan Women': Jazz, Blues, and Gender in On the Town and Wonderful Town," *American Music* 31, no. 1 (March 2013): 78.

77. A September 19, 1934, article in the *Denton Record-Chronicle* states that Al Kavla's orchestra was from Chicago, and that "Kavla played with Wayne King's orchestra at the Oriental Theater." I am not confident that the reporter spelled the orchestra leader's name correctly. Louise recalled that his name was spelled Kavali. I have not been able to find any information on "Kavali." I did, however, locate an Al Kavelin. According to Allmusic.com, Al Kavelin and His Orchestra was formed in 1933 and that the "30s and 40s saw the orchestra play most of the major hotels and ballrooms of the dance band circuit, including the Waldorf-Astoria, Essex House and the Biltmore (New York), the Blackstone Hotel (Chicago), the Mark Hopkins (San Francisco), the Baker (Dallas)." www.allmusic.com/artist/al-kavelin-mn0001009035/

biography. The article does not mention Kavelin working with Wayne King's orchestra in Chicago. The search continues.

78. Tobin interview, August 30, 2012.

79. The story of Louise joining Art Hicks and first meeting Harry is best recounted in her interview with Graham Pass for the BBC, September 3, 2009.

80. Tobin interview, September 11, 2014.

81. "Dining and Dancing," *Dallas Morning News*, August 5, 1934.

82. The *Dallas Morning News* first announced the opening on June 28, 1934.

83. *Dallas Morning News*, June 28 and 29, 1934.

84. *Dallas Morning News*, July 15, 1934.

85. Tobin interview by Graham Pass, September 3, 2009.

86. *Dallas Morning News*, July 23, 1934. Manny Harmon (d. 2003) was a violinist dance band leader who, through his Los Angeles connections, led the orchestra for the Republican National Conventions from 1956 through 1992. He was born in Philadelphia, and after playing dance music with hotel bands led by Earl Burtnett and Art Hickman, he formed and led his own orchestra, working hotels in the East and in Texas before settling in Los Angeles, California, in the early 1940s. For most of the 1940s and into the 1950s, he was orchestra manager for Howard Hughes's RKO Studio. "Manny Harmon, 93; Music Director for GOP Conventions," Obituary, *Los Angeles Times*, March 12, 2003.

87. *Dallas Morning News*, July 24, 1934. The Roddy Twins performed a Hawaiian dance sporting cellophane hula skirts. *Dallas Morning News*, July 29, 1934.

88. *Dallas Morning News*, September 10, 1934.

89. *Dallas Morning News*, September 27, 1934.

90. There is little information available on Hicks. Peter J. Levinson's *Trumpet Blues* includes a brief account of his orchestra. According to Levinson, citing Tobin, Hicks "had married into a wealthy family that owned the Lions Stores chain in the Toledo, Ohio, area, and formed his own band." Peter J. Levinson, *Trumpet Blues: The Life of Harry James* (Oxford: Oxford University Press, 1999), 20. Levinson also identifies Hicks as having been musical director for Paul Spector's band in New York (p. 20). Tom Lord's discography identifies Hicks as the violinist and vocalist of the Chubb-Steinberg Orchestra recording in Cincinnati, April 10, 1924, with an ensemble that included a young Wild Bill Davison on cornet. Hicks's vocals with Chubb-Steinberg included "Horsey, Keep Your Tail Up" and "Steppin' in Society," the latter of which was recorded with the same ensemble in Richmond, Indiana, April 30, 1925, and features a vocal by Hicks (Tom Lord's *The Jazz Discography*; Art Hicks, www.lordisco.com; both tracks can be heard on YouTube.com). Hal Willard's biography of "Wild" Bill Davison includes several references to Hicks. Hal Willard, *The Wildest One: The Life of Wild Bill Davison* (Monkton, MD: Avondale Press, 1996).

91. Willard, *Wildest One*, 40.

92. Willard, *Wildest One*, 43.

93. Willard, *Wildest One*, 29.

94. Willard, *Wildest One*, 29.

95. Tobin interview with Deborah Porter, September 8, 2013.

96. See Levinson, *Trumpet Blues*, 19. Levinson mentions "a photograph from the June 8, 1934, edition of the *San Antonio Evening News* [that] shows members of the Ligon Smith Orchestra posing amid a lineup of various shiny brand-new General Motors cars in front of the St. Anthony Hotel" (p. 19).

97. Tobin interview with Deborah Porter, September 8, 2013. Dennis M. Spragg, in his book *Glenn Miller Declassified* (Lincoln: University of Nebraska Press, 2017), distinguishes "copyist Sgt. Jimmy Jackson (piano)" from "arrangers M/Sgt. Norman Leyden and S/Sgt. Ralph Wilkinson ([arranger] S/Sgt. Jerry Gray went along to France)" (p. 275).

98. Tobin interview with Deborah Porter, September 8, 2013.

99. *Dallas Morning News*, October 12, 1934, announced that, "Louise Tobin, blues singer, is not with the club this week, but will be brought back for another engagement later."

100. Tobin interview with Deborah Porter, September 8, 2013.

101. *Dallas Morning News*, October 3, 1934.

102. Tobin interview by Graham Pass for BBC, September 3, 2009.

103. Tobin interview, July 16, 2009.

104. Tobin interview, July 16, 2009.

105. Letter mentioned in interview with Tobin, July 16, 2009.

106. *Plainview Daily Herald* (TX), Monday, November 8 (reprinted, Nov. 8, 2004, Section: Back in Time, Daily Retrospective to News from the Archives). "Louise Tobin, formerly of Plainview, will be heard from 10:45–11:45 tonight with the Art Hicks Orchestra from The Sylvan Club in Dallas on radio station WFAA."

107. Art Hicks poster advertising November 12, 1934, performance at the Hilton Hotel, San Angelo, Texas (LTPHJC). In the personals section of the *Breckenridge American*, Breckenridge, Texas, Tuesday, November 13, 1934, an announcement reads: "Misses Dora and Mary Louise Tobin who are entertainers with Art Hicks orchestra, visited their brother, Don Tobin, here Monday. The girls will leave soon with the orchestra to play engagements in Cincinnati and New York City. They have just finished an engagement at the Sylvan Club in Arlington."

108. The Mayo in Tulsa was a luxury hotel that opened in 1925.

109. *Tulsa Tribune*, December 14, 1934. See also, Levinson, *Trumpet Blues*, 21.

110. Tobin interview, July 16, 2012.

111. Tobin interview, July 16, 2012.

112. Betty Jo Lagman, "Entertainers Talk about Big Band Era," *Mobile Press Register*, Saturday, August 17, 1985.

113. *Toledo Blade*, January 23, 1935. Clipping, LTPHJC.

114. According to Hal Willard in his biography of Wild Bill Davison, Hicks ultimately left music and became "a highly successful businessman living in Jackson, Michigan" (p. 44).

115. Paul Levinson, *Trumpet Blues*, mistakenly has May 25 for their wedding date.

116. Tobin interview with Deborah Porter, September 8, 2013.

117. Tobin interview by Deborah Porter, February 10, 2016. (The author acknowledges and thanks Dr. Porter for transcribing and sharing this interview.)

118. Tobin interview with Deborah Porter, February 10, 2016.

119. Tobin interview (and transcription) by Deborah Porter, January 20, 2016.

Chapter 2

1. Eric Aasen, "At 91 Louise Tobin Recalls Singing with Jazz Giants," *Dallas Morning News*, May 24, 2010.

2. "Denton Girl Singer to Visit Here Soon," *Denton Record-Chronicle*, May 22, 1935.

3. "Dora was real good to me. She took care of me. I can remember her rubbing my feet at night." "I remember that she bought me formals for $3.99 at Lerner's. You would have thought I had gone to Saks Fifth Avenue. We were so excited." Dora went to work at their brother's pharmacy and later married. Louise sang at her wedding (see chapter 4). Interview June 2009.

4. Levinson, *Trumpet Blues*, 22. The secret was kept closer to three months than four as stated in Levinson, as the *Denton Record-Chronicle* reported on Thursday, July 25, 1935.

5. www.allmusic.com/artist/herman-waldman-mn0001010082.

6. Tobin interview, July 16, 2009.

7. www.allmusic.com/artist/herman-waldman-mn0001010082.

8. Levinson, *Trumpet Blues*, 23.

9. June 20, 1935, "Louise Tobin to Be Featured Saturday," *Campus Chat* (Denton, TX), Vol. 19, No. 34, Ed. 1, Thursday, June 20, 1935—"Although the entire bill for the Saturday night stage show it [*sic*] not yet complete, Director Bob Marquis was able to announce on Wednesday the return of Mary Louise Tobin to the Teachers College stage as the special feature of the evening. Miss Tobin has been presented as featured vocalist during the last year with Art Hicks and his orchestra, and has recently completed a tour of the East and the South with that organization."

10. *Denton Record-Chronicle*, June 18, 1935. KTAT was 1240 on the dial. Ft. Worth shares the frequency with WACO—Waco. It briefly exchanged frequencies in January with KGKO 570 in Wichita.

11. *Campus Chat* (Denton, TX), Vol. 19, No. 35, Ed. 1, Wednesday, June 26, 1935; Column: "Pick Ups" by Elizabeth Belcher of the Huey, Louisiana, Belchers.

12. *Amarillo Sunday News Globe*, July 28, 1935, 13.

13. *Denton Record-Chronicle*, June 18, 1935. KTAT was 1240 on the dial. Ft. Worth shares frequency with WACO—Waco. Briefly exchanged frequencies in January with KGKO 570 in Wichita.

14. *Denton Record-Chronicle*, July 25, 1935.

15. *Denton Record-Chronicle*, July 25, 1935.

16. That would put their departure for Chicago at about August 4–5, 1935.

17. *Denton Record-Chronicle*, July 25, 1935.

18. *Morning Avalanche*, July 25, 1935.

19. *Morning Avalanche*, July 27, 1935.

20. *Amarillo Globe*, July 23, 1935. The newspaper printed a featured article the following day: "Smith Is Very Proud of His Novelty Band," quoting Smith as stating that the band represents "the best group of musicians I have ever directed." The article

also states that, "During the past several months Ligon Smith's orchestra has been playing in leading hotels of the state, and the popularity of the orchestra has been continually increasing," *Amarillo Globe*, July 24, 1935.

21. Poster: "Dance to Ligon Smith and His Orchestra featuring the Lovely and Beautiful Miss Tobin"—Lake Cisco "Where West Texas Dances" 9:30–1:30 Admission $1.65; LTPHJC, Correspondence Folder, Harry James. Cisco Lake (also known as Williamson Dam) is located about four miles north of Cisco in Eastland County, on Sandy Creek, a tributary of Hubbard Creek, which is tributary to Clear Fork Brazos River, which is tributary to the Brazos River. See "Cisco Lake (Brazos River)," Texas Water Development Board, www.twdb.texas.gov/surfacewater/rivers/reservoirs/cisco/index.asp.

22. For more on the *Ice Parade* radio program, see W. E. Keys, "Radio Reports: Ice Parade," *Variety*, July 17, 1935, 51.

23. *Dallas Morning News*, August 5 and 12, 1935.

24. Tobin interview, July 16, 2009.

25. *Dallas Morning News*, September 29, 1935.

26. Charlie Davis, *That Band from Indiana* (Oswego, NY: Mathom Publishing, 1982).

27. Tobin interview, July 16, 2009.

28. Charlie Davis married Miriam Browne on May 19, 1924, "when Charlie agreed to play ten years and then quit." Davis, *That Band from Indiana*, 23.

29. Davis, *That Band from Indiana*, 151.

30. Davis, *That Band from Indiana*, 151.

31. Levinson, *Trumpet Blues*, 23.

32. Levinson, *Trumpet Blues*, 23. Charlie Barnet with Stanley Dance, *Those Swinging Years* (Baton Rouge: Louisiana State University Press, 1984), 14.

33. Tobin interview, July 16, 2009.

34. Levinson, *Trumpet Blues*, 23–25.

35. William Howland Kenney, *Chicago Jazz: A Cultural History, 1904–1930* (New York: Oxford University Press, 1993), 87. The "brash young whites" included such Chicago jazzmen as the McPartlands, Bud Freeman, Mezz Mezzrow, George Wettling, Gene Krupa, Max Kaminsky, and Muggsy Spanier. Kenney, *Chicago Jazz*, 88–90.

36. Kenney, *Chicago Jazz*, 90–91.

37. Jim Edwards and Wynette Edwards, *Chicago Entertainment between the Wars, 1919–1939* (Chicago Arcadia, 2003), 7.

38. For more on the distinctions between local and translocal music scenes, see Richard A. Peterson and Andy Bennett, "Introducing Music Scenes," in *Music Scenes: Local, Translocal, and Virtual*, ed. Bennett and Peterson (Nashville: Vanderbilt University Press, 2004), 1–16.

39. Tobin interview, July 16, 2009.

40. *Chicago Daily Tribune*, January 4 and 11, 1936. Back in Texas, Louise's older sisters continued to follow and support her career, starting a scrapbook with newspaper clippings as well as alerting the local newspaper of Louise's accomplishments. For example, the Denton newspaper included the headline on page four, "Former

Miss Tobin Singing over Radio," announcing that, "Mrs. Harry James, daughter of Mrs. Hugh Tobin, will sing over station WGN, Chicago at 7:30 tonight, according to word received here. She continues to sing under the name Louise Tobin," *Denton Record-Chronicle*, January 11, 1936.

41. Paul K. Damai, "The Air Angle," *Down Beat* 3, no. 4 (April 1936): 10.

42. Tobin interview, February 10, 2016.

43. January 21, *Daily Times*, Chicago, "Louise Tobin, singer of popular ballads, joins [Leonard] Keller's orchestra for week's personal appearances at Marbro Theater, opening Friday [Jan. 24]. She has been with Charlie Davis' orchestra in New York [*sic*]." Clipping scrapbook, LTPHJC. *Chicago Daily Tribune*, January 24, 1936, 18: Announcement: Leonard Keller "Tone Poet" and His NBC Orchestra with Lela Moore in her startling "Dance with the Lovers," Pinky Lee & Co., Four Robeys, and Louise Tobin.

44. H. Arlo Nimmo, *The Andrews Sisters: A Biography and Career Record* (Jefferson, NC: McFarland, 2007), 60.

45. Edwards and Edwards, *Chicago Entertainment between the Wars, 1919–1939*, 42.

46. "Leonard Keller at the Bismarck," *Down Beat* 1, no. 1 (July 1934): 4.

47. Tobin interview, July 16, 2009.

48. Levinson, *Trumpet Blues*, 26.

49. LeVere, a few years later, was Bing Crosby's accompanist (1939–47).

50. Tobin interview, July 16, 2009.

51. Tobin interview, July 16, 2009.

52. Tobin interview, February 27, 2014.

53. Tobin interview with Deborah Porter, October 25, 2014.

54. Tobin interview, February 27, 2014.

55. Tobin interview, February 27, 2014.

56. Art Cohn, *The Nine Lives of Michael Todd* (New York: Random House, 1958), 62.

57. Tobin interview, July 16, 2009.

58. *Amarillo Globe*, July 9, 1936, 11: Advertisement: Ligon Smith and His Orchestra featuring Louise Tobin and other entertainers at The Nat. 30 cents/person and 60 cents/stags. *Amarillo Globe*, July 29, 1935: "Louise Tobin Arrives," "Singer Comes from Chicago to Join Ligon Smith Band," "Louise Tobin, nationally known singer is joining Ligon Smith's band at The Nat tonight. She has been with Leonard Keller's orchestra in Chicago." See also, *Handbook of Texas Online*, Laurie E. Jasinski, "Amarillo Natatorium [The Nat]," accessed November 17, 2017, www.tshaonline.org/handbook/online/articles/xda06.

59. *Dallas Morning News*, August 9, 1936, 10: "Carlos Shaw and His Orchestra will follow Bobby Meeker at Chez Maurice . . . Shaw recently completed a seven-week engagement at the Tulsa Hotel in Tulsa, Okla., and has played such spots as the Brown Palace in Denver, the Club New Yorker and the Continental Club in Los Angeles. While in California Shaw played for a good many private parties for the gelatin gentry, including Shirley Temple, Nelson Eddy and Marion Davies. Shaw not only leads the band, but also sings with it, and his featured girl vocalist is Louise Tobin of Denton, Texas. Louise, who started her career at the Palace Theater several seasons

ago has also sung with Art Hicks, Ben Pollack, and Charlie Davis." A photo of Shaw is included with the announcement.

See also, *Dallas Morning News*, August 11, 1936, 11: "The orchestra opening at Chez Maurice on Tuesday evening will be Carlos Shaw and his band, with Louise Tobin, formerly of Denton, as the featured girl singer."

60. Levinson, *Trumpet Blues*, 28.

61. *New York Times*, October 3, 1936, 21: "News of the Stage." "Four Shows are Closing this Evening, but Four Will Arrive During Next Week." "Loew's State's new bill this week offers George Hall and his orchestra and Al Shayne, radio singer, as co-headliners. Dolly Dawn and Johnny McKeever, singers, hold important positions in Mr. Hall's concert arrangement. The rest of the cast includes Harry Savoy, comedian, in a skit assisted by Louise Tobin; Worth, Wyle, and Howe, comedy trio, and the Five Elgins, jugglers." (In an interview with Tobin recorded by Mike Kubiak, Louise recalled that she was "fill," threw lines, sang a couple of tunes.) This was at New York's Taft Hotel. Louise worked with Harry Savoy again in July 1937.

62. Bill Smith, "Loew's State, New York," *Billboard*, June 10, 1944, 25.

63. Levinson, *Trumpet Blues*, 28.

64. Levinson, *Trumpet Blues*, 29.

65. Eric Aasen, "At 91 Louise Tobin Recalls Singing with Jazz Giants," *Dallas Morning News*, May 24, 2010.

66. On Harry's Goodman years, see Levinson, *Trumpet Blues*, 31–57.

67. Tobin interview, February 10, 2016.

68. Levinson, *Trumpet Blues*, 54–55.

69. *New York Times*, July 9, 1937, 19.

70. Tobin interview, July 16, 2009.

71. Tobin interview, July 16, 2009. Robin D. G. Kelley, in a 2002 article in the *New York Times*, highlights several of the "great couples of modern jazz" and the influence the wives had on the careers of their male counterparts. Robin D. G. Kelley, "The Jazz Wife: Muse and Manager," *New York Times*, July 21, 2002, 24. Cited in *Big Ears: Listening for Gender in Jazz Studies*, ed. Nichole T. Rustin and Sherrie Tucker (Durham, NC: Duke University Press, 2008), 12.

72. Tobin interview, July 16, 2009.

73. George Spelvin, "General News: Broadway Beat," *Billboard*, October 1, 1938.

74. Nick Kenny (1895–1975) was also a poet and lyricist, later penning with his brother Charles, "There's a Goldmine in the Sky," recorded by Isham Jones and His Orchestra with Joe Martin, vocal, and many others including Horace Heidt, Bing Crosby, and the Sons of the Pioneers. Kenny also had success with "Love Letters in the Sand" (Patti Page), "Gone Fishin'" (Louis Armstrong and Bing Crosby), and "Drop Me Off at Harlem" (Duke Ellington and Louis Armstrong). See Nick Kenny's Facebook page for many family photos, links to YouTube recordings of his poetry readings, and more.

75. New York *Daily Mirror*, December 24 and 29, 1938, the latter titled "Louise Tobin Headlines Daily Mirror Road to Fame Tonight," clipping in Tobin scrapbook, LTPHJC.

Chapter 3

1. "There'll Be Some Changes Made," recorded Los Angeles, CA, August 11, 1939. Columbia 35210. Louise Tobin and Benny Goodman's "There'll Be Some Changes Made" tops Chuck Eddy's list of "Records that Say Selling Out Is a Virtue," followed by Chuck Berry's "Sweet Little Sixteen," the Kingston Trio's "Sold Out," Lesley Gore's "You Don't Own Me," Bob Dylan's "Positively Fourth Street," and more. For "Changes," Eddy writes: "New walk, new talk, new name. Strut your stuff." Chuck Eddy, *The Accidental Evolution of Rock-n-Roll: A Misguided Tour through Popular Music* (New York: Da Capo Press, 1997), 68.

2. Tobin interview, July 16, 2009.

3. Tobin interview, March 2, 2012. Levinson dates these sessions October 31 and November 9, 1938, in *Trumpet Blues*, 46.

4. Susan Carter, Scott Sigmund Gartner, Michael Haines, Alan Olmsted, Richard Sutch, and Gavin Wright, eds., *Historical Statistics of the United States: Millennial Edition*, (Cambridge: Cambridge University Press, 2006), http://hsus.cambridge.org/.

5. Levinson, *Trumpet Blues*, 57.

6. The $43,000 figure is from an interview with Louise Tobin, April 6, 2012. Ross Firestone, in *Swing, Swing, Swing: The Life and Times of Benny Goodman*, describes the agreement between Benny and Harry: "In exchange for a line of credit allowing Harry to borrow up to seven thousand dollars during the course of the year Benny was to receive one-third of Harry's net earnings over the next decade. The loan had to be repaid within twenty-four months (New York: W. W. Norton, 1993), 233. Levinson, *Trumpet Blues*, citing Firestone, *Swing, Swing, Swing*, recounts these details on p. 60.

7. Tobin interview, July 16, 2009.

8. For more on Nick's nightclub and owner Nick Rongetti, see Warren Vaché, "When the Steaks and Jazz Sizzled at Nick's," *Mississippi Rag* (May 1, 1999): 30–32.

9. Vaché, "When the Steaks and Jazz Sizzled at Nick's," 30.

10. Tobin interview, February 24, 2012.

11. Tobin interview, July 16, 2009.

12. George T. Simon, *The Big Bands* (New York: Schirmer, 1981), 265. On Tobin's role in the discovery of Sinatra, see also Levinson, *Trumpet Blues*, 67, and James Kaplan, *Frank: The Voice* (New York: Anchor Books, 2011), 65.

13. Tobin interview, February 24, 2012.

14. John Hammond, "J. Hammond Says," *Down Beat* 1, no. 10 (October 1938): 27.

15. For more on Hammond, see Dunstan Prial, *The Producer: John Hammond and the Soul of American Music* (New York: Farrar, Straus, and Giroux, 2006).

16. Tilton left the band in April 1939. Tilton and Vannerson married on April 1, 1940, according to an announcement in the *Los Angeles Times*. The notice titled "Goodman Business Manager Marries Former Soloist" was accompanied by a large wedding photo, under which reads: "They take vows—Mr. and Mrs. Leonard K. Vannerson just after their marriage yesterday at Glendale." Goodman was best man, and Tilton's sister, Elizabeth, was maid of honor. The announcement stated that, "The bride was given away by her father, Frederick S. Tilton" (April 2, 1940, A1). They divorced in 1947. See also Tom Oehme, "And the Angels Sing: The Career of Martha Tilton," http://marthatilton.com/index.html.

17. Tobin interview, February 24, 2012.

18. Louise was not able to recall the exact date when she first sang with Goodman. The May 10, 1939, issue of *Variety* reviewed a May 6 performance of Goodman's orchestra in St. Louis, Missouri, mentioning Goodman songstress Martha Tilton, who "swings a couple of numbers." The next week's issue of *Variety* reported that Goodman's performance on May 13, in Cleveland, Ohio, was "missing" Tilton and that Louise Tobin was "taking over her assignment." Hence, Tobin "auditioned" and joined the band some time during the second week of May 1939. See *Variety*, May 10 and 17, 1939.

19. Tobin interview, July 16, 2009.

20. Tobin interview, February 24, 2012.

21. Tobin interview, February 24, 2012.

22. See Alex Chilowicz, "A Career Retrospective of Eddie Sauter, Jazz's Overlooked Composer and Innovator" (master's thesis, Rutgers University, 2013). https://rucore. libraries.rutgers.edu/rutgers-lib/40386/. Tobin ultimately recorded the following Sauter arrangements: "Scatterbrain," "Rendezvous Time in Paree," "Comes Love," "I Didn't Know What Time It Was," and "Love Never Went to College." Unfortunately, Chilowicz did not address these works or Tobin's renditions.

23. See Paul Oliver, "Blues," in *The New Grove Dictionary of Jazz*, 2nd ed., ed. Barry Kernfeld (Oxford: Oxford University Press, 2002).

24. Tobin interview.

25. *Camel Caravan* broadcast, Cleveland, Ohio, May 16, 1939, Aircheck 32, Benny Goodman, G3848. See Appendix A for a complete list of Louise Tobin's performances with Benny Goodman on the Camel Caravan, compiled by Karl Wingruber.

26. *Camel Caravan* broadcast, Cleveland, Ohio, May 16, 1939.

27. Jeff Todd Titon writes: "freedom from mistreatment was the overarching theme in blues lyrics." Titon, *Early Downhome Blues* (Chapel Hill: University of North Carolina Press, 1994), 266.

28. Tobin interview, July 16, 2009.

29. Tobin interview, July 16, 2009.

30. Glenn C. Pullen, "House Reviews: Palace, Cleve," *Variety*, May 17, 1939, 37. The review was of a Palace Theater performance in Cleveland, May 13. Regarding the group, Pullen wrote: "Benny Goodman's jivers are again catching a heavy load of jitterbugs. This in spite of several changes in his band, an off-key opening and a show that isn't as compact as when it last showed here." George Simon's May 1939 issue of *Metronome* boasted the "exclusive" prediction of Louise Tobin replacing Tilton, writing "Miss Tobin, less well known as Mrs. Harry James, is an extremely attractive brunette who, during her engagement with Bobby Hackett's band last summer, displayed a grand style of warbling." See "Bernstein and Cornelius Join Benny Goodman . . . Martha Tilton May Retire," *Metronome* 55, no. 5 (May 1939): 7. The following month Simon's *Metronome* announced: "The pert and pretty Louise [Tobin] joined the band in Cleveland the second week in May, as predicted exclusively in *Metronome* last month." See "My Greatest Band's Coming—Benny," *Metronome* 55, no. 6 (June 1939): 8.

31. Joseph F. Laredo, liner notes, *Benny's Girls: Goodman's Rare Songbirds*, Sony Music, 2004.

32. *San Antonio Light*, May 23, 1939, and *Denton Record-Chronicle*, May 25, 1939, respectively.

33. See "Louise Remains," *Tempo*, 7, no. 1 (July 1939): 5.

34. See "Benny Goodman's Band Much Changed," *Variety*, May 24, 1939, 32.

35. For more on these changes related to the Goodman orchestra, see Jeffrey Magee, *The Uncrowned King of Swing: Fletcher Henderson and Big Band Jazz* (Oxford: Oxford University Press, 2005), 230–32; and Firestone, *Swing, Swing, Swing*, 260.

36. On the Sauter's salaries, see "Chilowicz, A Career Retrospective of Eddie Sauter, Jazz's Overlooked Composer and Innovator," 31–33.

37. Chilowicz, "A Career Retrospective of Eddie Sauter, Jazz's Overlooked Composer and Innovator," 113–14.

38. Martha Tilton sang "You and Your Love" with Goodman for a *Camel Caravan* broadcast from Asheville, NC, April 25, 1939, according to Tom Lord's *The Jazz Discography*.

39. For more background on "The Lamp Is Low," see Alex Johnson, "History of the Track The Lamp Is Low," October 15, 2017, https://blacksquirrelradio.com/history-of-the-track-the-lamp-is-low/.

40. "Around the Studios: A Gershwin Memorial Is Booked for July," *New York Times*, June 18, 1939, 122; "Nothing Done about Wish of Benny Goodman, Says MCA; Morris Seeks Band," *Variety*, June 28, 1939, 39; and, *Madison Capital Times*, July 8, 1939.

41. *Amarillo Sunday News Globe*, July 2, 1939.

42. "When Louise Tobin Swings the College Boys Swoon," Louise Tobin Scrapbook, Sunday, July 16, 1939, LTPHJC.

43. "When Louise Tobin Swings the College Boys Swoon," Louise Tobin Scrapbook, Sunday, July 16, 1939, LTPHJC.

44. LTPHJC, Box 9, folder 7.

45. "Goodman's Swing Concert Numbers Named," *Los Angeles Times*, August 3, 1939, A14.

46. "Goodman's Killer-Dillers Go Whacky in Bowl," *Los Angeles Times*, August 7, 1939, 8. "A cellist in the Women's Orchestra," *Los Angeles Times* critic Mark Swed wrote that Isabel Morse Jones "became the L.A. Times critic in 1925, a position she held for 22 years." See Swed, "Then and Now, L.A. Women Get Things Done," *Los Angeles Times*, December 19, 2014. Jones also authored *Hollywood Bowl* (New York: G. Schirmer, 1936).

47. Tobin interview, February 24, 2012.

48. Tobin interview, February 24, 2012.

49. Tobin interview, February 10, 2016.

50. Michael Taft, *Blues Lyric Poetry: A Concordance* (New York: Garland, 1984).

51. Other blues lyrics with "I was born in —— raised in ——" include Frankie Half Pint Jaxon (Tampa Red), "She Can Love So Good," Chicago circa mid-August 1930, record numbers: (C-6079-A) Vo-1540 Mel MLP-7324, "She was born in Kentucky,

raised in Tennessee"; Noah Lewis "New Minglewood Blues," Memphis, November 26, 1930, record numbers: (64737–2) Vi-23266 OJL-4, "I was born in the desert; I was raised in the lion's den"; include Ruby Glaze (Blind Willie McTell) "Lonesome Day Blues," Atlanta, February 22, 1932, record numbers: (7160–1) Vi-23353 RCA LPV-518, "I was born in Georgia, but I hangs around in Tennessee"; Georgia White "Pigmeat Blues," Chicago, May 12, 1936, record numbers: (90722-A) De—7209 AH-158, "I was born in the country but daddy I was raised in town"; and, Memphis Minnie, "Nothing Is Rambling," Chicago, June 27, 1940 (note later date than August 1939 recording of "Louise Tobin Blues"), record numbers: (WC-3167-A) OK-05670 BC-1.

52. Louise did not recall ever listening to Jimmie Rodgers's music. Tobin interview, March 2016.

53. Sharing Louise's views on the shortcomings of Fletcher Henderson's blues playing, Ethel Waters recalled "how she had to force Henderson to listen to player piano rolls so that he could understand how to accompany her properly on a blues recording." Reference made by Ted Gioia in his *The History of Jazz*, 2nd ed. (Oxford: Oxford University Press, 2011), 102. In Waters's autobiography, she recounted that "I kept having arguments with Fletcher Henderson about the way he was playing my accompaniments." This is quoted in Magee, *Uncrowned King of Swing*, 24. Magee's account of Waters's perspective on Henderson support Louise's perspective (see Magee, *Uncrowned King of Swing*, 23–25).

54. Tobin interview, March 2, 2012.

55. Tobin interview, March 2, 2012.

56. James Lincoln Collier, *Benny Goodman and the Swing Era* (New York: Oxford University Press, 1989), 196.

57. For more on torch singers performing resistance, see Stacy Holman Jones, *Torch Singing: Performing Resistance and Desire from Billie Holiday to Edith Piaf* (New York: Altamira Press, 2007).

58. Angela Davis, *Blues Legacies and Black Feminism* (New York: Random House, 1998), 20.

59. Daphne Duval Harrison, *Black Pearls: Blues Queens of the 1920s* (New Brunswick, NJ: Rutgers University Press, 2000), 147–64.

60. Prial, *Producer*, 140.

61. Tobin interview, March 2, 2012.

62. Tobin interview, February 24, 2012.

63. Tobin interview, August 30, 2012.

64. Victor Davis, "Versatile Lucas Here: Notes on New Records," *Dallas Morning News*, September 15, 1939, 1.

65. Bill Gottlieb, "Swing Sessions," *Washington Post*, September 17, 1939, A5.

66. Carnegie Hall, New York, October 6, 1939: Full Orchestra included Ziggy Elman-Jimmy Maxwell-Johnny Martell-t/Red Ballard-Vernon Brown-Ted Vesley-tb/ Benny Goodman-cl/Toots Mondello-Buff Estes-as/Jerry Jerome-Bus Bassey-ts/Fletcher Henderson-p-a/Arnold Covarrubias-g/Artie Bernstein-sb/Lionel Hampton-d/Eddie

Sauter-George Bassman-a/Louise Tobin-v. According to Brian Rust (*Jazz Records: 1897–1942* [New York: Arlington House, 1978], 653), "The occasion of Benny Goodman's second Carnegie Hall concert was recorded somewhat amateurishly on a 'bootleg' LP without matrix numbers or labels, and two numbers from it also were issued on a 78 rpm disc as shown."

The Goodman band performed "Don't Be That Way," "Sunrise Serenade" (Henderson, arr.), "'T Ain't What You Do" (Goodman vocal), "Bach Goes To Town," "One O'Clock Jump," "The Sheik of Araby" (Goodman Trio, with Henderson and Lionel Hampton), "Flying Home" (Goodman Sextet), "Star Dust" (Goodman Sextet), and "Sing, Sing, Sing." Louise Tobin was not mentioned in the *New York Times* review, October 7, 1939. *New York Times* review (see downloads; print), October 7, 1939.

67. See "Goodman Re-Chills Carnegie Cats!" *Metronome* 55, no. 11 (November 1939): 12 and 30.

68. Goodman performed at the Waldorf Astoria from October 1939 until New Year's Day, 1940. See "Waldorf Astoria" from "Nightclubs and other Venues," in *The New Grove Dictionary of Jazz*, 2nd ed., vol. 3 (2002), 130.

69. According to Russell Connor, "Louise left 25 October, while the band was at the Waldorf-Astoria, because of illness." Liner notes, *The Different Version Vol. 1, 40 Alternate Takes of Recordings, 1939–1940* (Sweden: Phontastic NCD 8821/2, 1993). Louise did not mention illness as a reason for her leaving Goodman. Her reason was that Harry wanted her to leave the band and for her to be "Mrs. Harry James." Tobin interview, January 20, 2016.

70. Tobin interview, January 20, 2016.

71. Tobin interview, July 16, 2009.

72. Tobin interview, March 2, 2012.

73. See "The News Goes 'Round and Round,'" *Metronome* 55, no. 11 (November 1939): 29, and "Mildred Bailey with Goodman," *Swing: The Guide to Modern Music* 2, no. 6 (November 1939): iv, respectively.

74. See "Tobin to Leave BG to Become Mother," *Down Beat* 6, no. 12 (November 1, 1939): 11.

75. See "Louise Tobin Leaves Benny," *Tempo* 8, no. 2 (November 13, 1939): 3.

76. "Stop the Press," *Down Beat* 6, no. 13 (November 15, 1939): 10.

77. "Names in the Swing News," *Swing: The Guide to Modern Music* 2, no. 7 (December 1939): 1.

78. "Mrs. Harry James Recovers," *Down Beat* 6, no. 14 (December 1, 1939): 1.

79. Goodman Gallops to Top Swing Poll: Wins in Three Divisions," *Swing: The Guide to Modern Music* 2, no. 8 (January 1940): 3.

80. "The Biggest News Stories of the Year," *Down Beat* 7, no. 1 (January 1, 1940): 11.

81. "Ear to the Ground Department—Rumors and Humors of Mad Musicians," *Swing: The Guide to Modern Music* 2, no. 7 (December 1939): 3 and 25.

82. Tobin interview, July 16, 2009.

83. Ibid.

Chapter 4

1. In an interview on February 10, 2016, Louise recalled that after she had quit singing with Benny Goodman, "Harry said, 'from now on she's going to be plain Mrs. Harry James.'"

2. Tobin interview, February 10, 2016.

3. Tobin interview, January 20, 2016.

4. Tobin interview, January 20, 2016. The next week, back in Texas, she told a *Denton Record-Chronicle* reporter that "it was the first and last time that I ever sang with his band." *Denton Record-Chronicle*, "Louise Tobin, Widely Known Vocalist, With Her Husband, Orchestra Leader Harry James, Visit Home Folk Here," March 11, 1940, 4.

5. *Port Arthur News*, "Orchestra Leader Is Visiting Parents," March 6, 1940. "Harry James, Beaumont boy who made good as big-time orchestra leader and noted trumpet player, arrived in town to visit his parents, Mr. and Mrs. Everette James, 635 Lea St., Monday night. With him was his attractive wife, Louise Tobin" (p. 9).

6. *Denton Record-Chronicle*, "Louise Tobin, Widely Known Vocalist, With Her Husband, Orchestra Leader Harry James, Visit Home Folk Here," March 11, 1940, 4. Curiously, thinking back over all of her performances up to that point in her career, the only other time that she experienced such stage fright was also in Texas, "about three years ago when she came back here and sang at a Teachers College Saturday night stage show."

7. *Denton Record-Chronicle*, "Louise Tobin, Widely Known Vocalist." *Captain Caution* was a 1940 United Artists American adventure film directed by Richard Wallace, staring Alan Ladd, Victor Mature, and Louise Platt.

8. Tobin interview, February 10, 2016.

9. His name is also listed under the spelling Jenny. He was born Truman Eliot Jenney, May 12, 1910, and died on December 16, 1945. See www.discogs.com/artist/322119-Jack-Jenney.

10. "Got No Time" was first recorded in the 1920s.

11. Tobin interview, May 24, 2014.

12. "Big Stage Show Saturday on Stage in Person Jack Jenn[e]y His Trombone and His Orchestra Featuring Louise Tobin (Lovely Singer of Songs)," Announcement, *Chester Times*, April 25 and 27, 1940.

13. Leonard Feather, "Louise Tobin, Well Again, Sings on Wax," *Down Beat* 7, no. 12 (June 15, 1940): 2.

14. For the Bradley discography, see Charles Garrod and Bill Korst, *Will Bradley and His Orchestra* (Zephyrhills, FL: A Joyce Music Publication, 1986). New York, July 16, 1940, Columbia 35607, Bandstand 1, Ajax 119; WCO 28022-A "Deed I Do" arr/Al Datz; "Don't Let It Get You Down" WCO 28023-A, Columbia 35629, Ajax 119 (p. 3).

15. See American Society of Music Arrangers, "Complete List of A.S.M.A. Members," *The Score*, 3, nos. 7 and 8 (July–August 1946): 4 and 6, www.asmac.org/wp-content/uploads/2013/06/ASMAC-Newsletter-1946–04.pdf, accessed September 29, 2013. For more on Al Datz [and Peanuts!], see Arthur Rollini, *Thirty Years*

with the Big Bands (Wheatley, Oxford: Bayou Press, 1989). See chapter 7 on Rollini joining Will Bradley's band. Al Datz also had a dance orchestra. Muggsy Spanier (1901–1967): see the Muggsy Spanier Collection, Rutgers University. Datz was a member of the New York chapter of the American Society of Music Arrangers (ASMA).

16. "Deed I Do" [in B♭ major], *Will Bradley and His Orchestra "Five O'Clock Whistle," 1939–1941* (Los Angeles: Aero Space Records, RACD 7101). Louise recorded "Deed I Do" in G major with Peanuts on *Tribute to Benny Goodman* (Timeless Records, 1986; available on YouTube: www.youtube.com/watch?v=pvR5Izm2y8U. Note: Ella Fitzgerald recorded "Deed I Do" with Basie July 1963 in the key of B♭ major, *Ella and Basie*. See YouTube: www.youtube.com/watch?v=Vj4gbky1QCU.

17. Members of the band included Steve Lipkins, Joe Weidman, Herbie Dell, trumpets; Will Bradley, Jimmy Emmert, Bill Corti, trombones; Artie Mendelsohn, Jo Jo Huffman, Bernie Billings, Sam Sachelle, saxophones; Freddy Slack, piano; Danny Perri, guitar; Delmar Kaplan, bass; Ray McKinley, drums; and Carlotta Dale, vocals. See Ian Crosbie, "Will Bradley and His Orchestra Featuring Ray McKinley," *Coda Magazine*, September 1976, 2–6.

18. Caiazza also played clarinet, and by the end of his career had played with Joe Haymes (1936–37); Muggsy Spanier's Ragtimers (November–December 1939); Woody Herman (early 1940); the band led by Will Bradley and Ray McKinley (autumn 1940); Bobby Hackett; Louis Armstrong; "Hot Lips" Page; Jack Teagarden; Hank D'Amico; and many others. According to Barry Kernfeld, Caiazza worked with Peanuts Hucko in 1957. See www.discogs.com/artist/939761-Nick-Caiazza, and Barry Kernfeld, "Caiazza, Nick." *The New Grove Dictionary of Jazz*, 2nd ed., online.

19. Tobin interview by Graham Pass for the BBC, July 1, 2010 (transcript by Deborah Porter in personal collection). According to Ian Crosbie in his article "Will Bradley and His Orchestra Featuring Ray McKinley," published in *Coda Magazine*, September 1976, "Nick Caiazza replaced Hucko on tenor sax and singer Jimmy Valentine was added. 'Peanuts was noted for his lack of punctuality, especially on the job,' Will recalled. 'We parted company several times because of that. The only date for which I remember him turning up on time was his wedding!'" (p. 3; inside quote from Bradley's correspondence with Crosbie). In an interview Louise commented on a question regarding Peanuts's punctuality. He was never late and was a very well organized person. She thought that Bradley's comment was perhaps an inside joke, February 10, 2016.

20. See announcement in the *Lowell* (MA) *Sun* (September 21, 1940, p. 46): "At the Merrimack Square tomorrow—Will Bradley 'The Boy with the Horn' who rated one of the greatest trombone profession, comes to the stage of the Merrimack Square theatre tomorrow with his famous orchestra and Louise Tobin, the famous ballad singer, as well as Jimmy Valentine, noted vocalist." This appears to have been her last performance until the birth of Harry Jr., March 3, 1941. She was about three months pregnant at this time. The LTPHJC includes an envelope postmarked September 20, 1940, from Harry to Mrs. H. James, c/o L. L. Jones, Fayetteville, Arkansas.

21. Bob Bach, "Midwest Function," *Swing: The Guide to Modern Music* 3, no. 2 (October 1940): 7.

22. Gordon Wright, "Bradley, Herman Add New Wax Life," *Metronome* 56, no. 11 (November 1940): 14.

23. "Contest Results," *Swing: The Guide to Modern Music* 3, no. 2 (August 1940): 24.

24. Telegram, Louise Tobin, private collection.

25. *Dallas Morning News*, February 19, 1941, "No. 1 Trumpet Man Is Texan by Adoption."

26. Wikipedia, "There'll Be Some Changes Made."

27. See Levinson, *Trumpet Blues*, 94.

28. Harry's letters, scans, envelopes and cards, Louise's personal collection.

29. Tobin interview, June 19, 2014.

30. Dorothy Kilgallen, "Broadway," *Mansfield* (Ohio) *News Journal*, March 12, 1941.

31. See Levinson, *Trumpet Blues*, 94.

32. Tobin interview with Mike Kubiak, June 19, 2014.

33. Tobin interview with Mike Kubiak, June 19, 2014.

34. Tobin interview with Mike Kubiak, June 19, 2014.

35. Tobin interview with Mike Kubiak, June 19, 2014.

36. Louise wrote two alternative titles to this poem: Song of Sorrow and Across Oceans of Tears.

37. Helen Forrest, with Bill Libby, *I Had the Craziest Dream* (New York: Coward, McCann and Geoghegan, 1982), 105. Prior to singing with Goodman, Forrest sang in Artie Shaw's orchestra. Kay Foster sang with Goodman briefly prior to Forrest. Forrest recalled, "had been done in by the Ray. Benny simply wasn't satisfied with her. I guess I satisfied him, but he never said so" (p. 107).

38. Forrest, *I Had the Craziest Dream*, 108.

39. Forrest, *I Had the Craziest Dream*, 111.

40. Forrest, *I Had the Craziest Dream*, 112.

41. *Denton Record-Chronicle*, September 6, 1941, "Denton's Big-Time Band Singer," 1-16-2009-128 clipping, LTPHJC.

42. *Denton Record-Chronicle*, "Denton's Big-Time Band Singer."

43. Scrapbook, undated clipping, LTPHJC.

44. *McAllen Daily Press*, November 28, 1941.

45. This ad ran in the *Kingsport Times* (TN), January 7, 1942; *McAllen Daily Press*, January 8, 1942; *Madison Wisconsin State Journal*, January 15, 1942; and the *Arcadian Tribune* and *Arcadia News*, January 22, 1942.

46. This ad ran in the *Corona Daily Independent*, July 24, 1942; *Butte Montana Standard*, August 1, 1942; *Wisconsin State Journal*, "Radio Stars Model Swimsuits," August 5, 1942; *Oxnard Press-Courier*, August 6, 1942; and *Bakersfield Californian*, September 14, 1942.

47. *The Ogden* (Utah) *Standard Examiner*, August 12, 1942. This ad also ran in *The Boone* (IA) *News-Republican*, August 17, 1942; *Kingsport* (TN) *Times*, August 19, 1942; *Oxnard Press-Courier*, August 20, 1942; and *Madison Wisconsin State Journal*, August 21, 1942.

48. Letter, Charles Enge to Mrs. Harry James, May 12, 1945.

49. "Harry James and Wife Plan Divorce Suit," *Los Angeles Times*, May 9, 1943.

50. "Betty Grable to Be Wed," *New York Times*, June 30, 1943, 23.

51. "Harry James and Wife Plan Divorce Suit," *Los Angeles Times*, May 9, 1943.

52. "Betty Grable to Be Wed," *New York Times*, June 30, 1943, 23.

53. "Grable Marriage Plans Reported," *Wichita Daily Times*, June 30, 1943, 2.

54. To calculate the inflation of the dollar value of 1944 (or any year), see www .dollartimes.com/inflation/.

55. A search of her name in the *Newspaper Archive* for the years 1947–50, 1951, 1954, 1956, and 1957 yielded no hits.

56. Tobin interview with Mike Kubiak, June 19, 2014.

57. Thanks to Karl Wingruber for alerting us to this source. The 1946 20th-Century Fox musical film *Centennial Summer* was directed by Otto Preminger and stars Jeanne Crain and Cornel Wilde. "All through the Day" was nominated for Best Original Song for the 1946 Academy Awards. Wikipedia: https://en.wikipedia.org/ wiki/Centennial_Summer.

58. Simon Ulanov and Leonard Feather, "Record Reviews: Tommy Jones," *Metronome* 62, no. 5 (May 1946): 27.

59. Maurie Orodenker, "Records on Review," *Band Leaders and Record Review* 3, no. 6 (August 1946): 10.

60. I do not have information on the members of his orchestra at that time. I learned this from an entry in the second edition of the *New Grove Dictionary of Jazz* in the entry on American guitarist Bob Lessey, who began his professional career playing with Jones (1931–33).

61. Karl Wingruber, email correspondence, December 12, 2014.

62. The Mocambo and Waldorf Astoria announced in *Down Beat* 12, no. 18 (September 15, 1945): 4.

63. These soundies can be viewed on YouTube: www.youtube.com/watch?v =HT2qrQLgWB0. (Note: the image is reversed.) Singer June Barton seems to have recorded a soundie during the same session with Coleman, singing "Gotta Be This or That," also available on YouTube: www.youtube.com/watch?v=I3Dgvpbz5Lo. (This image is also reversed.)

64. Hal Holly, "Los Angeles Band Briefs," *Down Beat* 13, no. 17 (August 12, 1946): 6. The Rhythm Note label is identified in a letter in the LTPHJC from Lars Westin, Sweden, to Peanuts, June 16, 1980. "A Cottage for Sale" is available on YouTube: www .youtube.com/watch?v=C0-maa5INRE&feature=related.

65. Tobin interview, February 10, 2016. For more on Hasselgard, see Leonard Feather, "The Changing of the Hasselgard," *Metronome* 64, no. 9 (September 1948): 20–21.

66. See William F. Lee, *American Big Bands* (Milwaukee: Hal Leonard, 2005), 311–12.

67. See Charles Garrod, *Ziggy Elman and His Orchestra* (Zephyrhills, FL: Joyce Record Club, 1990), 4.

68. See Christopher Popa, "Ziggy Ellman: 'Fralich in Spring,'" November 2005, www.bigbandlibrary.com/ziggyelman.html.

69. See Compilation; Side A—One Night Stand with Ziggy Elman, Hollywood Palladium, Hollywood, California, 1 cassette, 1948, 5 CS 372 (LTPHJC inventory, p. 171).

70. Lee, *American Big Bands*, 248.

71. Orchestra members included Ziggy Elman and Neal Hefti (tp/arr); Claude Bowen, Everett McDonald, Ray Horak (tp); Red Ballard, Moe Schneider, Norris Hurley, Neil Reid (tb); Jack Dumont, Kenny Olsen (as); Troy Parkinson, Everett McLaughlin (ts); Joe Koch (bar); Shelton Smith (p); Jimmy Stutz (b); Roy Harte (d); Bob Allen, Louise Tobin, Top Notchers (vo). See Garrod, *Ziggy Elman and His Orchestra*, 4.

72. Lee, *American Big Bands*, 326.

73. According to Garrod, Hollywood Palladium, August 27, 1948: AFRS One Night Stand 1771, Tobin vocals on: "A Boy from Texas," "September Song"; August 31, 1948: AFRS ONS 1759, Joyce 1059, Tobin vocals on: "A Boy from Texas," "You Turned the Tables on Me"; September 7, 1948: AFRS One Night Stand 1793, Tobin vocals on "If I Could Be with You," "You Turned the Tables on Me"; "From this period": AFRS One Night Stand 1807, "Details unknown"; September 10, 1948, AFRS One Night Stand 1821, "Details unknown" (Garrod, *Ziggy Elman and His Orchestra*, 4).

74. See YouTube, www.youtube.com/watch?v=ynLDAm5_6_o.

75. Garrod, *Ziggy Elman and His Orchestra*, 5 and 7.

76. Jack Tracy, "What's on Wax: Ziggy Elman," *Down Beat* 18, no. 25 (December 14, 1951): 14.

77. Barry Ulanov, "Record Reviews: Ziggy Elman," *Metronome* 68, no. 1 (January 1952): 26.

78. *Billboard*, November 27, 1954, Reviews of New Pop Records, Louise Tobin, "Hurry Home" and "Lonesome Road," MGM 11881, p. 40. LTPHJC, Box Correspondence: clipping. On MGM Records, see Alex Cosper, "History of Record Labels and the Music Industry: 1940s," www.playlistresearch.com/history/labels1940s.htm.

79. Letter, signed Marie, from Radio Corporation of America, RCA Building, 30 Rockefeller Plaza, NY 20, NY, January 12, 1955, addressed to Mr. George T. Simon, *Metronome Magazine*, 114 East 32nd Street, NY, NY. "Dear George: I appreciate your sending me the record by Louise Tobin James. I played it and she is still listed among my favorites. Thanks, George, for your thoughtfulness. Sincerely, Marie." LTPHJC, General Correspondence, Ser II A box 9 folder 9.

80. George Simon, "The Editors Speak: The Limp Dept.," *Metronome* 70, no. 3 (March 1954): 34.

81. *Dallas Morning News*, November 1, 1959.

Chapter 5

1. *Washington Post*, April 4, 1960. Statement from Dorothy Kilgallen's entertainment news column.

2. George T. Simon, *Simon Says: The Sights and Sounds of the Swing Era, 1935–1955* (New Rochelle, NY: Arlington House, 1971).

3. Tobin interview by Graham Pass for the BBC, July 1, 2010. Transcription by Deborah Porter.

4. For more on the fragmentation of jazz styles of the 1950s and '60s in contrast with the traditional jazz or revivalist jazz, see Ted Gioia's *The History of Jazz* (New York: Oxford University Press, 2011), 253–308.

5. This quote is from John S. Wilson's review of *Great Moments in Jazz Re-created at the Newport Jazz Festival* (RCA Victor LPM 3369; Stereo LSP 3369) titled "The Jazz Faithful," *New York Times*, October 31, 1965, 24. This recording of the Newport Jazz Festival in 1964 includes performances by Peanuts Hucko.

6. The jazz parties are covered in more detail in chapter 6.

7. See Charles H. Waters Jr., "Anatomy of a Cover," in *Annual Review of Jazz Studies* 6, ed. Edward Berger, David Cayer, Dan Morgenstern, and Lewis Porter (Metuchen, NJ: Scarecrow Press, 1993), 37.

8. John Gennari, "Hipsters, Bluebloods, Rebels, and Hooligans: The Cultural Politics of the Newport Jazz Festival, 1954–1960," in *Uptown Conversations: The New Jazz Studies*, ed. Robert G. O'Meally et al. (New York: Columbia University Press, 2004), 126–49.

9. Ernie Smith and colleagues describe this film as "a personal record of the 1958 Newport Jazz Festival. Although flawed, this rare and fascinating work was far ahead of the average effort to document jazz performance. It failed in the contrived excursions into beer parties, sailboat racing, and shots of Newport scenery, but it succeeded in the many intense close-ups of the artists, leaving an exciting first record, in color, of one of the most important and successful American jazz events." Ernie Smith et al., "Films," *Oxford Music Online*, https://doi.org/10.1093/gmo/9781561592630.article.J149900, published in print: January 20, 2002; published online: 2003.

10. Paul R. Laird, "Newport Jazz Festival," *Grove Music Online*, https://doi.org/10.1093/gmo/9781561592630.article.J327300, published in print: January 20, 2002; published online: 2003. Union Films, 1960, directed by Bert Stern.

11. David B. Bittan, "Newport Jazz Fest Reaches Maturity as Wave of Dignity Sinks 'Jazzniks,'" *Variety*, July 11, 1962, 227.

12. The details of Louise's performance and the program on July 8, 1962, at the Newport Festival outlined here are from Thomas P. Hustad, *Born to Play: The Ruby Braff Discography and Directory of Performances* (Lanham, MD: Scarecrow Press, 2012), 157–58; Whitney Balliett, "The Inheritors," in *Collected Works: A Journal of Jazz, 1954–2001* (New York: St. Martin's Griffin, 2002), 173–75; and David Bittan, "Newport Jazz Fest Reaches Maturity as Wave of Dignity Sinks 'Jazzniks,'" *Variety*, July 11, 1962, 227. Hustad notes that a tape recording of the performance is available in the Library of Congress and that "film clips may exist from WJAR-TV and WPRI-TV held at Rhode Island Historical Society Library," Hustad, *Born to Play*, 158.

13. *The 1962 Newport Jazz Festival*, DVD, directed by Buddy Bregman (Australia and New Zealand: Umbrella Entertainment, 2004), DAVID0419.

14. Bittan, "Newport Jazz Fest Reaches Maturity as Wave of Dignity Sinks 'Jazzniks,'" 227.

15. Balliett, "The Inheritors," 174. Balliett also did not mention that Aretha Franklin sang with the Monk Quartet.

16. Bittan, "The Inheritors," 227.

17. Bittan, "The Inheritors," 227.

18. Bittan, "The Inheritors," 227.

19. Original and copy of letter, Whitney Balliett, the *New Yorker*, to Louise, September 18, 1962. LTPHJC, General Correspondence, LT PH Col Ser II A box 9 folder 10. Written in ink on the envelope is "50 Copies" underlined twice. Louise was proud of Balliett's words and used copies of this in her promotional material.

20. Tobin interview by Graham Pass for the BBC, July 1, 2010. Transcription by Deborah Porter.

21. Tobin interview by Graham Pass for the BBC, July 1, 2010.

22. Balliett, "The Inheritors," 174.

23. John Pagones, "Jazzwise, You Needn't Be Starving Now," *Washington Post*, April 30, 1965, D14.

24. John Pagones, "Gwaltney Sets Blues Alley Flair from Front Office," *Washington Post*, August 15, 1965, G4.

25. Letter, Warren W. Hicks, 27 Friendly Road, Norwalk, Conn. 06850 to Tobin, 201 East 20th St. NY NY, May 17, 1966. Hicks with D. Russell Connor coauthored *BG On the Record: A Bio-discography of Benny Goodman* (New York: Arlington House, 1969).

26. For more on the Dick Gibson jazz parties, see chapter 6.

27. Designated as a cultural historic district in 2002, most recently the Five Points African American community has succumbed to gentrification. For more on this issue, see Alison Gregor, "In Denver, Beat Starts to Pick Up in a Once-Thriving Hub for Jazz," *New York Times*, August 21, 2013, B1.

28. Robert H. Byler Jr., "Jazz Is Back," *Historic Preservation* 28, no. 4 (July 1976): 24–29. Quote from p. 29. The Queen City Jazz Band, specializing in traditional jazz, still performs, and in 2018 celebrated their sixtieth anniversary, boasting only two new members within the past ten years. See https://queencityjazzband.com.

29. Tobin interview by Graham Pass for the BBC, July 1, 2010. Transcription by Deborah Porter.

30. "Entertainers Wed at Littleton," *Denver Post*, June 26, 1967, 23.

31. Sources for the music performed at Peanuts Hucko's Navarre are Pat Hanna, "Peanuts Swings at His Navarre," *Rocky Mountain News* (Denver), July 21, 1967; *Navarre Times*, single-issue paper given to guests at the Navarre, LTPHJC, Magazines and Newspapers.

32. For this quote and more on Hucko's view of Sutton, see James D. Shacter, *Loose Shoes: The Story of Ralph Sutton* (Chicago: Jaynar Press, 1994), 146.

33. Pat Hanna, "Peanuts Swings at His Navarre," *Rocky Mountain News* (Denver), July 21, 1967. They were married on June 25, 1967.

34. *Navarre Times* (1967) is in the LTPHJC, Magazines and Newspapers. For more on the history of the building, see https://anschutzcollection.org/about-us/navarre-building; https://www.theclio.com/web/entry?id=24109; and http://americashauntedroadtrip.com/tag/the-navarre-denver/.

35. Tobin interview by Graham Pass for the BBC, July 1, 2010. Transcription by Deborah Porter.

36. Letter: Michael Kelly, Memphis, TN, to Mr. Peanuts Hucko, Navarre Restaurant, LTPHJC, General Correspondence, Series II, A box 9 folder 10.

37. For more information on jazz parties, see chapter 6. A program included in the LTPHJC documents his performance at the Pinehurst Country Club on August 23, 1968.

38. Tobin interview by Graham Pass for the BBC, July 1, 2010. Transcription by Deborah Porter.

39. A program of this festival and set is included in the LTPHJC, Box: Programs, Folder 1969. See also "Red Norvo at Monterey," *Sacramento Observer*, August 21, 1969, 14.

40. "Red Norvo at Monterey," 14.

41. "33,600 at Monterey," *Oakland Post*, September 25, 1969, 16. Leonard Feather was less flattering of Sly and the Family Stone in his review of the festival. See "Monterey Jazz Fest Amplifies Rock Aspects," *Los Angeles Times*, September 22, 1969, E1 and p. 13.

42. Deborah Porter phone interview with Tobin, May 24, 2014. Transcription by Porter.

43. Edith Austin, "A Soul-Less Weekend in Monterey," *Sun Reporter*, September 27, 1969, 18.

44. Melvin Maddocks, "The Annual Identity Crisis: Self Renewing Barbaric Honk," *Christian Science Monitor*, September 26, 1969, 10.

45. Maddocks, "Annual Identity Crisis," 10.

Chapter 6

1. Quoted in Betty Jo Lagman, "Entertainers Talk about Big Band Era," *Mobile Press Register*, August 17, 1985, 7B.

2. Hollie I. West, "Some Unusual Insights into Jazz: The Men, the Music, the Era; Rhythm Mode," *Washington Post*, April 30, 1972, L3. Whitney Balliett, *Ecstasy at the Onion: Thirty-One Pieces on Jazz* (Indianapolis: Bobbs-Merrill, 1971).

3. Linda Dahl, *Stormy Weather: The Music and Lives of a Century of Jazzwomen* (New York: Proscenium Publishers, 1984), 135; 3rd ed., New York: Limelight Editions, 1995.

4. See Ted Gioia, *The History of Jazz*, 2nd ed. (Oxford: Oxford University Press, 2011), 345–68.

5. Alice Berthelsen, "Peanuts Hucko: Walking Tall in the World of Jazz," *Odessa American*, May 24, 1981.

6. Nat Hentoff, "Jazz: An Exceedingly Hard Vocation to Grow Old In?" *New York Times*, March 8, 1970, M6.

7. Hentoff, "Jazz: An Exceedingly Hard Vocation to Grow Old In?" M6.

8. Hollie I. West, "Not 'Greatest'; Not Humblest, Either," *Washington Post*, May 14, 1970, B17. "The nine-man World's Greatest Jazz Band, playing through Saturday at the Shoreham's Blue Room, did not live up to its name in its opening performance. It is professional, energetic and loose. But it is also unoriginal and not very striking in the solo work of most of its members, or in the group's arrangements." "The band is sponsored by Dick Gibson, a wealthy fan businessman who is responsible for the group title. ('I think it's the greatest. The guys don't like it [the title], but they

deserve it')." West concludes: "It is pleasant and sometimes very spirited. But except for Freeman and [Vic] Dickerson, the group's soloists are not engaging. The color contrasts and textures of the arrangements (mostly Haggart's) are pretty simple and lackluster. If this group is called The World's Greatest Jazz Band, what superhuman honors can we accord Duke Ellington, the master orchestrator and bandleader?"

9. Al White, *Jazz Party: A Photo Gallery of Great Jazz Musicians* (Little Rock, AR: August House Publishers, 2000), 3.

10. There is little documentary evidence on the Dick Weyrich, Denver, Colorado, jazz parties at which Peanuts performed for several years in the early 1970s. For some home recordings of Peanuts at these events, see December 1973, Recording, LTPHJC, Box 5, Reel [no identification], Dick Weyrich Jazz Party at Cosmopolitan, Denver, Colorado, Peanuts, Sutton, Gus Johnson, Bill Basten. December 29, 1974—Recording, LTPHJC, Box 2, Reel 51, Dick Weyrich and Peanuts, Continental, Denver, Colorado. Jazz Party Live, most likely; and December 30, 1974—Recording, LTPHJC, Box 1, Reel 33, Dick Weyrich Jazz Party Live, Peanuts, Continental, Denver, Colorado.

11. Leonard Feather, "Wealthy Man Likes Staging 'Jazz Party,'" *Austin Statesman*, September 21, 1971, 10.

12. Feather, "Wealthy Man Likes Staging 'Jazz Party,'" 10.

13. "Gibson almost never hires singers," Leonard Feather concurred with Louise in his 1984 review, "The Finest Musicians for Great Get-Together," *Los Angeles Times*, September 16, 1984, 68.

14. Letter: Dick Gibson, 1061 Humbolt, Denver, CO 80218 to Mr. and Mrs. Peanuts Hucko, 13336 Huston ST Apt. C, Sherman Oaks, CA 91403, Sept. 26, 1973. See General Correspondence, LTPHJC, Ser II A box 9 folder 12.

15. Nat Hentoff, "Jazz: An Exceedingly Hard Vocation to Grow Old In?" *New York Times*, March 8, 1970, M6.

16. Leonard Feather, "Celebration of Maturity in Music," *Los Angeles Times*, September 23, 1973, n49.

17. Feather, "Celebration of Maturity in Music," n49.

18. Feather, "Celebration of Maturity in Music," n49.

19. Feather, "Celebration of Maturity in Music," n49.

20. Feather, "Celebration of Maturity in Music," n49.

21. Leonard Feather, "Rambling in the Rockies," *Los Angeles Times*, October 13, 1974, 62.

22. Leonard Feather, "Jazz Parties Catch Attention of Patrons," *American Statesman*, December 6, 1970, E26.

23. On the Fulcher-Gibson connection, see John Sliney, "All That Jazz: Odessa Is Becoming a Jazz Oasis in a Musical Desert," *Austin Statesman*, August 22, 1971, A8, 11.

24. For more on the history of the West Texas Jazz Party and recent happenings of the West Texas Jazz Society, see https://wtjs.org.

25. Feather, "Jazz Parties Catch Attention of Patrons," E26.

26. Feather, "Jazz Parties Catch Attention of Patrons," E26.

27. Stanley Dance, "Jazz," *Music Journal* 28, no. 2 (February 1, 1970): 44.

28. Dance, "Jazz," 44. This article also addressed the challenge to find record stores that stock jazz and blues records of small and obscure labels.

29. Ian Dove, "Talent: Jazz Band, Venuti Group Plays It Like Old 52d St," *Billboard*, January 17, 1970, 26.

30. Jose, "Night Club Reviews: Roosevelt Grill, N.Y.," *Variety*, January 28, 1970, 59.

31. Ian Dove, "Talent: WGJB Spurs New Swing Jazz at Roosevelt Grill," *Billboard*, February 28, 1970 26.

32. "Roosevelt Grill Serves Jazz at 5 P.M. to Counter Late Night Café Biz Eclipse," *Variety*, April 29, 1970, 219. The Bobby Hackett Quintet recorded numerous live performances at the Roosevelt Grill in March and April 1970, released as *Live at the Roosevelt Grill—The Bobby Hackett Quintet* (volumes 1–4) for Chiaroscuro label and two additional releases from the same time period titled *Melody Is a Must: Live at the Roosevelt Grill* (volumes 1 and 2) for the Phontastic label. Also in April (17 and 18) of 1970, the World's Greatest Jazz Band recorded several live tracks that were released as *Live at Roosevelt Grill—World's Greatest Jazz Band* for Atlantic, SD 1570.

33. Mike Griffith, "Jazz Fest and Newport," *New Orleans Magazine* 50, no. 7 (2016): 70–71.

34. Irving Kolodin, "Music to My Ears: Jazz in Brubecksville" *Saturday Review* (September 5, 1970): 42. For more on the Concord Summer Festival, see "Concord Jazz Festival," http://cowellhistoricalsociety.org/html/jazz.html, and P. Elwood, "Concord Jazz: The Festival and the Founder," *JazzTimes* (1985). The first Concord Summer Festival was held at the Concord Boulevard Neighborhood Park on August 26, 1969.

35. Letter: Red Norvo to Peanuts, August 1, 1970, Santa Monica, CA. "My dear Peanuts, Got your letter, the group for the concert sounds great. It should be a 'buster.' Am really looking forward to it. . . . My regards, Norvo." This is a very personal letter suggesting that Red Norvo and his wife Eve were close to the Huckos. General Correspondence, LTPHJC, Ser II A box 9 folder 11.

36. Kolodin, "Music to My Ears," 42.

37. Kolodin, "Music to My Ears," 42.

38. Kolodin, "Music to My Ears," 42.

39. LTPHJC: Box Programs, folder 1971: Program, 3rd Annual Concord Summer Festival, August 7, 1971.

40. Feather, Leonard. *Los Angeles Times*, December 1981, j52.

41. Leonard Feather, "Dixieland Show Scores in Capital," *Los Angeles Times*, May 2, 1986, pp. 1 and 9.

42. Feather, "Dixieland Show Scores in Capital," 9.

43. Feather, "Dixieland Show Scores in Capital," 9.

44. Feather, "Dixieland Show Scores in Capital," 9. Peanuts and Louise continued to perform in festivals in the 1980s and 1990s. In August 1989 Louise sang with Peanuts's Quintet for the eleventh anniversary of the Edinburgh International Jazz Festival, and almost ten years later, in June 1998, Louise sang with Peanuts's large orchestra featured in the Texas Big Band Jazz Festival, to name just a few.

45. Tobin interview by Graham Pass for the BBC, July 1, 2010.

46. Tobin interview by Graham Pass for the BBC, July 1, 2010.

47. Letters, LTPHJC: Box Correspondence.

48. Letter: Teddy Wilson to Peanuts, September 12, 1971. LTPHJC: Box Correspondence.

49. LTPHJC: Box Programs, folder 1971: February 20; and, LTPHJC: Box Programs, folder 1972: February 11.

50. Letter: Steve Allen, California, to Louise and Peanuts Hucko, 13102 Otsego, Sherman Oaks, CA 91403, December 30, 1971. "Thanks so much for your thoughtful holiday message." Sends best wishes for 1972, Cordially, Steve Allen. General Correspondence, LTPHJC, Ser II A box 9 folder 11. There is a photo in the T/H Collection of Sandra Dee, Louise, Elmer Turner (Louise's sister Lucille's husband), Rose Marie and Jerry Van Dyke. Louise's recollections from an interview with Deborah Porter, February 27, 2014.

51. Tobin interview by Graham Pass for the BBC, July 1, 2010. Transcription by Deborah Porter.

52. LTPHJC: Box Correspondence, folder in folder "records," Tobin handwritten list of engagements (Louise performances? "Casual Club Dates not listed."): 1973—"Some single club dates."

53. Tobin interview by Graham Pass for the BBC, July 1, 2010. Transcription by Deborah Porter.

54. LTPHJC: Box Programs, folder 1973, September 29; Peanuts with the Big Band Cavalcade performed with Frankie Carle, Bob Crosby, Freddy Martin, or Margaret Whiting. LTPHJC: Box Programs, folder 1973, November 4, Carnegie Hall, Peanuts with the Big Band Cavalcade performed with Frankie Carle, Bob Crosby, Freddy Martin, or Margaret Whiting. Peanuts: "Guest Star."

55. Tobin interview by Graham Pass for the BBC, July 1, 2010. Transcribed by Deborah Porter.

56. Tobin interview by Graham Pass for the BBC, July 1, 2010.

57. Tobin interview by Graham Pass for the BBC, July 1, 2010.

58. "Glenn Miller Band under Hucko's Baton," *Variety*, January 16, 1974, 76.

59. Letter: Lawrence Welk to Peanuts, January 14, 1974. Eleven Western Union telegrams were sent on January 18, 1974, to Peanuts, Glenn Miller Band, Kahler Plaza Hotel, wishing him well, including one from Red Norvo. General Correspondence, LTPHJC, Ser II A box 9 folder 12.

60. Letter: W. Alexander to Mrs. Louise Hucko, 1336 Huston St, Sherman Oaks, CA 91403, Jan 24, 1974. General Correspondence, LTPHJC, Ser II A box 9 folder 12.

61. Letter: John J. Meehan, President/Chairman The Glenn Miller Society—American Branch #2, Wyckoff, NJ to David McKay, Esq. Attorney, NY, NY, undated. General Correspondence, LTPHJC, Ser II A box 9 folder 12.

62. John S. Wilson, "Miller Band Given a Broader Scope by Peanuts Hucko," *New York Times*, August 7, 1974, 21.

63. Tobin interview by Graham Pass for the BBC, July 1, 2010. Transcribed by Deborah Porter.

64. Buddy Morrow took his place as leader.

65. Zan Stewart, "Army Made Hucko into Clarinetist," *Los Angeles Times*, September 7, 1987, 1.

66. Leonard Feather, "Rambling in the Rockies," *Los Angeles Times*, October 13, 1974, 62.

67. Geoff Millerman, "Review: San Diego Jazz Club, Sound of Jazz," *Cadence* 3, no. 4 (October 1977): 45–46. This album was retitled as *The New Orleans Jazz Ensemble Plays the Sound of Jazz* and reissued in 1984 by Murray Hill Enterprises.

68. Shirley Klett, "Review: Peanuts Hucko, Tribute to Louis Armstrong–Benny Goodman," *Cadence* 12, no. 10 (October 1986): 88.

69. Shirley Klett, "Review: Peanuts Hucko, Tribute to Louis Armstrong–BGoodman," *Cadence* 14, no. 8 (August 1988): 89.

70. Leonard Feather, "Joe Williams: Good Feel, No Hit," *Los Angeles Times*, September 8, 1974, 56.

71. Feather, "Joe Williams: Good Feel, No Hit," 56.

72. Mary Lee Hester, "Peanuts," *Mississippi Rag* 16, no. 6 (April 1989): 1–3.

73. Deborah Porter to author, personal correspondence, February 27, 2016.

74. Deborah Porter to author, personal correspondence, February 27, 2016.

Appendix A

1. For complete scripts to these and other *Camel Caravan* broadcasts, see www.otrr.org/FILES/Scripts_pdf/Benny%20Goodman%27s%20Camel%20Caravan/.

Appendix B

1. Michael Taft, *Blues Lyric Poetry: A Concordance* (New York: Garland, 1984).

References

Louise Tobin Interviews
Mike Kubiak
Kevin Mooney
Graham Pass
Deborah Porter

Newspapers
Amarillo Globe
Amarillo Sunday News Globe
American Statesman
Arcadian Tribune
Arcadia News
Austin Statesman
Bakersfield Californian
Boone News-Republican
Breckenridge American
Butte Montana Standard
Campus Chat
Chester Times
Chicago Daily Times
Chicago Daily Tribune
Christian Science Monitor
Corona Daily Independent
Daily Mirror (New York)
Dallas Morning News
Denton Record-Chronicle
Denver Post
Houston Post
Kingsport Times
Los Angeles Times
Lowell Sun
Madison Capital Times

Madison Wisconsin State Journal
Mansfield News Journal
McAllen Daily Press
Mobile Press Register
Morning Avalanche
New York Times
Oakland Post
Odessa American
Ogden Standard Examiner
Oxnard Press-Courier
Plainview Daily Herald
Port Arthur News
Rocky Mountain News
Sacramento Observer
San Antonio Light
Saturday Review
Sun Reporter
Toledo Blade
Tulsa Tribune
Washington Post
Wichita Daily Times
Wisconsin State Journal

Archival Collections

The Hoblitzelle & Interstate Theater Collection, Harry Ransom Center, the University of Texas at Austin.

Interstate Theatre Collection, Texas Archival Resources Online, https://legacy.lib.utexas.edu/taro/dalpub/07701/dpub-07701p1.html.

Louise Tobin and Peanuts Hucko Jazz Collection, Northeast Texas Digital Collections, Velma K. Waters Library Special Collections Department, Texas A&M University–Commerce, Commerce, Texas.

Muggsy Spanier Collection, Rutgers University.

Old Time Radio Researchers Group, Camel Caravan, Benny Goodman, Broadcast Scripts, http://www.otrr.org/FILES/Scripts_pdf/Benny%20Goodman%27s%20Camel%20Caravan/.

Secondary Sources

American Society of Music Arrangers. "Complete List of A.S.M.A. Members." *The Score* 3, nos. 7 and 8 (July–August 1946): 4 and 6.

Aubrey, Denton County, Texas. Accessed July 27, 2012. www.usacitiesonline.com/txcountyaubrey.htm.

Baber, Katherine. "'Manhattan Women': Jazz, Blues, and Gender in On the Town and Wonderful Town." *American Music* 31, no. 1 (March 2013): 73–105.

Bach, Bob. "Midwest Function." *Swing: The Guide to Modern Music* 3, no. 2 (October 1940): 7.

Balliett, Whitney. *Ecstasy at the Onion: Thirty-One Pieces on Jazz*. Indianapolis: Bobbs-Merrill, 1971.

———. "The Inheritors." In *Collected Works: A Journal of Jazz, 1954–2001*, 173–75. New York: St. Martin's Griffin, 2002.

Billings, Molly. "The Influenza Pandemic of 1918." June 1997. Last modified February 2005. https://virus.stanford.edu/uda/.

Bittan, David B. "Newport Jazz Fest Reaches Maturity as Wave of Dignity Sinks 'Jazzniks.'" *Variety*, July 11 1962, 227.

Bregman, Buddy, dir. *The 1962 Newport Jazz Festival*. DVD. Australia and New Zealand: Umbrella Entertainment, 2004, DAVID0419.

Byler, Robert H., Jr. "Jazz Is Back." *Historic Preservation* 28, no. 4 (July 1976): 24–29.

Caiazza, Nick. http://www.discogs.com/artist/939761-Nick-Caiazza.

Carter, Susan, Scott Sigmund Gartner, Michael Haines, Alan Olmsted, Richard Sutch, and Gavin Wright, eds. *Historical Statistics of the United States: Millennial Edition*. Cambridge: Cambridge University Press, 2006. http://hsus.cambridge.org/.

Chilowicz, Alex. "A Career Retrospective of Eddie Sauter, Jazz's Overlooked Composer and Innovator." Master's thesis, Rutgers University, 2013. https://rucore.libraries.rutgers.edu/rutgers-lib/40386/.

"Cisco Lake (Brazos River)." Texas Water Development Board. www.twdb.texas.gov/surfacewater/rivers/reservoirs/cisco/index.asp.

Cohn, Art. *The Nine Lives of Michael Todd*. New York: Random House, 1958.

Collier, James Lincoln. *Benny Goodman and the Swing Era*. New York: Oxford University Press, 1989.

Connor, D. Russell. *Benny Goodman: Listen to His Legacy*. Studies in Jazz 6. Metuchen, NJ: Scarecrow Press, 1988.

———. Liner notes. *The Different Version Vol. 1, 40 Alternate Takes of Recordings, 1939–1940*. Sweden: Phontastic NCD 8821/2, 1993.

Connor, D. Russell, and Warren W. Hicks. *BG On the Record: A Bio-discography of Benny Goodman*. New York: Arlington House, 1969.

Cosper, Alex. "History of Record Labels and the Music Industry: 1940s." www.playlistresearch.com/history/labels1940s.htm.

Crosbie, Ian. "Will Bradley and His Orchestra Featuring Ray McKinley." *Coda Magazine*, September 1976, 2–6.

Dahl, Linda. *Stormy Weather: The Music and Lives of a Century of Jazzwomen*. New York: Pantheon Books, 1984. 3rd ed., New York: Limelight Editions, 1995.

Dance, Stanley. "Jazz." *Music Journal* 28, no. 2 (February 1, 1970): 44.

———. *Those Swinging Years*. Baton Rouge: Louisiana State University Press, 1984.

Davis, Angela. *Blues Legacies and Black Feminism*. New York: Random House, 1998.

Davis, Charlie. *That Band from Indiana*. Oswego, NY: Mathom Publishing, 1982.

Discogs.com. 2019.

Dove, Ian. "Talent: Jazz Band, Venuti Group Plays It Like Old 52d St." *Billboard*, January 17, 1970, 26.

Eddy, Chuck. *The Accidental Evolution of Rock-n-Roll: A Misguided Tour through Popular Music*. New York: Da Capo Press, 1997.

Edwards, Jim, and Wynette Edwards. *Chicago Entertainment between the Wars, 1919–1939*. Chicago: Arcadia, 2003.

Enstam, Elizabeth York. "Women and the Law." *Handbook of Texas Online*. https://tshaonline.org/handbook/online/articles/jsw02. Accessed July 27, 2012. Published by the Texas State Historical Association.

Evans, Arthur, ed. *The Yucca: Yearbook of North Texas State Teachers College*. Denton: North Texas State Teachers College, 1940. http://texashistory.unt.edu/ark:/67531/metapth61014. Accessed May 17, 2010.

Feather, Leonard. "The Changing of the Hasselgard." *Metronome* 64, no. 9 (September 1948): 20–21.

———. "Louise Tobin, Well Again, Sings on Wax." *Down Beat* 7, no. 12 (June 15, 1940): 2.

Field, William T. "Swiss." *Handbook of Texas Online*. www.tshaonline.org/handbook/online/articles/pns01. Accessed September 16, 2017.

Firestone, Ross. *Swing, Swing, Swing: The Life and Times of Benny Goodman*. New York: W. W. Norton, 1993.

Forrest, Helen, with Bill Libby. *I Had the Craziest Dream*. New York: Coward, McCann and Geoghegan, 1982.

Fuller, Jackie Balthrop. "Aubrey, TX," *Handbook of Texas Online*. www.tshaonline.org/handbook/online/articles/hla28. Accessed July 27, 2012. Published by the Texas State Historical Association.

Garrod, Charles. *Ziggy Elman and His Orchestra*. Zephyrhills, FL: Joyce Record Club, 1990.

Garrod, Charles, and Bill Korst. *Will Bradley and His Orchestra*. Zephyrhills, FL: A Joyce Music Publication, 1986.

Gennari, John. "Hipsters, Bluebloods, Rebels, and Hooligans: The Cultural Politics of the Newport Jazz Festival, 1954–1960." In *Uptown Conversations: The New Jazz Studies*, edited by Robert G. O'Meally et al., 126–49. New York: Columbia University Press, 2004.

Gioia, Ted. *The History of Jazz*. 2nd ed. Oxford: Oxford University Press, 2011.

"Governors of Texas, 1846–Present." Published by the Texas State Library and Archives Commission. www.tsl.state.tx.us/ref/abouttx/governors.html. Accessed July 27, 2012.

Griffith, Mike. "Jazz Fest and Newport." *New Orleans Magazine* 50, no. 7 (2016): 70–71.

Hammond, John. "J. Hammond Says." *Down Beat* 1, no. 10 (October 1938): 27.

Harrison, Daphne Duval. *Black Pearls: Blues Queens of the 1920s*. New Brunswick, NJ: Rutgers University Press, 2000.

Hester, Mary Lee. "Peanuts." *The Mississippi Rag*. 16, no. 6 (April 1989): 1–3.

History of Aubrey, Texas, compiled by the Aubrey Historical Society. 2nd printing, December 2012.

"The History of Pageants: 1930–1939." 1998. PageantCenter.com. http://pageantcenter.com/history-30s.html. Accessed August 23, 2010.

Hobby, William P., Jr. "Hobby, William Pettus." *Handbook of Texas Online*. www.tshaonline.org/handbook/online/articles/fh004. Accessed July 27, 2012. Published by the Texas State Historical Association.

Holly, Hal. "Los Angeles Band Briefs." *Down Beat* 13, no. 17 (August 12, 1946): 6.

Hustad, Thomas P. *Born to Play: The Ruby Braff Discography and Directory of Performances*. Lanham, MD: Scarecrow Press, 2012.

Jasinski, Laurie E. "Amarillo Natatorium [The Nat]." *Handbook of Texas Online*. www.tshaonline.org/handbook/online/articles/xda06. Accessed November 17, 2017.

"Jenny, Jack." www.discogs.com/artist/322119-Jack-Jenney.

Johnny Mercer Foundation website, www.johnnymercerjoundation.org.

Johnson, Alex. "History of the Track: The Lamp Is Low." https://blacksquirrelradio.com/history-of-the-track-the-lamp-is-low/. Accessed October 15, 2017.

Jones, Isabel Morse. *Hollywood Bowl*. New York: G. Schirmer, 1936.

Jones, Stacy Holman. *Torch Singing: Performing Resistance and Desire from Billie Holiday to Edith Piaf*. New York: Altamira Press, 2007.

Jose, [unknown]. "Night Club Reviews: Roosevelt Grill, N.Y." *Variety*, January 28, 1970, 59.

Kaplan, James. *Frank: The Voice*. New York: Anchor Books, 2011.

"Kavelin, Al." Allmusic.com. www.allmusic.com/artist/al-kavelin-mn0001009035/biography.

Kenney, William Howland. *Chicago Jazz: A Cultural History, 1904–1930*. New York: Oxford University Press, 1993.

Kernfeld, Barry. "Caiazza, Nick." *The New Grove Dictionary of Jazz*. 2nd ed. Online.

Keys, W. E. "Radio Reports: Ice Parade." *Variety*, July 17, 1935, 51.

Kimball, Robert, et al., eds. *The Complete Lyrics of Johnny Mercer*. The Johnny Mercer Foundation. New York: Alfred A. Knopf, 2009.

Klett, Shirley. "Review: Peanuts Hucko, Tribute to Louis Armstrong-Benny Goodman." *Cadence* 12, no. 10 (October 1986): 88.

———. "Review: Peanuts Hucko, Tribute to Louis Armstrong-B Goodman." *Cadence* 14, no. 8 (August 1988): 89.

Laird, Paul R. "Newport Jazz Festival." *Grove Music Online*. https://doi.org/10.1093/gmo/9781561592630.article.J327300, published in print: January 20, 2002; published online: 2003.

Laredo, Joseph F. Liner notes. *Benny's Girls: Goodman's Rare Songbirds*. Sony Music, 2004.

Lee, William F. *American Big Bands*. Milwaukee: Hal Leonard, 2005.

Legacies: A History Journal for Dallas and North Central Texas, vol. 21, no. 2 (Fall 2009), Dallas, Texas. texashistory.unt.edu/ark:/67531/metapth66965/m1/26/. Accessed September 16, 2017. University of North Texas Libraries. The Portal to Texas History, texashistory.unt.edu; crediting Dallas Historical Society.

Levinson, Peter J. *Trumpet Blues: The Life of Harry James*. Oxford: Oxford University Press, 1999.

Lord, Tom. *The Jazz Discography Online*. West Vancouver, BC: Lord Music Reference, 2010. www.lorddisco.com/.

Magee, Jeffrey. *The Uncrowned King of Swing: Fletcher Henderson and Big Band Jazz*. Oxford: Oxford University Press, 2005.

Metropolitan Theater, Houston, TX. www.houstondeco.org/1920s/metro.html.

Millerman, Geoff. "Review: San Diego Jazz Club, Sound of Jazz." *Cadence* 3, no. 4 (October 1977): 45–46.

Montgomery, R.C. "Victor 19644-Lloyd Finlay and His Orchestra-1925." Website: "Old Time Blues: Electrically Recorded." June 5, 2015. http://oldtimeblues.net/2015/06/05/victor-19644-lloyd-finlay-and-his-orchestra-1925/.

Mooney, Kevin. "As Big as All of Texas: An Overview of Music in the Lone Star State." Unpublished keynote address. Texas Music Conference. Dallas Public Library. Dallas, Texas. May 31, 2009.

Nimmo, H. Arlo. *The Andrews Sisters: A Biography and Career Record*. Jefferson, NC: McFarland, 2007.

Oehme, Tom. "And the Angels Sing: The Career of Martha Tilton." http://marthatilton.com/index.html.

Oliver, Paul. "Blues." *The New Grove Dictionary of Jazz*, 2nd ed. Barry Kernfeld, ed. Oxford: Oxford University Press, 2002.

"One O'Clock Jazz Band." Wikipedia. https://en.wikipedia.org/wiki/One_O%-27Clock_Lab_Band.

Orodenker, Maurie. "Records on Review." *Band Leaders and Record Review* 3, no. 6 (August 1946): 10.

Pagones, John. "Jazzwise, You Needn't Be Starving Now." *Washington Post*, April 30, 1965, D14.

Peerless, Brian. Liner notes. *Benny Goodman, Roll 'Em, Volume 1*. Columbia Records/CBS Inc., 1987.

Peterson, Richard A., and Andy Bennett. "Introducing Music Scenes." In *Music Scenes: Local, Translocal, and Virtual*. Edited by Bennett and Peterson, 1–16. Nashville: Vanderbilt University Press, 2004.

Popa, Christopher. "Big Bands at Disneyland." bigbandlibrary.com (2016). www.bigbandlibrary.com/bigbandsatdisneyland.html.

———. "Collector's Checklists: Benny Goodman 33s." bigbandlibrary.com (2004). www.bigbandlibrary.com/collectorschecklists33sgoodmanbenny.html.

———. "Ziggy Ellman: 'Fralich in Spring.'" November 2005. www.bigbandlibrary.com/ziggyelman.html.

Prial, Dunstan. *The Producer: John Hammond and the Soul of American Music*. New York: Farrar, Straus, and Giroux, 2006.

Pullen, Glenn C. "House Reviews: Palace, Cleve." *Variety*, May 17, 1939, 37.

Rogers, James L. *The Story of North Texas*. Denton: North Texas State University, 1965.

Rollini, Arthur. *Thirty Years with the Big Bands*. Wheatley, Oxford: Bayou Press, 1989.

Roy, James V. "Scotty Moore—Official Website: Cotton Bowl." February 10, 2008. http://www.scottymoore.net/CottonBowl.html. Accessed September 12, 2009.

Rusch, Bob. "Interview with Peanuts Hucko." Transcribed by Kea D. Rusch. *Cadence: The American Review of Jazz and Blues* 11, no. 5 (May 1985): 13–18.

Rust, Brian. *Jazz Records: 1897–1942.* New York: Arlington House, 1978.

Rustin, Nichole T., and Sherrie Tucker, eds. *Big Ears: Listening for Gender in Jazz Studies.* Durham, NC: Duke University Press, 2008.

Scoppa, Bud. "Western Studios—Hollywood (1966): The Beach Boys—Pet Sounds." *Paste Magazine* (June 1, 2004). https://www.pastemagazine.com/articles/2004/06/western-studios-hollywood-1966.html.

Shacter, James D. *Loose Shoes: The Story of Ralph Sutton.* Chicago: Jaynar Press, 1994.

Simon, George. "The Editors Speak: The Limp Dept." *Metronome* 70, no. 3 (March 1954): 34.

Simon, George T. *The Big Bands.* New York: Schirmer, 1981.

———. *Simon Says: The Sights and Sounds of the Swing Era, 1935–1955.* New Rochelle, NY: Arlington House, 1971.

Smith, Bill. "Loew's State, New York." *Billboard,* June 10, 1944, 25.

Smith, Ernie, et al. "Films." *Oxford Music Online.* https://doi.org/10.1093/gmo/9781561592630.article.J149900, published in print: January 20, 2002; published online: 2003.

Spelvin, George. "General News: Broadway Beat." *Billboard* October 1, 1938.

Spragg, Dennis M. *Glenn Miller Declassified.* Lincoln: University of Nebraska Press, 2017.

Stokes, W. Royal. *The Jazz Scene: An Informal History from New Orleans to 1990.* New York: Oxford University Press, 1991.

Stowe, David W. *Swing Changes: Big Band Jazz in New Deal America.* Cambridge, MA: Harvard University Press, 1996.

Storm, Rick. "Business @marillo Globe-News: WDAG Made First Broadcast with 10 Watts of Power." *Amarillo Globe News,* May 18, 1997. http://amarillo.com/stories/051897/first.html#.Wb0VHzlukfE.

Taft, Michael. *Blues Lyric Poetry: A Concordance.* New York: Garland, 1984.

Titon, Jeff Todd. *Early Downhome Blues.* Chapel Hill: University of North Carolina Press, 1994.

Tracy, Jack. "What's on Wax: Ziggy Elman." *Down Beat* 18, no. 25 (December 14, 1951): 14.

Ulanov, Barry. "Record Reviews: Ziggy Elman." *Metronome* 68, no. 1 (January 1952): 26.

Ulanov, Simon, and Leonard Feather. "Record Reviews: Tommy Jones." *Metronome* 62, no. 5 (May 1946): 27.

Vaché, Warren. "When the Steaks and Jazz Sizzled at Nick's." *Mississippi Rag* (May 1, 1999): 30–32.

Waters, Charles H., Jr. "Anatomy of a Cover." In *Annual Review of Jazz Studies,* vol. 6. Edited by Edward Berger, David Cayer, Dan Morgenstern, and Lewis Porter. Metuchen, NJ: Scarecrow Press, 1993.

White, Al. *Jazz Party: A Photo Gallery of Great Jazz Musicians*. Little Rock, AR: August House, 2000.

Willard, Hal. *The Wildest One: The Life of Wild Bill Davison*. Monkton, MD: Avondale Press, 1996.

Wilson, John S. "The Jazz Faithful." *New York Times*, October 31, 1965, 24.

Wright, Gordon. "Bradley, Herman Add New Wax Life." *Metronome* 56, no. 11 (November 1940): 14.

Index